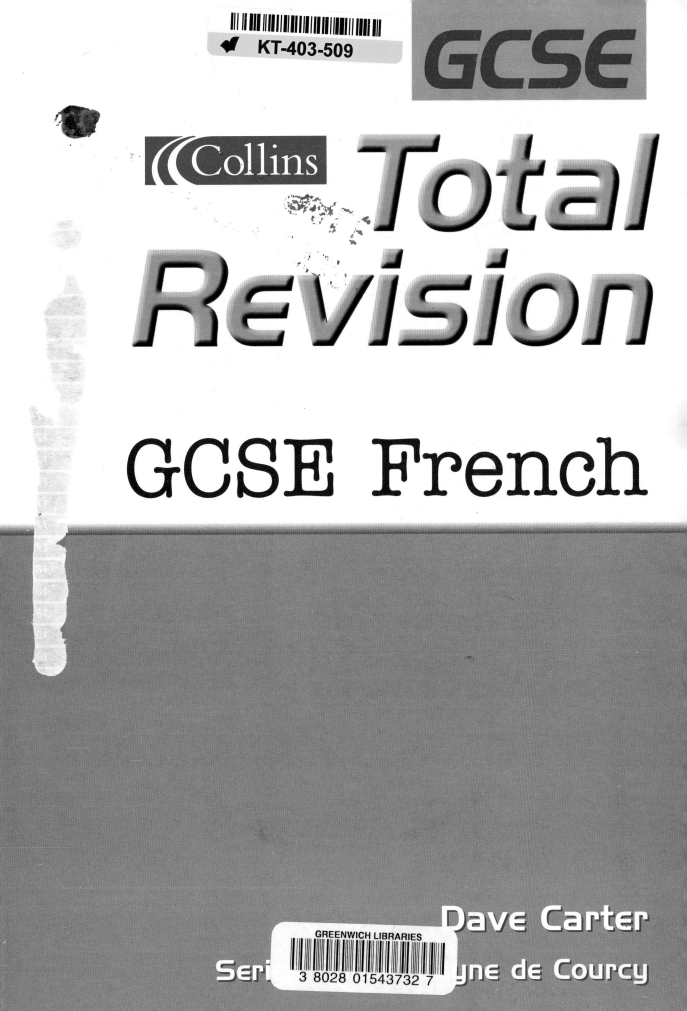

GCSE

Collins

Total Revision

GCSE French

Dave Carter

Seri... ...yne de Courcy

Contents

How this book will help you...   iii

About your GCSE French course   vi

1 *L'école*   *1*

2 *A la maison/les média*   *10*

3 *La santé, la forme et la nourriture*   *18*

4 *Moi, ma famille et mes amis*   *26*

5 *Le temps libre, les loisirs, les vacances et les fêtes*   *34*

6 *Les rapports personnels, les activités sociales et les rendez-vous*   *42*

7 *La ville, les régions et le temps*   *50*

8 *Les courses et les services publics*   *57*

9 *La route, les voyages et les transports*   *65*

10 *L'enseignement supérieur, la formation et l'emploi*   *74*

11 *La publicité, les communications et les langues au travail*   *81*

12 *La vie à l'étranger, le tourisme, les coutumes et le logement*   *88*

13 *Le monde*   *96*

14 *Listening and responding*   *104*

15 *Speaking*   *117*

16 *Reading and responding*   *134*

17 *Writing*   *152*

18 *Grammar summary*   *167*

Nouns   *167*

Articles   *168*

Adjectives   *168*

Demonstratives   *169*

Possessives   *170*

Indefinites   *171*

Adverbs   *172*

Intensifiers   *172*

Comparative   *173*

Superlative   *174*

Pronouns   *174*

Numbers   *176*

Quantities   *177*

Dates   *178*

Time   *179*

Prepositions   *179*

Conjunctions   *180*

Interrogatives   *181*

Verbs   *181*

List of common verbs   *191*

Answers   *194*

Index   *246*

How this book will help you...

It doesn't matter whether you're heading for mocks in Year 11, or in the final run-up to your GCSE exam – **this book will help you to produce your very best.**

Whichever approach you decide to take to revision, this book will provide everything you need:

1. Total revision support
2. Quick revision check-ups
3. Exam practice

1 Total Revision Support

Everything you need to know

This book contains all the topics you'll have studied at school. **It covers all the main topics set by all the Exam Boards.**

Short sections of vocabulary and grammar

The vocabulary and grammar you need to know are divided between the 13 topic chapters. **This means you don't have to wade through pages and pages of grammar and vocabulary when you're revising.**

The 'What you need to know section' in each chapter contains the vocabulary and structures you need to get a **Grade C**. The 'Going Further' section gives additional language which will help you **move up the grades to an A or A*.**

Revising the 'four skills'

Reading, Writing, Listening and Speaking are in every chapter. But we've also included one whole chapter on each skill. **Read through each of these as revision before each of your specific skill exams.**

...Turn over for QUICK REVISION CHECK-UPS and EXAM PRACTICE...→

Quick Revision Check-ups

Check yourself questions

It can be really hard knowing where to start when you're revising. Sitting down and wading through pages of text isn't easy. You're probably asleep before the third page! This book makes it easy to stay awake – **because it makes revising ACTIVE.**

We came up with the idea of putting **'Check yourself'** questions into each chapter. **The questions test your understanding of all the important vocabulary and structures** in each chapter. In this way, you can find out quickly and easily just how much you know. You don't need to read through all the chapter first – just try the questions. If you get all the questions right, you can move straight on to the next section. If you get several of the questions wrong, you know you need to read through the vocabulary and grammar sections carefully. **This really cuts down on revision time – and helps you focus on where you need to put most effort.**

Answers and Tutorials

If you want the 'Check yourself' questions to be a genuine test of how much you know, then you need to cover up the answers. But, if you'd rather, you can read through a question, then the answer and then the **'tutorial'**. This will still do you a lot of good – and doesn't require quite as much effort!

We've included 'tutorials', as well as answers, to give you even more help with your revision. The tutorials point out common mistakes that the author knows candidates make, and give you hints on answering similar questions in exams.

3 Exam Practice

Exam technique

Knowing your vocabulary and grammar is important. But **it's even more important to know how to use them to answer exam questions properly.** The author sees hundreds of exam scripts a year and students very often lose marks because **they haven't understood how to tackle exam questions.**

Foundation and Higher

You will be sitting either the Foundation or Higher tier papers. If you are doing **Foundation**, practise the questions marked **F** and **F/H**; if you are doing **Higher**, practise the questions marked **F/H** and **H**.

The audio CD

This contains the Listening questions and sample answers for the Speaking questions. We use this symbol  in the book to show when you need to use the CD.

Questions to Answer and Examiner's comments

We've included **lots of past exam questions from different Exam Boards for you to have a go at.** The answers are at the back of the book so it's easy not to cheat. Have a go at the questions yourself and then compare them with the answers.

We've provided comments on the answers to give you extra help. The comments highlight what is good about the answers and what an examiner looks for in order to award a high grade.

Three final tips:

1. Work as consistently as you can during your whole GCSE French course. If you don't understand something, ask your teacher straight away, or look it up in this book. You'll then find revision much easier.

2. Plan your revision carefully and focus on the areas you know you find hard. The 'Check yourself' questions in this book will help you do this.

3. Try to do some exam questions as though you were in the actual exam. Time yourself and don't cheat by looking at the answers until you've really had a good go at working out the answers.

About your GCSE French course

Exam Boards

This book has been produced to help you to study and revise for the French exams set by all the Exam Boards of England, Northern Ireland and Wales.

Grammar

The grammatical content of all the French syllabuses is very similar. The final chapter of the book is a summary of the grammar required in the GCSE exam. This can be used as a reference section to help you find the answer to any problems you may have in the exercises in the rest of the book. It can also form the basis of a revision programme, as each grammar point refers you to the appropriate chapter, where you will find further examples as well as *Check yourself* exercises that test your recall and understanding.

Vocabulary

The core vocabulary defined by each board as a minimum for the lower grades differs between boards. There is no upper limit on the amount of vocabulary, and therefore no guide can give a comprehensive list of what might be in any given exam paper. However, if you learn all the vocabulary in this guide you are likely to encounter relatively few unknown words in the exam, and for this reason the use of a dictionary is now allowed by all boards for some parts of the exam.

Types of questions

The *Exam practice* sections include examples of the types of questions set by all the groups. In Listening and Reading, many of the question-types are very similar for all the groups. In the Speaking and Writing chapters, a note has been included to tell you which group is likely to use each type of task.

All the groups use role-plays and conversation in the Speaking test. NEAB and MEG (and Edexcel in the coursework option) also require candidates to give a prepared presentation.

Use of dictionaries

All Exam Boards allow the use of dictionaries during Reading and Writing tests and for the preparation of the Speaking test. You will need to consult your board's syllabus for the exact details regarding the use of a dictionary in the Listening test. NEAB and WJEC allow the use of a dictionary for part of the test, while other boards do not.

Foundation and Higher tiers

All Exam Boards offer the GCSE papers at Foundation and Higher tiers, and candidates can choose – in consultation with their teachers – to enter at either of the two levels in each of the four skills. You can, for example, take Higher level papers in Listening and Reading, but Foundation level papers in the Speaking and Writing tests. The arithmetic of the points awarded on papers and their conversion to grades goes like this: on each of the four Foundation papers you can score up to 5 points. on each of the four Higher papers you can score between 4 and 8 points. You can 'mix and match' the papers you take.

Number of Foundation papers taken	Number of Higher papers taken	Maximum Number of points that this can give you	Best overall grade that you can get
4	0	20	C
3	1	23	B
2	2	26	A
1	3	29	A
0	4	32	A*

Candidates who take all four Foundation papers can reach a maximum of a Grade C, while those who offer all four Higher papers will normally be awarded a minimum of a Grade D.

WHAT YOU NEED TO KNOW

Levez-vous.	Stand up.
Asseyez-vous.	Sit down.
Ouvrez la fenêtre/vos cahiers.	Open the window/your exercise books.
Fermez la porte/le livre.	Close the door/the book.
Taisez-vous.	Be quiet.
Je (ne) comprends (pas).	I (don't) understand.
Pouvez-vous répéter (plus lentement), s'il vous plaît.	Can you say it again (more slowly), please.
Mon école est très grande.	My school is very large.
Il y a mille cinq cents élèves.	There are 1,500 pupils.
Il y a beaucoup de salles de classe.	There are lots of classrooms.
Il n'y a pas de laboratoire de langues.	There is no language laboratory.
La rentrée, c'est le mardi deux septembre.	We go back to school on Tuesday the 2nd of September.
Les grandes vacances commencent le 23 juillet.	The summer holidays start on the 23rd of July.
On est en vacances du 8 au 12 février.	We are on holiday from the 8th to the 12th of February.
Le premier cours commence à neuf heures vingt.	The first lesson begins at 9.20.
Il y a une récréation de 10h20 à 10h45.	There is a break from 10.20 to 10.45.
Le déjeuner est à midi vingt.	Lunch is at 12.20.
Je mange à la cantine.	I eat in the canteen/dining hall.
Chaque cours dure quarante minutes.	Each lesson lasts for 40 minutes.
Les cours finissent à 3h30.	Lessons finish at 3.30.
Le soir, j'ai deux heures de devoirs.	In the evening, I have two hours' homework.
Le mercredi, je n'ai pas cours.	I don't have school on Wednesdays.
Je viens au collège à pied.	I walk to school.
Je suis membre du club de gym.	I'm a member of the gym club.
L'uniforme scolaire est affreux.	The school uniform is awful.
Je porte une jupe grise.	I wear a grey skirt.
Les garçons portent une cravate/un pantalon.	The boys wear a tie/trousers.
Je fais partie de l'équipe d'athlétisme.	I'm in the athletics team.
Je suis en seconde.	I'm in Year 11.
Mon frère est en quatrième.	My brother is in Year 9.
Je fais de l'histoire, de l'EMT.…	I do history, design technology.…
Ma matière préférée, c'est la physique.	My favourite subject is physics.
Le prof d'anglais s'appelle M. Martin.	The English teacher is called Mr Martin.
Je n'aime pas le professeur de gymnastique.	I don't like the gym teacher.
Je suis bon(ne) en espagnol.	I'm good at Spanish.
Je parle bien l'allemand.	I speak German well.
Je suis nul(le) en sciences.	I'm useless at science.
J'ai de bonnes notes.	I get good marks.
La technologie, c'est facile.	Technology is easy.

LES MOIS

janvier	juillet
février	août
mars	septembre
avril	octobre
mai	novembre
juin	décembre

DES ADJECTIFS

intelligent	intelligent
stupide	stupid
bête	silly
fort en	good at
doué	clever
amusant	amusing/funny
difficile	difficult
facile	easy
passionnant	fascinating
intéressant	interesting
ennuyeux/euse	boring
fatigant	tiring
utile	useful
inutile	not useful

QUESTIONS UTILES

Comment ça s'écrit?	How do you spell it?
Comment dit-on X en français?	How do you say X in French?
C'est quoi en français?	What is it in French?
Qu'est-ce que ça veut dire?	What does that mean?

LES MATIERES

l'anglais   le français   la chimie   la physique   la biologie

l'EPS (le sport)   la musique   le dessin   les mathématiques   la géographie

l'espagnol   l'informatique   l'histoire   l'EMT (la technologie)

QUAND?

le matin	in the morning
l'après-midi	in the afternoon
le soir	in the evening
par jour	per day
par semaine	per week
jeudi	on Thursday
le dimanche	on Sundays

QUESTIONS/PROMPTS

Parlez-moi de votre école.
Les cours commencent à quelle heure?
C'est quand, les vacances de Noël?
Décrivez votre uniforme.
Vous êtes en quelle classe?
Quelle est votre matière préférée?
Vous êtes membre d'un club?

Check yourself

QUESTIONS

Q1 **How would you say in French?**
a) My favourite subject is maths.
b) On Wednesdays, lessons begin at 9.45.
c) My sister is in Year 7.
d) I like the science teacher.
e) There are a lot of pupils at my school.

Q2 **C'est quelle matière?**
a) On utilise des ordinateurs.
b) Langue parlée à Berlin.
c) On étudie les plantes.
d) On fait beaucoup d'activités sportives.
e) On apprend beaucoup de dates.

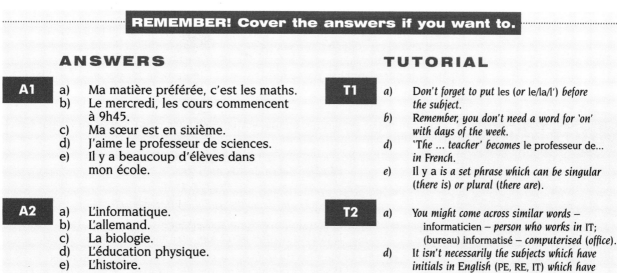

ANSWERS

A1
a) Ma matière préférée, c'est les maths.
b) Le mercredi, les cours commencent à 9h45.
c) Ma sœur est en sixième.
d) J'aime le professeur de sciences.
e) Il y a beaucoup d'élèves dans mon école.

A2
a) L'informatique.
b) L'allemand.
c) La biologie.
d) L'éducation physique.
e) L'histoire.

TUTORIAL

T1
a) *Don't forget to put* les *(or* le/la/l'*) before the subject.*
b) *Remember, you don't need a word for 'on' with days of the week.*
d) *'The ... teacher' becomes* le professeur de... *in French.*
e) Il y a *is a set phrase which can be singular (there is) or plural (there are).*

T2
a) *You might come across similar words –* informaticien *– person who works in* IT; *(bureau)* informatisé *– computerised (office).*
d) *It isn't necessarily the subjects which have initials in English (*PE, RE, IT*) which have initials in French (*l'EPS, l'EMT*).*

GOING FURTHER

A L'ECOLE

sixième	Year 7
cinquième	Year 8
quatrième	Year 9
troisième	Year 10
seconde	Year 11
première	Year 12
terminale	Year 13
le bac(calauréat)	exam taken at end of *terminale*

QUELLE ECOLE?

le collège	school (Years 7–10)
le lycée	school (Years 11–13)
une école mixte	a mixed school
une école de filles	a girls' school
une école publique	a state school
une école privée	a private school
un(e) pensionnaire	a boarder
un(e) demi-pensionnaire	a half-boarder (stays at school for lunch)

Je déteste les maths parce que c'est trop difficile.	I hate maths because it's too difficult.
Je ne suis pas bon(ne) élève, car je ne travaille pas assez.	I'm not a good student, because I don't work hard enough.
J'attends les grandes vacances avec impatience.	I can't wait for the summer holidays.
J'espère réussir au bac l'année prochaine.	I hope to pass the 'bac' next year.
Je ne supporte vraiment pas l'école.	I really can't stand school.
Les profs me critiquent toujours.	The teachers are always criticising me.
Je voudrais bien apprendre d'autres langues.	I'd love to learn (some) other languages.
J'apprends le français depuis cinq ans.	I've been learning French for 5 years.
L'année passée je n'ai pas travaillé, mais maintenant je fais des progrès.	Last year I didn't work, but now I'm making progress.

Je préfère les écoles mixtes parce que ça ressemble plus à la vie normale.

I prefer mixed schools because they're more like real life.

J'ai choisi ce collège car il est près de chez moi.

I chose this school because it's near where I live.

Je suis pensionnaire, parce que j'habite loin du lycée.

I'm a boarder because I live a long way from school.

EXTRA DETAILS

mais	but
et	and
puis	then
donc	therefore
alors	so
car	for
parce que	because
à cause de	because of
malgré	in spite of

You can make even quite simple statements earn extra marks for Higher Level, by adding extra information:

- Say how long you've been doing something:
  J'étudie l'italien **depuis deux ans**.

- Express opinions and give a reason:
  J'aime le prof de maths, **car** il est très sympa.

- Say why you do/have done something:
  Je fais des sciences **parce que** c'est une matière passionnante.

- Use linking words to avoid a series of very short sentences:
  Je suis intelligente. Je ne travaille pas assez. → Je suis intelligente **mais** je ne travaille pas assez.

- To make a change from car or parce que followed by a verb, try another linking phrase:
  J'aime les langues parce que le prof est bon. → J'aime les langues **à cause du** prof.

HOW THE GRAMMAR WORKS

DATES

Unlike in English, the date is always expressed in the same way in French – le + number + month:
  le dix-neuf mars – March 19th

An exception is the 1st of the month, when you use le premier:
  le premier mai

The French do not use a word for 'on' with days or dates:

Les cours commencent le six janvier. – Lessons begin on the 6th of January.

Vendredi, j'ai un examen. – I have an exam on Friday.

To use dates to say how long something lasts, use du + date + au + date:

On est en vacances du trois au vingt avril. – We're on holiday from the 3rd to the 20th of April.

TIME

The time can be expressed very simply in French by using number (hours) + heures + number (minutes):
  trois heures dix – 3.10/ten past three.
On notices, this will usually be written as 3h10.

Remember that heure will be singular after une:
  une heure vingt.

You may, however, hear some rather different expressions:
  midi – 12 o'clock (midday)
  minuit – 12 o'clock (midnight)

et quart – quarter past (*six heures et quart* – 6.15)
et demie – half past (*huit heures et demie* – 8.30)
moins le quart – quarter to (*onze heures moins le quart* – 10.45)
moins cinq/dix/vingt/vingt-cinq – five/ten/twenty/twenty-five to (*quatre heures moins vingt* – 3.40)

For timetables, the French always use the 24-hour clock. So, on a school timetable you might find:

Quatorze heures trente: anglais – 14.30 (2.30pm): English.

To say what time something happens, use *à* followed by the time:

J'arrive à l'école à neuf heures moins le quart.	– I get to school at quarter to nine.

To indicate how long something lasts, you can use *de* with a time, followed by *à* with a later time:

La pause déjeuner est de midi vingt à une heure dix.	– Lunchtime is from twelve twenty to one ten.

Or, if you want to avoid a particular time you can use the verb durer:

La récréation dure vingt minutes.

Remember that as well as being used in times, *heure* also means 'hour':

Les cours durent une heure.

HOW LONG FOR

To say how long you have been doing something for, use *depuis*. It is important to use the right tense, and it's not what you might expect.

To say how long you have been doing something, use *depuis* with the present tense:

Je fais de l'anglais depuis trois ans. – I have been doing English for three years.

To say how long you had been doing something, use *depuis* with the imperfect tense:

Avant de venir ici, j'étais à l'école à Paris depuis deux ans.	– Before coming here, I had been at school in Paris for two years.

Depuis can also mean 'since':

Je suis là depuis une heure trente. – I have been here since 1.30.

COMMANDS

You can often identify when someone is telling you to do something by listening for the *-ez* ending on the verb:

attendez	wait	*entrez*	come in
choisissez	choose	*fermez*	close
continuez	continue	*finissez*	finish
dessinez	draw	*ouvrez*	open
écoutez	listen	*prenez*	take
écrivez	write	*sortez*	go out

Remember that if the verb is reflexive, you will also hear the *vous*:

asseyez-vous	sit down	*levez-vous*	stand up

If your teacher calls you *tu*, then he/she will simply use the *tu* form of the verb without *tu* (for er verbs minus the final *-s*):

attends	wait	*choisis*	choose	*entre*	come in

If the verb is reflexive, you will also hear *toi*:

lève-toi

QUESTIONS

Q1 **How would you say in French?**

a) I like science because I find it interesting.
b) I chose English because the teacher is amusing.
c) I have been studying geography for one year.
d) I can't stand history because of the homework.
e) I'm useless at music in spite of the good teacher.

Q2 **Match the sentence with the right person.**

a) L'école, ça va. Mais je ne crois pas que je vais réussir à mes examens, car je n'ai pas assez travaillé.
b) Je ne supporte pas les profs, et je trouve les cours ennuyeux. Puis on a trop de devoirs.
c) Je fais toujours mes devoirs. Tous les soirs, de huit heures à onze heures, je suis dans ma chambre.

> **Marc**, qui n'aime pas l'école.
> **Anne**, qui travaille beaucoup.
> **Sandrine**, qui n'est pas bonne élève.

REMEMBER! Cover the answers if you want to.

ANSWERS

A1
a) J'aime les sciences parce que je trouve ça intéressant.
b) J'ai choisi l'anglais car le professeur est amusant.
c) J'étudie la géographie depuis un an.
d) Je ne supporte pas l'histoire à cause des devoirs.
e) Je suis nul(le) en musique, malgré le bon professeur.

A2
a) Sandrine
b) Marc
c) Anne

TUTORIAL

T1
a) *If you wrote* J'aime les sciences parce que je les trouve intéressantes, *that is quite correct, but the French often use* ça *in this way, especially to refer to an idea rather than an object.*
c) *Present tense with* depuis.
d) *You can only use* parce que *before a verb. You need* des *because* devoirs *is plural.*
e) *Remember that* bon *comes before the noun.*

T2
a) *Thinks school is all right, so it can't be Marc. Hasn't worked, so it can't be Anne.*
b) *All negative comments, but it implies working (trop de devoirs) so it can't be Sandrine.*

General: *In this sort of item, it isn't just a matter of recognising key words, since none of the people actually says* Je n'aime pas l'école. *You must get the gist, then draw your conclusion.*

EXAM PRACTICE

1 Find Chapter 1 – Exam Practice Listening on the CD. Listen to the French (Track 1) twice, then answer this question.

LISTENING F H

Alain et Floriane parlent de l'école. Remplissez la grille en français.

	aime	n'aime pas	Attitude envers l'école 1 = adore 5 = déteste
Alain	1 .... 2	1	1 2 3 4 5
Floriane	1 .... 2	1	1 2 3 4 5

You will find the transcript, with answers and examiner's comments, on page 194.

2 First, look at the situation below, and think what you might say. Then find Chapter 1 – Exam Practice Speaking on the CD and listen to a student doing the role-play with his teacher (Track 2). Don't forget, most role-plays will include an unexpected part – one that you have not been able to prepare in advance. In this case, it is **d)**. For this, you need to understand what the teacher asks you.

SPEAKING F H

You will find the transcript and examiner's comments on page 194.

You are speaking to a teacher at a school in France.
You are in Year 11.
Your favourite subjects are maths and chemistry.
You don't like the English teacher.

a) Votre classe
b) Vos préférences
c) Les profs
d) Répondez à la question.

F H READING

3 Look at this timetable, then answer the question which follows it.

Regardez l'emploi du temps, puis répondez à la question.

	lundi	mardi	jeudi	vendredi	samedi
1	français	maths	histoire	informatique	biologie
2			chimie		anglais
3	espagnol	biologie		géo	espagnol
4		anglais	physique	maths	
5	géo	français			
6	histoire		EMT	EPS	
7		physique			

You will find the answers and examiner's comments on page 195.

Hélène: adore les maths, mais déteste les sciences.

Alexandre: aime les maths et le sport; est nul en langues.

Julie: ne comprend rien aux ordinateurs, mais adore le prof de chimie.

Quels jours préfèrent-ils?

	aime	n'aime pas
Hélène		
Alexandre		
Julie		

F H WRITING

4 Vous écrivez à votre correspondante Dominique. Parlez de votre école.

Parlez:

– de l'école (où, nombre d'élèves et de profs, etc.)

– des matières

– de la journée scolaire

– des professeurs

– de votre attitude envers l'école

Ecrivez environ 100 mots.

Sample Student's Answer

Chère Dominique

Mon école est assez grande.
Il y a huit cents élèves et
cinquante professeurs.
L'école est à cinq minutes
de chez moi, <u>alors</u> j'y vais
à pied.
Mes matières préférées sont
le français, l'histoire et la
géographie. J'aime aussi les
langues, <u>mais</u> je suis nul(le)!
Je ne suis pas bon(ne) en
sciences <u>non plus</u>, mais pour
les maths, ça va.
Les cours commencent à
neuf heures, et nous avons
cinq ou six cours par jour.
L'école finit à cinq heures,
mais il y a aussi les
devoirs – <u>trop de devoirs</u>!
Les profs sont assez sympa
en général, mais je n'aime
pas le prof d'anglais.
J'aime assez l'école, et je
suis bon(ne) élève, <u>car</u> je
veux réussir à mes
examens, <u>donc</u> il faut
travailler!

EXAMINER'S COMMENTS

● This answers all the tasks set, which is most important.

● The candidate makes a good effort to develop ideas, and does not just stick to basic statements – see the words and phrases underlined.

● There is quite a lot of repetition: être is used six times, j'aime three times and il y a twice. The candidate could have used se trouve instead of est in line 5, and je trouve les profs instead of les profs sont in line 21.

● This letter is of about Grade C standard. To get really high marks, you need greater variety of constructions, more complex expressions of opinion (look back at GOING FURTHER for examples) and, in particular, a mix of tenses. Even to get a Grade C you need to refer to past, present and future in your written exam. There could easily have been reference to the past (for example l'année passée j'ai étudié l'espagnol) and/or the future (for example en première je vais faire les sciences) when writing about school subjects.

You may now like to try writing your own letter, using the above sample and the other examples in this chapter for help.

CHAPTER 2

A LA MAISON/ LES MEDIA

HOME LIFE & MEDIA

LA MAISON

les pièces	rooms
la cuisine	kitchen
la salle à manger	dining room
la salle de séjour	sitting room
les WC	toilet
la cave	cellar
le rez-de-chaussée	ground floor
le premier étage	first floor

LE MENAGE

faire...	to do...
la cuisine	the cooking
les courses	the shopping
le jardinage	the gardening
le ménage	the housework
la vaisselle	the washing-up
le lit	(to make) the bed
laver	to wash
passer l'aspirateur	to vacuum
aider	to help

LES REPAS

le petit déjeuner	breakfast
le déjeuner	lunch
le goûter	tea
le dîner	dinner

WHAT YOU NEED TO KNOW

J'habite une petite maison.	I live in a small house.
Tu habites près du collège?	Do you live near school?
C'est pratique.	It's convenient/handy.
Mon frère habite un grand appartement.	My brother lives in a big flat.
Son adresse est trente-six rue de la Gare.	His address is 36 rue de la Gare.
Ma sœur habite un village à la campagne.	My sister lives in a village in the country.
Nous habitons en centre-ville.	We live in the town centre.
Mon ami habite à côté de chez moi.	My friend lives next door to me.
C'est une maison à deux étages.	It's a two-storey house.
C'est une vieille maison.	It's an old house.
L'appartement est neuf.	The flat is new.
Derrière la maison, il y a un jardin.	Behind the house there is a garden.
Devant la villa, il y a un garage.	In front of the villa there is a garage.
Nous avons trois chambres.	We have three bedrooms.
Dans le salon, nous avons une télévision.	In the living-room, we have a television.
Les murs sont bleus.	The walls are blue.
Je range ma chambre.	I tidy my room.
Elle fait le ménage.	She does the housework.
J'aide ma mère.	I help my mother.
Tous les dimanches, je lave la voiture.	Every Sunday, I wash the car.
Ma sœur débarrasse la table.	My sister clears the table.
Je peux téléphoner en France?	Can I telephone France?
Le déjeuner est à quelle heure?	What time is lunch?
J'ai oublié ma brosse à dents.	I've forgotten my toothbrush.
J'ai besoin de dentifrice.	I need toothpaste.
Tu as du savon/une serviette?	Do you have any soap/a towel?
Je n'ai plus de shampooing.	I have no shampoo left.
La douche ne marche pas.	The shower doesn't work.
Où est ma chambre?	Where is my bedroom?
Elle est en face de la salle de bains.	It's opposite the bathroom.
Tu prends le petit déjeuner?	Are you having breakfast?
Tu veux mettre la table?	Will you set the table?
Où se trouvent les assiettes?	Where are the plates?
D'habitude, je me lève à sept heures.	Usually, I get up at seven o'clock.
Elle se couche à onze heures.	She goes to bed at eleven.
Tu as vu le film à la télé?	Did you see the film on TV?
J'ai regardé le match.	I watched the match.
Il écoute souvent la radio.	He often listens to the radio.
Qu'est-ce qu'il y a à la télé?	What's on TV?

QUESTIONS/PROMPTS

Où habites-tu?	Décris ta chambre.
Tu habites une maison ou un appartement?	Que fais-tu dans ta chambre?
Où se trouve ta maison?	Que fais-tu pour aider à la maison?
Parle-moi de ta maison.	Tu regardes souvent la télévision?
Il y a combien de chambres?	Quelles sont tes émissions préférées?

LES MEUBLES

une armoire	wardrobe	un placard	cupboard	un lave-vaisselle	dishwasher
un canapé	a settee	une table	table	une machine à laver	washing machine
une chaise	chair	un congélateur	freezer	une chaîne-stéréo	hi-fi
un fauteuil	armchair	une cuisinière	cooker	un magnétoscope	video
une lampe	lamp	un four	oven	une radio	radio
un lit	bed	(à micro-ondes)	(microwave)	un réveil	alarm clock
un miroir	mirror	un frigo	fridge		

Check yourself

QUESTIONS

Q1 Write in the missing word. (Look at pages 13–14 before you do this.)

a) Mon frère _____ l'aspirateur.
b) Tu _____ ta chambre?
c) Nous _____ papa dans le jardin.
d) Ma sœur _____ les fenêtres.
e) J'_____ une télévision dans ma chambre.
f) Tu _____ la vaisselle?
g) Tu _____ besoin d'une serviette?
h) Tu _____ le dîner à quelle heure?

Q2 Put the items (in the box) in the right room.

LA CHAMBRE
a) _____
b) _____

LA CUISINE
c) _____
d) _____
e) _____

LA SALLE DE SEJOUR
f) _____

| le frigo   un fauteuil   un placard |
| la cuisinière   une armoire   un réveil |

REMEMBER! Cover the answers if you want to.

ANSWERS

A1
a) passe
b) ranges/nettoies
c) aidons
d) lave
e) ai
f) fais
g) as
h) prends

A2 LA CHAMBRE
a) une armoire
b) un réveil

LA CUISINE
c) le frigo
d) un placard
e) la cuisinière

LA SALLE DE SEJOUR
f) un fauteuil

TUTORIAL

T1
a) A singular er verb will always end in -e except after tu.
b/f/g/h) After tu, any er verb will end in -es, and all verbs will end in -s.
c) Apart from être, all verbs end in -ons after nous.
e) It is a very common mistake to write (or say) je when you mean j'ai.
g) If you don't know the present tense of avoir, learn it now.

T2 You will often need to interpret pictures and other visuals. You have to do this carefully, taking account of all the information you have. You need to make sure that you don't allow one mistake to lead to another. If you are copying words into the right place, make sure you spell them correctly.

LES OPINIONS

C'est/c'était...	It is/it was...
affreux/affreuse	awful
drôle	funny
formidable	great
génial	wonderful

GOING FURTHER

L'école est à deux cents mètres de chez moi.	School is two hundred metres from home.
Le centre-ville est à deux kilomètres.	The town centre is two kilometres away.
J'ai une très belle chambre. Elle est verte et blanche.	I have a lovely room. It is green and white.
Dans ma chambre, je fais mes devoirs et je regarde la télé.	In my (bed)room, I do my homework and I watch TV.
Mes deux petites sœurs partagent une chambre.	My two little sisters share a room.
Je partage ma chambre avec mon frère.	I share my room with my brother.
Tous les dimanches, je dois faire le repassage. J'ai horreur de ça!	Every Sunday I have to do the ironing. I hate it!
Nous aidons tous à la maison – mes frères, ma sœur et mon père.	We all help with the housework – my brothers, my sister and my father.
Mon frère n'aide jamais à la maison. Il dit que c'est le travail des filles.	My brother never helps in the house. He says it's girls' work.
Et mes parents sont d'accord!	And my parents agree!
Il me reste très peu de savon.	I haven't got much soap left.
A la télé, je préfère les émissions sportives.	On TV I prefer sports programmes.
Je peux allumer la télé? Ça ne vous gêne pas?	Can I put the TV on? Do you mind?
Dans le journal, je lis des articles sur la politique.	In the newspaper, I read articles about politics.
Je trouve les films sous-titrés très ennuyeux.	I find sub-titled films very boring.
Hier, j'ai vu une émission sur les lions. C'était passionnant.	Yesterday, I saw a programme on lions. It was fascinating.
Je regarde toujours le journal de vingt heures.	I always watch the eight o'clock news.
Chaque semaine, j'achète un magazine de mode.	Every week I buy a fashion magazine.

LES EMISSIONS DE TELE/DE RADIO

les informations	the news
un jeu télévisé	quiz show
un documentaire	documentary
une émission comique	a comedy programme
une émission musicale	a music programme
la météo	weather forecast
une publicité	an advert
un feuilleton	a soap/serial
un dessin animé	a cartoon
une pièce de théâtre	a play
en version française (en VF)	in French
en version originale (en VO)	in original soundtrack

les informations

un documentaire

la météo

un dessin animé

une pièce de théâtre

When you are talking about your favourite programmes, try to use words like these, rather than English titles – *J'adore EastEnders* won't mean much to most French people, but *J'aime les feuilletons* will!

HOW THE GRAMMAR WORKS

One of the clear differences between a Grade C/D piece of writing and a Grade A piece is the accuracy of the verbs. The more verbs you can use correctly, the higher the mark you will get, not only for accuracy but also for Use of Language, where you get credit for the variety of your language. If you are limited to half a dozen verbs which you know well, your work is likely to be repetitive.

VERBS – PRESENT TENSE

In English we can say:

1 **I eat** chocolate.
2 **I am** eating some chocolate.
3 **I do eat** chocolate sometimes.

The verb in each of these sentences in French would be the same:

1 *Je mange* du chocolat.
2 *Je mange* du chocolat.
3 *Je mange* quelquefois du chocolat.

The present tense in French works by a system of endings.
There are three main types of verbs:

● *er* verbs, like *regarder* (to watch)

● *ir* verbs, like *finir* (to finish)

● *re* verbs, like *vendre* (to sell)

As well as making sure you use the right personal pronoun (*je*, *tu*, etc.), you need to get the ending right too. This is most important when you are writing, as it will affect your accuracy mark. In speaking, the question of endings doesn't make as much difference, since in the singular, whatever the ending, the sound will be the same for most verbs.

Look at these examples. Notice that the underlined words all sound the same for each verb:

er verbs

regarder	to watch
je <u>regarde</u>	I watch, I am watching, I do watch
*tu <u>regardes</u>	you watch, you are watching, you do watch
il/elle/on <u>regarde</u>	he/she/one watches, etc.
nous regardons	we watch, we are watching, we do watch
*vous regardez	you watch, you are watching, you do watch
ils/elles <u>regardent</u>	they watch, they are watching, they do watch

**For the difference between *tu* and *vous*, see Chapter 6 (page 45).
Note:

● Verbs ending in *-ger* add *-e* in front of the *-ons* ending:
   nous mangeons

● Verbs ending in *-cer* add a cedilla under the *c* before the *-ons* ending:
   nous commençons

ir verbs

finir	to finish
je <u>finis</u>	I finish, etc.
tu <u>finis</u>	you finish, etc.
il/elle/on <u>finit</u>	he/she/one finishes, etc.
nous finissons	we finish, etc.
vous finissez	you finish, etc.
ils/elles finissent	they finish, etc.

re verbs

vendre	to sell
je <u>vends</u>	I sell, etc.
tu <u>vends</u>	you sell, etc.
il/elle/on <u>vend</u>	he/she/one sells, etc.
nous vendons	we sell, etc.
vous vendez	you sell, etc.
ils/elles vendent	they sell, etc.

Some *er* verbs with minor irregularities

acheter	to buy

j'achète – tu achètes – il/elle achète – nous achetons – vous achetez – ils/elles achètent

Some other verbs which gain an accent except after *nous* and *vous*:

geler	to freeze
mener	to lead
se lever	to get up
se promener	to go for a walk

....

espérer	to hope

j'espère – tu espères – il/elle espère – nous espérons – vous espérez – ils/elles espèrent

Some other verbs where the accent *é* changes to *è* except after *nous* and *vous*:

répéter	to repeat
s'inquiéter	to worry

....

jeter	to throw

je jette – tu jettes – il/elle jette – nous jetons – vous jetez – ils/elles jettent

Some other verbs where a consonant doubles except after *nous* and *vous*:

appeler	to call
s'appeler	to be called

....

envoyer	to send

j'envoie – tu envoies – il/elle envoie – nous envoyons – vous envoyez – ils/elles envoient

Some other verbs where the *y* changes to *i* except after *nous* and *vous*:

appuyer	to lean/press
balayer	to sweep
essayer	to try
essuyer	to wipe

COMMON REFLEXIVE VERBS

se baigner	to bathe
se coucher	to go to bed
se débrouiller	to cope/get by
se dépêcher	to hurry
se déshabiller	to get undressed
se détendre	to relax
se fâcher	to get angry
s'habiller	to get dressed
se moquer (de)	to make fun (of)
se raser	to have a shave
se reposer	to rest
se réveiller	to wake up
se terminer	to end
se tromper	to make a mistake
se tromper (de)	to get the wrong number (train, etc.)
se trouver	to be (situated)

REFLEXIVE VERBS

A slightly different group of verbs, many of which we use in order to talk about our daily routine, is reflexive verbs. Most of these follow the pattern of *er* verbs, but they have an extra pronoun. Look at this example:

se laver	**to have a wash**
je me lave	I have a wash
tu te laves	you have a wash
il/elle/on se lave	he/she/one has a wash
nous nous lavons	we have a wash
vous vous lavez	you have a wash
ils/elles se lavent	they have a wash

The reflexive pronoun always changes with the subject pronoun:
je me ; tu te; il/elle se; nous nous; vous vous; ils/elles se.

The verb endings are the same as for ordinary *er* verbs.

COMMON IRREGULAR VERBS

Unfortunately, there are a lot of verbs in French which don't really follow any pattern, and which therefore need to be learnt individually. You will find a list of those you are likely to meet on pages 182–184, but here are a few you absolutely cannot do without.

avoir – to have
j'ai
tu as
il/elle/on a
nous avons
vous avez
ils/elles ont

être – to be
je suis
tu es
il/elle/on est
nous sommes
vous êtes
ils/elles sont

aller – to go
je vais
tu vas
il/elle/on va
nous allons
vous allez
ils/elles vont

faire – to make/do
je fais
tu fais
il/elle/on fait
nous faisons
vous faites
ils/elles font

prendre – to take
je prends
tu prends
il/elle/on prend
nous prenons
vous prenez
ils/elles prennent

sortir – to go out
je sors
tu sors
il/elle/on sort
nous sortons
vous sortez
ils/elles sortent

venir – to come
je viens
tu viens
il/elle/on vient
nous venons
vous venez
ils/elles viennent

vouloir – to want
je veux
tu veux
il/elle/on veut
nous voulons
vous voulez
ils/elles veulent

Note that there are groups of verbs which follow a similar pattern:

Like **prendre:**
apprendre — to learn
comprendre — to understand

Like **sortir:**
partir — to leave

Like **venir:**
devenir — to become
revenir — to come back
se souvenir (de) — to remember

Check yourself

QUESTIONS

Q1 | **You are staying with a French family. How would you find out...?**

a) ...where the bathroom is.
b) ...how far away the town centre is.
c) ...if you can phone home.
d) ...if you can have a bath.
e) ...what time lunch is.

Q2 | **Put these sentences in the right order. Then add linking words and extra detail to make them into a full account.**

a) Je me lave.
b) Je prends le petit déjeuner.
c) Je me lève à sept heures et demie.
d) Je vais à l'école.
e) Je m'habille.

REMEMBER! Cover the answers if you want to.

ANSWERS

A1 |
a) Où se trouve la salle de bains?
b) Le centre-ville, c'est à quelle distance?
c) Je peux téléphoner chez moi?
d) Je peux prendre un bain?
e) Le déjeuner, c'est à quelle heure?

A2 | Best order: c - a - e - b - d

Full account:
Le matin, je me lève à sept heures et demie et je me lave <u>dans la salle de bains</u>. <u>Puis</u> je m'habille <u>dans ma chambre</u>, <u>et</u> je prends <u>mon</u> petit déjeuner <u>dans la cuisine</u>. <u>A huit heures et demie</u> je vais à l'école.

TUTORIAL

T1 |
a) When asking where places are, the French will often use *Où se trouve?* rather than *Où est?*
b/e) In questions, the French will often use *c'est* or *ce sont* as well as the noun.
c/d) After *Je peux* (*or any other part of* pouvoir) *the next verb will always be in the infinitive* (er/ir/re).

T2 | The addition of the underlined items, especially in the Speaking Test, will improve your marks by turning a series of brief answers into a full, though still simple, account.

EXAM PRACTICE

 **LISTENING**

1 Find Chapter 2 – Exam Practice Listening on the CD. Listen to the French (Track 3) twice, then answer the following questions.

Réponds à ces questions en français.

1 Que fait Salim pour aider à la maison? [2 marks]

2 Pourquoi est-ce que Noëlle ne fait rien à la maison? [1 mark]

3 Pourquoi est-ce que c'est le frère de Michel qui fait le ménage? [2 marks]

You will find the transcript and answers,
with examiner's comments, on page 195.

You will find the transcript and answers, with examiner's comments, on page 195.

READING

2 Look at this extract from a television magazine, then answer the questions which follow.

TF1	A2	FR3
18h15 LA ROUE DE LA FORTUNE Jeu télévisé	18h00 LE GRAND MATCH Film 1974 sous-titré	19h10 LE CHEF D'ORCHESTRE Bande dessinée
18h40 LE FLIC Film 1987 avec Jean-Paul Belmondo	20h40 USHUAIA Les forêts du Brésil. Vont-elles disparaître à jamais? Reportage	19h30 ADIEU POULET Policier 1952 en noir et blanc avec Jean Gabin
21h45 TARATATA Emission spéciale sur la chanson française – présentée par Nagui	22h30 CULTIVEZ VOTRE JARDIN Comment réussir un tout petit terrain en ville	23h10 LA COUPE DU MONDE Les meilleurs moments du tournoi 78

Remplis les blancs dans les phrases suivantes avec la chaîne (TF1/A2/FR3) et l'heure.

1 Marie s'intéresse à l'environnement. Elle regarde _____ à _____ .

2 Alexandre adore tout ce qui est sport. Il regarde _____ à _____ .

3 Maryse aime les émissions musicales. Elle regarde _____ à _____ .

4 Luc adore les vieux films français. Il regarde _____ à _____ .

You will find the answers and examiner's comments on page 196.

 3 Find Chapter 2 – Exam Practice Speaking on the CD. Listen to the conversation (Track 4). Think for a moment about what you have heard. Then read the examiner's comments. Did any of the comments made occur to you?

 **SPEAKING** **H**

*You will find the transcript and
examiner's comments on page 196.*

Now think about some of the things you might want to say in French about your house. The following questions will help you to plan your answers.

Où habites-tu?
Parle-moi de ta maison.
Décris ta chambre.

Look back at the previous sections for help. You may also want to play the CD again, or look at the transcript on page 196.

---

4 Answer the following question in French, then compare your version with the sample answer on page 197.

WRITING **H**

Tu viens de déménager. Ecris une lettre à ton/ta correspondant(e) français(e) Dominique pour lui décrire ta nouvelle maison.

Parle:

– de ta chambre

– des autres pièces

– du jardin

– de la situation de la maison

– d'une chose que tu vas acheter pour ta nouvelle maison

Fais une comparaison entre ta nouvelle maison et la maison où tu habitais.

Pose à ton/ta correspondant(e) une question sur sa chambre.

*You will find the sample student's answer and
examiner's comments on page 197.*

CHAPTER 3

LA SANTE, LA FORME & LA NOURRITURE

HEALTH, FITNESS & FOOD

AVOIR

avoir besoin (de)	to need
avoir chaud	to be warm/hot
avoir faim	to be hungry
avoir de la fièvre	to have a temperature
avoir froid	to be cold
avoir mal (à)	to have a pain (in)
avoir raison	to be right
avoir soif	to be thirsty
avoir sommeil	to be sleepy
avoir tort	to be wrong

WHAT YOU NEED TO KNOW

La santé

Ça va (mieux).
J'ai mal à la tête.

Ma sœur a mal au bras.
Tu as mal aux dents?
Je me suis cassé le nez.
Elle s'est cassé le doigt.
Je me suis fait mal à la jambe.
Il s'est fait mal au pied.
Ça fait mal, (là).
Elle est enrhumée.
Il a la grippe.
Hé! Attention!
Au secours! Aidez-moi!
Il faut aller chez le médecin.
Ma mère va à la pharmacie.
Je voudrais un rendez-vous avec le dentiste.
Je suis allergique à l'aspirine.

La nourriture

J'adore le poulet.
Je n'aime pas tellement le chou.
Tu me passes le sel/le poivre, s'il te plaît?
Je n'ai pas de fourchette.
Monsieur/Mademoiselle/Madame, s'il vous plaît.

Je voudrais une table pour quatre personnes.
Je voudrais le menu à 75 francs.
Vous pouvez me donner la carte, s'il vous plaît?
Le service est compris?
Où sont les toilettes/les téléphones?

L'addition, s'il vous plaît.
Pour commencer, je prends du jambon.
Comme plat principal, je voudrais la truite.
Qu'est-ce que vous avez comme dessert?

Health

I'm fine (better).
I have a headache (a pain in my head).
My sister's arm hurts.
Do you have toothache?
I've broken my nose.
She's broken her finger.
I've hurt my leg.
He's hurt his foot.
It hurts, (there).
She has a cold.
He has flu.
Hoy! Watch out!
Help! Help me!
You must go to the doctor's.
My mother's going to the chemist's.
I'd like an appointment with the dentist.
I'm allergic to aspirin.

Food

I love chicken.
I don't much like cabbage.
Will you pass the salt/pepper, please?
I haven't got a fork.
(to attract the waiter's attention)

I'd like a table for four.

I'd like the 75 franc menu.
Can you give me the menu, please?

Is the service charge included?
Where are the toilets/the telephones?
Can I have the bill, please.
To start, I'll have some ham.
For my main course, I'll have trout.
What sort of puddings do you have?

A TABLE

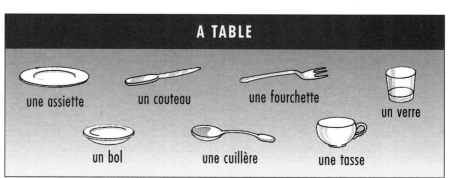

une assiette   un couteau   une fourchette   un verre

un bol   une cuillère   une tasse

LE CORPS HUMAIN

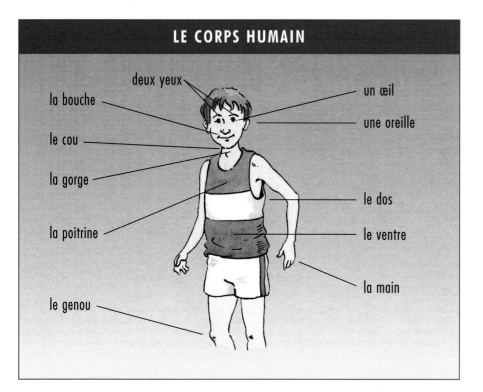

deux yeux

un œil

une oreille

la bouche

le cou

la gorge

la poitrine

le dos

le ventre

la main

le genou

A LA CARTE

un croque-monsieur	a toasted ham & cheese sandwich
les crudités	salad of raw vegetables
les fruits de mer	sea-food
un hors-d'œuvre	starter
le plat du jour	today's special
le potage du jour	soup of the day

QUESTIONS/PROMPTS

Qu'est-ce que vous aimez manger?
Il y a quelque chose que vous n'aimez pas?
Quel est votre plat préféré?
Que faites-vous pour garder la forme?
Est-ce que vous mangez sain?
Vous aimez la cuisine française?
Vous allez souvent au restaurant?

Check yourself

QUESTIONS

`Q1` **Tell the doctor what the problem is.**

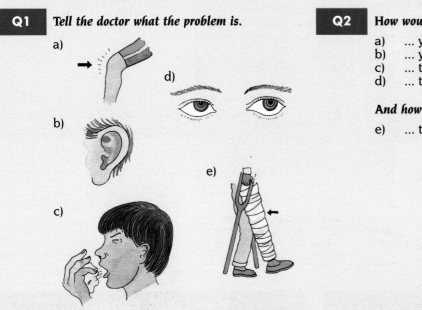

a)

b)

c)

d)

e)

`Q2` **How would you tell your penfriend ...?**

a)   ... you haven't got a knife.
b)   ... you don't really like chicken.
c)   ... that you are not hungry.
d)   ... that you need an aspirin.

And how would you ask him/her ...?

e)   ... to pass you a spoon.

REMEMBER! Cover the answers if you want to.

ANSWERS

`A1`
a)   J'ai mal au genou.
b)   J'ai mal à l'oreille.
c)   Je suis enrhumé(e).
d)   J'ai mal aux yeux.
e)   Je me suis cassé la jambe.

`A2`
a)   Je n'ai pas de couteau.
b)   Je n'aime pas vraiment le poulet.
c)   Je n'ai pas faim.
d)   J'ai besoin d'une aspirine.
e)   Tu me passes une cuillère, s'il te plaît?

TUTORIAL

`T1`
a)   Use au *because* genou *is masculine.*
b)   Remember l' *before a vowel.*
c)   Symptoms are not always expressed by avoir mal. *You need the correct part of* être *here – and remember, if you are female, to add an -e to* enrhumé.
d)   Did you remember the unusual plural of œil?
e)   Because of the reflexive pronoun me, *don't use the possessive* ma *in front of* jambe.

`T2`
a)   Remember to use de *after* ne ... pas.
b)   Don't forget that you need to include the definite article (le) *here.*
d)   J'ai besoin *is always followed by* de.
e)   Use tu (*and therefore* s'il te plaît) *to your penfriend. To his/her mother you would say* Vous me passez une cuillère, s'il vous plaît?.

GOING FURTHER

Je me suis fait mal au genou en jouant au tennis.	I hurt my knee while playing tennis.
Prenez ces comprimés trois fois par jour, après les repas.	Take these tablets 3 times a day after meals.
Je vais vous donner une ordonnance. Prenez deux cuillerées du sirop avant de vous coucher.	I'll give you a prescription. Take two spoonfuls of the linctus before you go to bed.
Qu'est-ce que c'est exactement, la bouillabaisse?	What is bouillabaisse exactly?
C'est une spécialité de la région.	It's a speciality of the area.
C'est une soupe de poisson.	It's a fish soup.
Tu en veux encore?	Would you like some more?
Non, merci. Ça suffit.	No, thank you. I've had enough.
Oui, je veux bien. C'était vraiment délicieux.	Yes, I'd love some. It was really delicious.
On se met dehors, à la terrasse?	Shall we sit outside, on the terrace?
Mon steak n'est pas assez cuit.	My steak isn't cooked enough.
Pour la santé, il faut manger équilibré – du pain, des céréales et pas trop de matières grasses, ni de choses sucrées.	For your health, you must eat a balanced diet – bread, cereals and not too much fat, or sweet things.
Il faut aussi mener une vie active.	You also have to lead an active life.

One of the skills which you are expected to have at Higher Level is the ability to cope with problems, and to handle the unexpected. This is particularly important in the role-plays, where you might have to return something you have bought, complain about something, or choose something else because your first choice is unavailable. Make sure you know ways of:

● apologising: *Je regrette, .../Excusez-moi, .../Je suis désolé(e), ... mais ...* .

● complaining: *Je voudrais voir le patron./Je voudrais me plaindre./Je ne suis pas satisfait(e)*.

● saying what is wrong: *... ne marche pas./Il y a un trou./... est de la mauvaise couleur (taille)*.

● negotiating: *Vous pouvez me faire une réduction?/Je voudrais un autre café*.

● choosing alternatives: *Alors, je prendrai une glace au citron./Bien, donnez-moi un sandwich au fromage*.

A LA PHARMACIE

Le médicament	medicine
la crème (solaire)	(sun) cream
le sparadrap	sticking plaster

SE PLAINDRE

brûlé	burnt
froid	cold
immangeable	uneatable
lent	slow
sale	dirty

COMMENT?

bien cuit	well done
à point	medium, just right
saignant	rare
nature	plain
à la française	French-style
grillé	grilled
vapeur	boiled

HOW THE GRAMMAR WORKS

NOUNS

Most French nouns, like most English nouns, make their plural by adding *-s*:
  une tasse – a cup
  deux tasses – two cups

There are exceptions to this rule.
Nouns ending in *-al* make their plural in *-aux*:
  un journal – a newspaper
  deux journaux – two newspapers

Nouns ending in *-eau* make their plural by adding *-x*:
  un gâteau – a cake
  deux gâteaux – two cakes

Nouns which end in *-s* stay the same in the plural:
  un tas – a heap
  des tas – heaps

However, the most important thing to remember about French nouns is that they are always either masculine or feminine. Since the gender affects all the words that go with nouns (adjectives, pronouns, articles), you should always learn any new nouns together with a word (*un/une* or *le/la*) which tells you whether the noun is masculine or feminine:

> *le lait* (masculine) – milk
> *la viande* (feminine) – meat
> *un abricot* (masculine) – apricot
> *une assiette* (feminine) – plate

When you are using a dictionary to find a noun you don't know or have forgotten, it will always tell you whether the noun is masculine or feminine – though sometimes it may be in code:

> *ananas nm* – pineapple (*nm* = masculine noun)
> *poire nf* – pear (*nf* = feminine noun)

It's worth remembering that nouns referring to male people are masculine:

> *un neveu* – a nephew

and that those referring to female people are feminine:

> *une nièce* – a niece

Otherwise, you simply have to learn the gender of nouns.

INDEFINITE ARTICLES

Un/une (a) and the plural *des* (some) are used in the same way as their English equivalents, but you have to remember to use *un* before masculine singular nouns, and *une* before feminine singular nouns. Also, when 'some' is singular, you need to use:

- *du* before masculine words:
  Vous voulez du sucre? – Do you want some sugar?

- *de la* before feminine words:
  Je vais acheter de la confiture. – I'm going to buy some jam.

- *de l'* before words which begin with a vowel:
  Je voudrais de l'eau minérale. – I'd like some mineral water.

Un/une are, however, usually left out when talking about someone's job:

> *Mon frère est chef de cuisine.*

All the above words are replaced by *de* after a negative:

> *Je n'ai pas de chien/de frères/de café.*   – I haven't a dog/any brothers/
>   any coffee.

DEFINITE ARTICLES

In most cases where the English would use 'the', the French would use:
le before a masculine singular noun
> *le menu*

la before a feminine singular noun
> *la table*

l' before a singular noun (masculine or feminine) beginning with a vowel
> *l'oreille* [f]; *l'œil* [m]

les before a plural noun (masculine or feminine)
> *les yeux* [m]; *les jambes* [f]

However, the French also use the definite article to talk about something in general, while in English we leave it out:

> *J'adore le chocolat.* – I love chocolate.
> *Je n'aime pas les animaux.* – I don't like animals.

When the words *à* (to/at) and *de* (of) come in front of the definite article, they combine in the following way:

> *à + le = au*   *de + le = du*
> *à + les = aux*   *de + les = des*

PRESENT PARTICIPLE

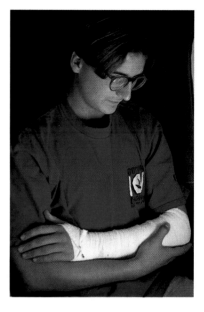

This form of the verb is used to show that one action happens at the same time as another:

> Je me suis cassé le bras en faisant du ski.
> – I broke my arm while I was skiing.

> En rentrant au bureau, j'ai trouvé beaucoup de messages.
> – On going back to the office, I found lots of messages.

The present participle is formed by removing *-ons* from the present tense of the verb, and adding *-ant*.

> REGARDER: (*nous*) regardons – regardant
> FAIRE: (*nous*) faisons – faisant

As in the examples above, the present participle usually has *en* in front of it.

Check yourself

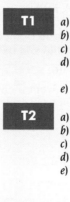

QUESTIONS

Q1 *In a restaurant, you have some complaints. What do you say when ...?*

a) ... your trout isn't cooked enough.
b) ... the service was very slow.
c) ... your coffee is cold.
d) ... there is a mistake in the bill.
e) ... the chips are burnt.

Q2 *Complete the following sentences.*

a) Je vais aller _____ cinéma ce soir.
b) Nous n'avons pas _____ carottes.
c) Vous avez _____ sandwichs?
d) Je voudrais _____ confiture.
e) Donnez-moi une glace _____ vanille.

REMEMBER! Cover the answers if you want to.

ANSWERS

A1
a) Ma truite n'est pas assez cuite.
b) Le service était très lent.
c) Mon café est froid.
d) Il y a une erreur dans l'addition.
e) Les frites sont brûlées.

A2
a) au
b) de
c) des
d) de la
e) à la

TUTORIAL

T1
a) Truite *is feminine, so* ma *and* cuite *must agree.*
b) *Remember to use a past tense.*
c) Café *is masculine, so use* mon.
d) *When you check a word in the dictionary, make sure you check its gender.*
e) Frites *is feminine plural, so* brûlées *must agree.*

T2
a) *It's* le cinéma, *and* à + le = au.
b) *After a negative,* des *becomes* de.
c) *'Some' (plural) =* des.
d) Confiture *is feminine.*
e) *To describe a flavour or a filling, use* à:
(glace) à la menthe – *mint (ice-cream)*
(tarte) aux fraises – *strawberry (tart)*
(sandwich) au jambon – *ham (sandwich)*
(saucisson) à l'ail – *garlic (sausage)*

EXAM PRACTICE

F **H** **LISTENING**

1 Find Chapter 3 – Exam Practice Listening on the CD.
Listen to the French (Track 5) twice, then answer the questions.

Pour chaque personne, indiquez le symptôme (choisissez la bonne
image et écrivez la lettre), et donnez un autre détail.

Personne	Symptôme	Autre détail
1		
2		
3		

You will find the transcript and answers,
with examiner's comments, on page 198.

F **H** **SPEAKING**

2 Look at the situation below, and think what you might say. Then find
Chapter 3 – Exam Practice Speaking on the CD and listen to the role-play
(Track 6). Don't forget, most role-plays will include an unexpected bit –
one that you have not been able to prepare in advance. Here, it is **c)**.

You are speaking to the waiter in a café.

– You want a cup of coffee.
– You want to know if they do meals.
– You want to know where the toilets are.

a) café

b) manger?

c) Répondez à la question.

d) toilettes?

You will find the transcript and
examiner's comments on page 198.

3 Read this article, then answer the questions which follow it.

Mangez sain!

Après de longues recherches, voici les conseils des médecins en ce qui concerne votre régime quotidien:

Le petit déjeuner:
C'est le premier repas de la journée – il vous donne de l'énergie pour bien travailler, il vous aide à vous concentrer. De préférence, vous prendrez une boisson à base de lait, et des tartines avec de la confiture, ou un bol de céréales, mais l'important, c'est de manger quelque chose.

Le déjeuner:
Prenez un repas équilibré – viande ou poisson et légumes – si possible, mais sinon, un bon sandwich, ça va!

Le repas du soir:
D'abord, essayez de manger de bonne heure – pas après huit heures – et assez légèrement. Il est plus difficile de brûler les calories quand vous dormez!

En dehors des repas:
Buvez de l'eau plusieurs fois par jour!

Si vous devez grignoter, prenez un fruit!

A éviter: excès de café et d'alcool; les boissons gazeuses; les choses sucrés.

Enfin, un peu d'exercice tous les jours, et vous dépasserez facilement les cent ans!

Maintenant, répondez à ces questions en français.

D'après l'article:

1 Quel est le repas le plus important?
2 A quel repas doit-on manger le plus?
3 Quand est-ce qu'on doit dîner?
4 En plus de la nourriture, qu'est-ce qui est important pour se maintenir en forme?

Maintenant, cochez les bonnes cases dans la grille.

	à éviter	modérément	important
biscuits			
vin			
eau			
lait			
coca cola			

You will find the answers and examiner's comments on page 199.

4 Read the article in Question 3 again, and write to the newspaper in French. Compare your version with the sample answer on page 199.

Vous avez lu l'article M*angez sain!*. Vous écrivez une lettre au journal.

– Parlez de ce que vous mangez tous les jours.
– Dites si vous mangez sain (ou pas). Pourquoi?
– Quelles sont les autres choses qui sont bonnes ou mauvaises pour la santé?
– Dites si vous êtes en forme. Si oui, qu'est-ce que vous faites? Sinon, qu'est-ce que vous allez faire?

Ecrivez environ 150 mots.

You will find the sample answer, and examiner's comments, on page 199.

CHAPTER 4

MOI, MA FAMILLE ET MES AMIS

SELF, FAMILY & FRIENDS

LA FAMILLE

un bébé	baby
un cousin	cousin (male)
une cousine	cousin (female)
le mari	husband
la mère	mother
un neveu	nephew
une nièce	niece
les parents	parents
le père	father
le beau-père	step-father

LES CHEVEUX

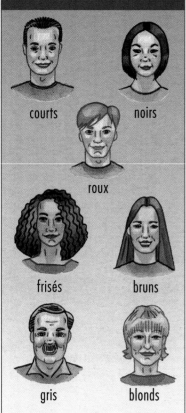

courts / noirs / roux / frisés / bruns / gris / blonds

WHAT YOU NEED TO KNOW

Je m'appelle Claire.	My name is Claire.
J'ai seize ans.	I am 16.
Mon anniversaire est le 9 juin.	My birthday is the 9th June.
Je suis né(e) à Bruges.	I was born in Bruges.
Je suis belge.	I am Belgian.
Je suis fille unique.	I am an only daughter.
Je suis fils unique.	I am an only son.
J'ai un frère et une sœur.	I have a brother and a sister.
Mon frère est plus jeune que moi.	My brother is younger than me.
Il est marié.	He is married.
Sa femme s'appelle Ghislaine.	His wife's name is Ghislaine.
Ça s'écrit G-H-I-S-L-A-I-N-E.	It's spelled G-H-I-S-L-A-I-N-E.
Aujourd'hui c'est leur anniversaire de mariage.	Today it's their wedding anniversary.
Ma sœur est plus âgée que moi.	My sister is older than me.
Elle est divorcée.	She is divorced.
Elle a deux enfants, un garçon et une fille de six mois.	She has two children, a six-month-old boy and girl.
Ce sont des jumeaux.	They are twins.
Dans ma famille il y a cinq personnes.	In my family, there are five people.
Ma grand-mère habite chez nous.	My grandmother lives with us.
Je porte des lunettes.	I wear glasses.
Je suis grand(e).	I am tall.
Mon oncle est mince.	My uncle is thin.
Il a les cheveux longs.	He has long hair.
J'ai les yeux bleus.	I have blue eyes.
Ma tante est petite.	My aunt is small.
Mon grand-père est de taille moyenne.	My grandfather is medium/average height.
Il est très vieux.	He is very old.
Elle est assez vieille.	She is quite old.
Ma demi-sœur est sympa.	My half-sister is nice.
Mon demi-frère est agressif.	My half-brother is aggressive.
Ma belle-mère est aimable.	My step-mother is pleasant.
Ma sœur aînée est méchante.	My older sister is nasty.
Je m'entends bien avec ma famille.	I get on well with my family.
J'aime les sports.	I like sport.
Ma mère déteste la télévision.	My mother hates television.
Elle adore les animaux.	She loves animals.
Nous avons un chat, un chien et deux souris blanches.	We have a cat, a dog and two white mice.

LES ANIMAUX

un cheval	horse
un cobaye	guinea-pig
un lapin	rabbit
un oiseau	bird

DESCRIPTION

beau (belle)	good-looking
gentil(le)	nice/kind
jeune	young
mignon(ne)	cute

LES YEUX

bleus	blue
verts	green
marron	brown

LES NATIONALITES

écossais

gallois

anglais

allemand

français

irlandais

belge

italien(ne)

suisse

américain

QUESTIONS/PROMPTS

Comment t'appelles-tu?
Quel âge as-tu?
C'est quand, ton anniversaire?
Parle-moi de ta famille.
Il y a combien de personnes dans ta famille?
Quel âge a ton frère?
Tu t'entends bien avec ta mère?
Comment est ta sœur?
Tes parents sont séparés?
Tu habites avec ton père?

Check yourself

QUESTIONS

Q1 **How would you say in French?**

a) My aunt lives with us.
b) He was born on the 23rd September.
c) She wears glasses.
d) I get on well with my parents.
e) She has grey hair.

Q2 **Correct the errors in the English.**

a) Ma sœur a quinze ans. — My sister is five.
b) Elle n'est pas mariée. — She is married.
c) Il s'appelle Louis. — My name is Louis.
d) Mon grand-père a quatre-vingts ans. — My grandfather is 24.

REMEMBER! Cover the answers if you want to.

ANSWERS

A1
a) Ma tante habite chez nous.
b) Il est né le 23 septembre.
c) Elle porte des lunettes.
d) Je m'entends bien avec mes parents.
e) Elle a les cheveux gris.

A2
a) My sister is 15.
b) She is not married.
c) His name is Louis.
d) My grandfather is 80.

TUTORIAL

T1
a) Use *ma* because aunt is female.
b) You don't need to write out numbers, but you do need to know them!
d) Use *mes* because parents are plural.
e) Don't add -s to gris; it already has one.

T2
a/d) Numbers are very easy to confuse, especially in listening:
cinq (5) and quinze (15)
quatre-vingts (80) and vingt-quatre (24).
b) Make sure you don't miss negatives. Again, this is especially easy to do in listening.
c) Pronouns are very important:
je (I); il (he); elle (she)

EXTRA DETAILS

toujours	always
tout le temps	all the time
de temps en temps	from time to time
souvent	often
trop	too
vraiment	really
beaucoup	much/a lot
si	if
parce que	because

GOING FURTHER

Je ne m'entends pas avec mon père. Il est beaucoup trop strict.
I don't get on with my father. He's much too strict.

Ma mère est adorable. Je peux lui parler de tout.
My mother is adorable. I can talk to her about anything.

Mon petit frère m'énerve! On se dispute tout le temps.
My little brother gets on my nerves! We're always arguing.

Nous n'avons pas les mêmes goûts.
We don't have the same tastes.

Je dois toujours rentrer à onze heures. Ce n'est pas juste!
I always have to be home by 11. It's not fair!

Mon frère est vraiment gâté – il peut faire ce qu'il veut.
My brother is really spoilt – he can do as he likes.

Il est plus facile de parler avec mes amis, si j'ai un problème.
It's easier to talk to my friends, if I have a problem.

Ils ont le même âge et ils s'intéressent aux mêmes choses que moi.
They are the same age as me and they are interested in the same things.

Ma petite sœur emprunte toujours mes affaires. Ça m'énerve!
My little sister is always borrowing my things. It drives me mad!

To do well at Higher Level, in both speaking and writing, you must express opinions. Make sure you have some ready-made phrases with which you can say how you feel about things:

> C'est super (great); C'est cool (super); C'est génial (brilliant); C'est nul (rotten); J'en ai marre (I'm fed up with it).

or about people:

> Il est casse-pieds (He gets on my nerves); Elle est égoïste (She's selfish).

HOW THE GRAMMAR WORKS

ADJECTIVES

Adjectives usually come after the word they describe:

> Il a les yeux bleus.

A few adjectives come before the word they describe:

> petit; grand; beau; gros; vieux; jeune

When adjectives are used to describe a female person, or a feminine object, you usually add an -e to the adjective:

> ma petite sœur

However, if the adjective already ends in -e, do not add another:

> Ma sœur est plus jeune que moi.

BUT   Ma sœur est plus âgée que moi (because of the accent é).

When adjectives are used to describe more than one person or thing, you usually add an -s to the adjective:

> J'ai les cheveux courts.

However, if the adjective already ends in -s, do not add another:

> Grand-père a les yeux gris.

Note that nationalities do not have a capital letter in French.

Some adjectives are irregular and do not follow the rules above:

Feminine		Plural	
agressif	agressive	beau	beaux
italien	italienne	vieux	vieux
marron	marron	marron	marron
beau	belle		
gentil	gentille		
gros	grosse		
mignon	mignonne		
vieux	vieille		
blanc	blanche		

MY / YOUR / HIS / HER

Remember to say:

> mon père but ma mère or mes parents
> ton frère but ta sœur or tes cousins

Remember that:

> son oncle can be **his** uncle or **her** uncle.
> sa belle-mère can be **his** step-mother or **her** step-mother.
> ses amis can be **his** friends or **her** friends.

Check yourself

QUESTIONS

Q1 **How would you say in French?**

a) We don't like the same music.
b) I can't come home after half past ten.
c) I get on quite well with my father, but I can't really talk to him.
d) My step-mother is older than my father.
e) Do you get on well with your brothers and sisters?
f) My best friend is called Marie. She is seventeen and she lives with her father. Her parents are divorced.

Q2 **Do these people get on well (✔) or badly (✗) with their family?**

a) Mes parents préfèrent toujours ma sœur – ce n'est pas juste!
b) Je suis fille unique, et mes parents me gâtent. Ils sont vraiment sympa.
c) Moi, je fais partie d'une famille nombreuse – quatre frères et trois sœurs – et c'est une famille très heureuse. Il n'y a jamais de disputes.
d) Ma mère, c'est aussi ma meilleure amie – mais on se dispute de temps en temps.
e) A la maison, c'est vraiment affreux. Heureusement que j'ai mes amis au collège.

REMEMBER! Cover the answers if you want to.

ANSWERS

A1
a) Nous n'aimons pas la même musique.
b) Je ne peux pas rentrer après dix heures et demie.
c) Je m'entends assez bien avec mon père, mais je ne peux pas vraiment lui parler.
d) Ma belle-mère est plus âgée que mon père.
e) Tu t'entends bien avec tes frères et sœurs?
f) Ma meilleure amie s'appelle Marie. Elle a dix-sept ans, et elle habite avec son père. Ses parents sont divorcés.

A2
a) ✗
b) ✔
c) ✔
d) ✔
e) ✗

TUTORIAL

T1
a) *The adjective* même *doesn't change in the singular.*
b) *Note:* il peut *but* je peux.
c) *Little words like* assez *and* vraiment *can really improve your work.*
d) Agée *goes with* belle-mère. *Remember, when you are comparing, put* plus *(or* moins – *less, or* aussi – *as) in front of the adjective, and* que *after it.*
f) *Did you get the adjectives right?*
   Ma meilleure amie; son père; ses parents divorcés.

T2
a) *Even if you didn't understand the rest,* ce n'est pas juste *gives you the answer.*
b) *Use any clues you can: you may never have seen* gâtent, *but look in GOING FURTHER and find* gâté.
c) *Watch for negatives when people are expressing opinions, but be careful.* Il n'y a jamais de disputes *isn't really a negative thing to say.*
d) *Opinions aren't always black or white – people sometimes express both sides of the argument, and you have to draw a conclusion. Are the disputes more important than the* meilleure amie?
e) *Again, you will often hear things which are not relevant to the question – you have to sort it out.*

EXAM PRACTICE

1 Find Chapter 4 – Exam Practice Listening on the CD.
Listen to the French (Track 7) twice, then answer the following question.

Ecoute l'interview avec Eric et Lorraine qui parlent de leur famille.
Complète la grille en français.

	Frères/Sœurs	**Avantage**	**Inconvénient**
Eric			
Lorraine			

*You will find the transcript and answers,
with examiner's comments, on page 200.*

2 Find Chapter 4 – Exam Practice Speaking on the CD. Listen to the
conversation (Track 8). Think for a moment about what you have
heard. Then read the examiner's comments. Did any of these points
occur to you?

You will find the transcript and examiner's comments on page 200.

---

*Now think about some of the things you might want to say in French about your
family. The following questions will help you to plan your answers:*

Tu as des frères et sœurs?
Tu t'entends bien avec eux?
Tu t'entends avec tes parents?

*Look back at the examples in the previous sections for help. You may also want to
play the CD again, or look at the transcript.*

 **H** **READING**

3 Read these two articles, then answer the following questions.

Lis ces deux articles sur la vie de famille. D'après les auteurs, quelles sont les différences entre la vie familiale d'il y a cent ans, et celle d'aujourd'hui?

— LA FAMILLE 1898 —

Quand j'étais petite, nous étions treize à la maison – mes parents, sept sœurs et trois frères, et moi. Pas question, alors, de disputes – et en tout cas on était trop fatigué, car on travaillait à la ferme, même les plus petits, avant et après l'école. Mais malgré l'entassement on s'amusait bien le soir. Maman jouait du piano, et papa chantait, et l'été on faisait des promenades ensemble dans les collines. On vivait vraiment en famille. C'était normal, car on ne voyageait pas – c'était assez rare d'aller au village voisin.

— LA FAMILLE 1998 —

Nous sommes une famille assez typique, je crois, mon père, ma sœur et moi. Maman habite à Paris avec son nouveau mari et ses enfants. Ma sœur est vraiment gâtée – sa chambre est beaucoup plus grande que la mienne, et elle a une télévision. Aussi, elle vient de passer un mois aux Etats-Unis – pour améliorer son anglais, dit-elle! Moi, je suis seulement allé en Bretagne à vélo avec mon ami Luc. Et puis, elle n'aime pas les mêmes disques que moi, et elle me traite comme un enfant. Bref, on se dispute sans cesse, et on se voit le moins possible.

Dans la case, écris **V** (vrai), **F** (faux) ou **?** (on ne sait pas).

1 Les familles étaient plus nombreuses en 1898. ☐
2 Les frères et sœurs s'entendent mieux en 1998. ☐
3 L'école était moins importante en 1898. ☐
4 En 1898 on n'avait pas de distractions. ☐
5 Les enfants sont plus heureux en 1998. ☐

You will find the answers and examiner's comments on page 201.

H **WRITING**

4 Write a short article about the ideal family.

Ecris un petit article sur 'la famille idéale'. N'oublie pas de donner des raisons pour tes opinions.

Sample Student's Answer

Dans ma famille idéale, il y a sept personnes: mes parents, mes grand-parents, mon frère, ma sœur et moi. J'aime habiter avec mes grands-parents. Mon grand-père est plus gentil que mon père.

Puis je voudrais un frère et une sœur – la sœur plus âgée que moi, le frère un peu plus jeune. J'aime avoir un petit frère. Avec une sœur plus agée, je peux parler de mes problèmes, et elle m'aide à faire mes devoirs.

Enfin, mes parents sont compréhensifs, et me donnent beaucoup de liberté et beaucoup d'argent. C'est ma vraie famille? Non. Je suis fils unique, et je ne m'entends pas bien avec mes parents.

EXAMINER'S COMMENTS

- As it stands, this is a good Grade C piece of work, mainly because of its accuracy, but it's rather simple, and all in the present tense. In this sort of piece, think about using the conditional tense: il y aurait (there would be); j'aimerais (I would like). It's useful too if you need to write about what you would do if ....

- Try not to over-use basic constructions like j'aime. In the second paragraph, it would be better to say Ce serait bien d'avoir un petit frère.

- This piece does not include enough reasons and explanations. Say why you like living with your grandparents (Quelquefois je me dispute avec mes parents au sujet de mes résultats scolaires, mais grand-père dit que lui aussi, il était faible en maths) or why you'd like a younger brother (parce qu'on pourrait lui donner des ordres).

- The use of extra words like d'habitude and quelquefois makes your work seem a lot less boring, as well as being more realistic. Parents might be compréhensifs but surely not all the time!

- There are some good things here. It is very accurate for a start, and there are some descriptions and comparisons (Mon grand-père est plus gentil que mon père). It's also well organised, leading from an introduction to an interesting ending.

- However, trying some of the ideas above would give it more variety, and make it a little longer – you should probably aim for 120 to 150 words in this sort of piece.

You may now like to try writing your own letter, using the above sample and the other examples in this chapter to help.

33

CHAPTER 5

LE TEMPS LIBRE, LES LOISIRS, LES VACANCES ET LES FETES

FREE TIME, LEISURE, HOLIDAYS AND SPECIAL OCCASIONS

WHAT YOU NEED TO KNOW

Mon passe-temps préféré, c'est la lecture.	My favourite pastime is reading.
Le sport ne m'intéresse pas.	I'm not interested in sport.
Ça me passionne vraiment.	I'm a real fan.
Je collectionne les timbres.	I collect stamps.
J'adore le bricolage.	I love do-it-yourself.
Le théâtre m'intéresse beaucoup.	I'm very interested in the theatre.
Je passe tout mon temps libre à écouter des disques.	I spend all my free time listening to records.
J'adore les vacances d'hiver.	I love winter holidays.
L'année dernière, je suis allé(e) en Italie.	Last year, I went to Italy.
J'ai passé les vacances de Pâques à Londres.	I spent the Easter holidays in London.
On va à la montagne, ou au bord de la mer?	Shall we go to the mountains, or to the sea-side?
Je préfère aller à l'étranger.	I prefer to go abroad.
Hier, je suis allé(e) au complexe sportif.	Yesterday, I went to the sports centre.
Il y a une piscine, des courts de tennis et un terrain de foot.	There is a swimming pool, tennis courts and a football pitch.
Le soir, j'aime m'amuser.	In the evening, I like to have fun.
Si on allait à la foire?	How about going to the fair?
Au club de jeunes, on peut jouer au tennis de table.	At the youth club, you can play table-tennis.
En été, il est ouvert jusqu'à dix heures du soir.	In summer, it's open till 10 o'clock in the evening.
Les billets coûtent combien?	How much do the tickets cost?
Ce n'est pas cher.	It's not expensive.
Ça coûte quinze francs.	It costs 15 francs.
Ce week-end, c'est la fête du village.	This weekend it's the village festival.
Il y a un 'son et lumière' au château.	There's a 'son et lumière' (sound & light show) at the castle.
Il y a un cirque sur la place.	There is a circus on the square.
Les zoos sont cruels.	Zoos are cruel.
Je ne suis pas d'accord avec toi.	I don't agree with you.
Mes parents me donnent de l'argent de poche.	My parents give me pocket money.
Je reçois cent francs par semaine/par mois.	I get 100 francs a week/a month.

LES PASSE-TEMPS

les cartes	cards
les échecs	chess
les jeux-vidéo	video games
aller à une boum	to go to a party
aller en boîte	to go to a night-club
danser	to dance
faire du camping	to go camping

LES PRIX

enfants	children
adultes	adults
moins de treize ans	under 13
étudiants	students
réductions	reductions
dix pour cent	10 per cent
groupe	group

LES FETES

le jour de Noël	Christmas Day
le jour de l'an	New Year's Day
la fête	person's 'name day'/saint's day (e.g. St David's Day for people called David)
la fête nationale (le quatorze juillet)	the (French) national holiday (14th July)

LES SPORTS

le cyclisme

le foot(ball)

la natation

la planche

les sports d'hiver

le rugby

le ski (nautique)

les sports nautiques

le tennis

la voile

le volley

QUESTIONS/PROMPTS

Quel est ton passe-temps préféré?

Tu préfères le sport ou la musique?

Pourquoi?

Qu'est-ce qu'il y a à faire?

Où as-tu passé les vacances l'été dernier?

Tu reçois combien d'argent de poche?

Check yourself

QUESTIONS

Q1 *Read the following information, then put 'vrai' or 'faux' next to each sentence.*

Au complexe sportif

❖ Prix normal d'entrée 15F par personne.
❖ Offres spéciales ce week-end seulement.
❖ Trois entrées pour le prix de deux.
❖ Réduction de cinquante pour cent pour les groupes de dix.
❖ Etudiants – moins trente pour cent.
❖ Enfants de moins de quinze ans – 5F.

a) Cette offre est valable tous les week-ends.
b) Trois adultes paient 10F par personne.
c) Dix adultes paient 75F en tout.
d) Les étudiants paient 5F par personne.
e) Un enfant de seize ans paie 5F.

Q2 *Match the two halves of the sentences.*

1) Ma passion, c'est les sports nautiques ...
2) Je n'aime pas la lecture ...
3) Je préfère les vacances d'été ...
4) J'adore faire du ski, alors ...
5) Je ne suis pas sportif, ...

a) car j'adore aller à la plage.
b) j'aime mieux lire un roman.
c) j'adore le ski nautique.
d) je trouve les livres ennuyeux.
e) je prends toujours mes vacances en hiver.

ANSWERS

A1
a) faux
b) vrai
c) vrai
d) faux
e) faux

A2
1) – c)
2) – d)
3) – a)
4) – e)
5) – b)

TUTORIAL

T1
a) *You need to spot the word* seulement *(only) to get this right.*
b) *3 for price of 2 = 30F.*
c) *50% off for a group of 10.*
d) *Students only get 30% (5F) off – they pay 10F.*
e) *You have to be under 15 to pay only 5F.*

You need to study the detail very carefully in this sort of question.

GOING FURTHER

Hier, mon oncle nous a emmenés au parc d'attractions.	Yesterday, my uncle took us to the theme park.
Je n'aime pas tellement jouer au foot, mais je vais souvent aux matchs.	I don't much like playing football, but I often go to matches.
Moi, c'est le contraire. Je préfère participer que regarder – ça m'ennuie.	For me, it's the opposite. I'd rather play than watch – it bores me.
J'ai passé d'excellentes vacances en Suisse avec mes amis.	I spent an excellent holiday in Switzerland with my friends.
Moi, je suis allé(e) en vacances avec mes parents. Je ne me suis pas amusé(e) du tout.	I went on holiday with my parents. I didn't enjoy myself at all.
Mes copains/copines reçoivent plus d'argent que moi.	My friends get more money than I do.
Mes parents ne me donnent que cinquante francs par semaine. Ce n'est pas assez!	My parents only give me 50 francs a week. It's not enough!
Je dois acheter tous mes vêtements avec.	I have to buy all my clothes with it.
Il me faut travailler pour gagner mon argent de poche.	I have to work to earn my pocket money.
Si j'avais l'argent, j'irais aux Etats-Unis.	If I had the money, I'd go to the United States.

Create extra impact by stressing what you say. It makes it much
more interesting.

- Change the impact of a negative by adding: *du tout* (at all); *tellement* (particularly); *souvent* (often).

- Point to a contrast by adding *par contre* (on the contrary) or simply *moi* (which stresses 'I').

- Use a variety of negatives: *ne ... jamais* (never); *ne ... que* (only).

HOW THE GRAMMAR WORKS

THE INFINITIVE

This is an important part of the verb in a number of ways. First, it is what you will find in the dictionary. If you come across, for example, *il a expédié* in a reading passage, the nearest thing you will find in the dictionary will be the infinitive *expédier*. The infinitive of all French verbs ends in *-er*, *-ir* or *-re*. It is often translated as 'to ...' (for example *expédier* – to send).

The most common use of the infinitive in a sentence is to enable you to use two verbs together. The second verb will be in the infinitive.

Many common French verbs can be followed immediately by the infinitive:

ADORER	*Elle adore lire.*	She loves reading.
AIMER	*J'aime jouer au football.*	I like playing football.
ALLER	*Il va regarder la télé.*	He's going to watch TV.
DETESTER	*Je déteste faire la vaisselle.*	I hate doing the washing up.
DEVOIR	*Je dois partir maintenant.*	I must go now.
PREFERER	*Je préfère participer.*	I prefer to take part.
SAVOIR	*Tu sais nager?*	Can you swim?
POUVOIR	*Je ne peux pas sortir.*	I can't go out.
VOULOIR	*Elle ne veut pas venir.*	She doesn't want to come.

Some verbs need *à* before the infinitive:

COMMENCER	*Il a commencé à pleuvoir.*	It began to rain.
CONTINUER	*Je continue à travailler.*	I am continuing to work.
REUSSIR	*Nous avons réussi à ouvrir la boîte.*	We succeeded in opening the box.

Some verbs need *de* before the infinitive:

DECIDER	*Nous décidons d'aller au cinéma.*	We're deciding to go to the cinema.
ESSAYER	*Il essaie de trouver un emploi.*	He's trying to find a job.
FINIR	*J'ai fini de manger.*	I've finished eating.
OUBLIER	*Elle a oublié de faire ses devoirs.*	She's forgotten to do her homework.

Note also the following expressions which use the infinitive:

J'ai quelque chose à faire.	– I have something to do.
Il est allé en ville pour acheter des vêtements.	– He went to town to buy some clothes.
J'ai dit au revoir avant de partir.	– I said goodbye before I left.

Note 1: If the verb is reflexive, think carefully about the reflexive pronoun:

Je me brosse les dents avant de me coucher.	– I clean my teeth before I go to bed.
BUT *Elle se brosse les dents avant de se coucher.*	– She cleans her teeth before she goes to bed.
Après avoir mangé, je suis sorti(e).	– When I had eaten, I went out.

Note 2: With the verbs listed under B on page 38:

*Après **être** descendu(e) du train, je suis allé(e) en ville.*	– When I had got off the train, I went into town.

THE PERFECT TENSE

This is the tense which is used to refer to events in the past. It consists of two parts.

A

1   The present tense of *avoir*:
j'ai   *nous avons*
tu as   *vous avez*
il/elle/on a   *ils/elles ont*

2   The past participle:
This will end in *-é* for er verbs (e.g. *mangé*), or in *-i* for ir verbs (e.g. *fini*), or in *-u* for re verbs (e.g. *vendu*).
J'ai regardé la télé hier soir. – I watched TV last night.
Tu as fini ton petit déjeuner? – Have you finished your breakfast?
Elle a rendu le livre à Marie. – She gave the book back to Marie.
Nous avons attendu le car. – We waited for the bus.
Vous avez choisi? – Have you chosen?
Ils ont parlé avec le professeur. – They spoke to the teacher.

The following verbs have irregular past participles, but otherwise follow the same pattern.

Infinitive	Past participle	
avoir	**eu**	*J'ai eu* – I had
boire	**bu**	*J'ai bu* – I drank
devoir	**dû**	*J'ai dû* – I had to
dire	**dit**	*J'ai dit* – I said
écrire	**écrit**	*J'ai écrit* – I wrote
être	**été**	*J'ai été* – I was
faire	**fait**	*J'ai fait* – I did
lire	**lu**	*J'ai lu* – I read
mettre	**mis**	*J'ai mis* – I put (on)
ouvrir	**ouvert**	*J'ai ouvert* – I opened
pouvoir	**pu**	*J'ai pu* – I could/was able to
prendre	**pris**	*J'ai pris* – I took
recevoir	**reçu**	*J'ai reçu* – I received
rire	**ri**	*J'ai ri* – I laughed
voir	**vu**	*J'ai vu* – I saw
vouloir	**voulu**	*J'ai voulu* – I wanted

B

For a limited number of verbs, *avoir* is replaced by *être* when forming the perfect tense:
je suis   *nous sommes*
tu es   *vous êtes*
il/elle/on est   *ils/elles sont*

These verbs are:

ALLER	*Je suis allé(e)* – I went
ARRIVER	*Tu es arrivé(e)* – You arrived
DESCENDRE	*Il est descendu* – He went down
DEVENIR	*Elle est devenue* – She became
ENTRER	*Nous sommes entré(e)s* – We went in
MONTER	*Vous êtes monté(e)s* – You went up
MOURIR	*Ils sont morts* – They died
NAITRE	*Elles sont nées* – They were born
PARTIR	*Je suis parti(e)* – I left
RENTRER	*Tu es rentré(e)* – You went back/went home
RESTER	*Il est resté* – He stayed
RETOURNER	*Elle est retournée* – She returned
REVENIR	*Nous sommes revenu(e)s* – We came back
SORTIR	*Vous êtes sorti(e)s* – You went out
TOMBER	*Elles sont tombées* – They fell
VENIR	*Ils sont venus* – They came

For all these verbs, the past participle agrees with the subject of the verb.

C

All reflexive verbs also use *être* to form the perfect tense:

SE LEVER	*Je me suis levé(e)*	– I got up
SE LAVER	*Tu t'es lavé(e)*	– You had a wash
SE RASER	*Il s'est rasé*	– He had a shave
S'HABILLER	*Elle s'est habillée*	– She got dressed
SE DESHABILLER	*Nous nous sommes déshabillé(e)s*	– We got undressed
S'ARRETER	*Vous vous êtes arrêté(e)s*	– You stopped
S'AMUSER	*Ils se sont amusés*	– They had a good time
S'ASSEOIR	*Elles se sont assises*	– They sat down

Check yourself

QUESTIONS

Q1 *Choose the right word(s) to fit the blank.*

a) Il est tard, je dois _____ tout de suite.
b) J'ai commencé _____ froid.
c) Elle a essayé _____ à son frère.
d) Tu as décidé _____ de bonne heure?
e) Elle _____ à la gare à huit heures.

1	de téléphoner	2	te coucher
3	est arrivée	4	partir
5	à être	6	à parler
7	à avoir	8	est arrivé
9	à me coucher	10	de te lever

Q2 *How would you say in French?*

a) Last weekend, I went to Paris.
b) My grandfather gave me fifty francs.
c) I have to do the housework to earn money.
d) I like watching television.
e) Yes, I agree with you.

REMEMBER! Cover the answers if you want to.

ANSWERS

A1
a) 4
b) 7
c) 1
d) 10
e) 3

A2
a) Le week-end dernier, je suis allé(e) à Paris.
b) Mon grand-père m'a donné cinquante francs.
c) Je dois faire le ménage pour gagner de l'argent.
d) J'aime regarder la télévision.
e) Oui, je suis d'accord avec toi.

TUTORIAL

T1
a) Devoir *is followed simply by the infinitive.*
b) Commencer *takes* à *before the infinitive – and remember, to be cold is* avoir froid.
c) Essayer *takes de before the infinitive.*
d) Décider *takes de before the infinitive – and remember, you need to use the right reflexive pronoun, even with the infinitive, in this case* te.
e) *If the verb uses être for the perfect tense, the past participle must agree (*arrivée*).*

T2
a) Aller *is one of the verbs which uses être. Remember to add en extra -e if you are female.*
b) *The pronoun me loses its e before a vowel.*
c) *Two infinitives here; the first after* devoir, *the second after* pour *(in order to).*
d) Aimer *is followed simply by the infinitive.*
e) *To agree =* être d'accord.

EXAM PRACTICE

 **H** **LISTENING**

1 Find Chapter 5 – Exam Practice Listening on the CD.
Listen to the French (Track 9) twice, then complete the grid and
complete the sentence in French.

Ecrivez V (vrai) ou F (faux), et donnez une raison.

Marie	vrai/faux	raison
ne veut pas aller au cinéma.		
veut aller au complexe sportif.		
ne veut pas aller au café.		

A la fin, ils décident de _____ .

*You will find the transcript, with answers and
examiner's comments, on page 202.*

 **H** **SPEAKING**

2 Find Chapter 5 – Exam Practice Speaking on the CD. Listen to the
presentation (Track 10). Think about what you have heard. Then read
the examiner's comments.

You will find the transcript and examiner's comments on page 203.

> *You might then like to prepare your own presentation on your favourite
> hobby. When you are practising your presentation, it's a good idea to
> record it on cassette, so you can listen to it and spot errors, and areas
> for improvement.*

3 Read this extract from a brochure, and fill in the blanks.

Ecrivez une lettre chaque fois.

Bienvenue à Thuir

Située au cœur du Roussillon, la vieille ville de THUIR vous offre un ___1___ chaleureux. Ses 6 500 ___2___ partageront volontiers avec vous leurs cafés et restaurants – du modeste au gastronomique – ainsi que leurs stades. Vous trouverez des ___3___ enchantantes, et vous pourrez visiter nos caves et notre musée du vin.

ENTRE MER ET MONTAGNE

Si vous voulez aller un peu plus loin, THUIR est à une petite demi-heure de la Méditerranée avec les ___4___ dorées de St Cyprien et de Canet à l'est. Ou, au nord-ouest, vous êtes à une heure du Mont Canigou.

LES COURSES ET L'HISTOIRE

Nous sommes à seulement 14km de Perpignan (chef-lieu du département) où vous pourrez faire vos ___5___ dans les grands magasins, visiter le Palais des rois de Majorque (XIIème siècle) ou simplement vous ___6___ dans les rues de cette magnifique ville ___7___.

a) promenades   b) vieille   c) accueil   d) promener
e) commerces   f) achats   g) habitants   h) historique
i) montagnes   j) plages

You will find the answers and examiner's comments on page 203.

4 Write an account of last weekend in French, then compare your version with the sample answer on page 204.

Ecrivez le récit de ce que vous avez fait le week-end dernier.

Ecrivez environ 150 mots.

You will find the sample answer, and examiner's comments, on page 204.

LES RAPPORTS PERSONNELS, LES ACTIVITES SOCIALES ET LES RENDEZ-VOUS

PERSONAL RELATIONSHIPS, SOCIAL ACTIVITIES AND MEETINGS

LES SALUTATIONS

Bonjour.	Hello.
Bonsoir.	Good evening.
Bonne nuit.	Good night.
Bonne journée.	Have a nice day.
Bonne soirée.	Have a nice evening.
Bon appétit.	Enjoy your meal.
Au revoir.	Goodbye.
Salut.	Hi!/Cheerio.
A tout à l'heure.	See you soon.
A la semaine prochaine.	See you next week.

AU CINEMA/THEATRE

au balcon	in the balcony (upstairs)
à l'orchestre	in the stalls (downstairs)
la séance	the performance
le spectacle	the show
l'entracte	the interval
une place assise	a seated place
une place debout	a standing place

WHAT YOU NEED TO KNOW

Enchanté(e).	Pleased to meet you.
Je vous présente M. Leblanc.	May I introduce M. Leblanc.
Voici ma sœur, Lucie.	This is my sister Lucie.
Entrez. Asseyez-vous.	Come in. Sit down.
Soyez le/la bienvenu(e).	Welcome!
Je vais te montrer ta chambre.	I'll show you your room.
Merci de votre hospitalité.	Thank you for your hospitality.
A demain.	See you tomorrow.
Ça te dit d'aller au concert?	Do you fancy going to the concert?
Si on allait au match?	How about going to the match?
Tu veux venir au cinéma avec moi?	Do you want to come to the cinema with me?
Je veux bien.	I'd love to.
Ce serait super.	That would be great.
Avec plaisir.	With pleasure.
Non, je regrette, je ne peux pas.	No, I'm sorry, I can't.
J'ai des devoirs à faire.	I have homework to do.
Je n'ai pas le temps.	I haven't got time.
Je dois me laver les cheveux.	I have to wash my hair.
On se rencontre à x heures.	Let's meet at x o'clock.
Si on se voyait devant la gare?	Shall we meet outside the station?
Rendez-vous au café.	Let's meet at the café.
Qu'est-ce qu'il y a au cinéma?	What's on at the cinema?
C'est un film d'aventures.	It's an adventure film.
C'est quel genre de concert?	What sort of concert is it?
Le concert commence/finit à quelle heure?	What time does the concert start/finish?
Je voudrais deux places, s'il vous plaît.	I'd like two seats, please.
C'était bien/intéressant/amusant?	Was it good/interesting/fun?
Non, moi, je l'ai trouvé ennuyeux.	No, I found it boring.
Mon acteur préféré est Gérard Depardieu.	My favourite actor is Gérard Depardieu.
Mon actrice préférée est Isabelle Adjani.	My favourite actress is Isabelle Adjani.

LES FILMS

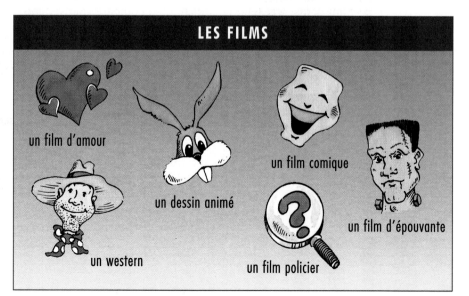

un film d'amour

un dessin animé

un film comique

un western

un film policier

un film d'épouvante

QUESTIONS/PROMPTS

C'est la première fois que tu viens en Angleterre?

Tu es déjà allé(e) en France?

Tu sors souvent avec tes amis?

Où vas-tu?

Qu'est-ce qu'il y a à faire à Paris?

Qu'est-ce que tu aimes comme films?

LES OPINIONS

moche	awful
chouette	brilliant
super	excellent

Check yourself

QUESTIONS

Q1 *Your French friend has asked you to go out. How would you say the following in French?*

a) Say you don't like detective films.
b) Say you have to do the housework.
c) Suggest meeting outside the cinema.
d) Suggest meeting at 7.30.
e) Ask if he/she would like to go to the football match on Saturday.

Q2 *Complete the following conversation.*

a) Tu veux sortir ce soir? (Accept the invitation.)
b) On va au cinéma? (Find out what's on.)
c) Un western. (Check what time it starts.)
d) A vingt heures quinze. (Ask where you will meet.)
e) On va au café après? (Say you have to be home before midnight.)

REMEMBER! Cover the answers if you want to.

ANSWERS

A1
a) Je n'aime pas les films policiers.
b) Je dois faire le ménage.
c) On se rencontre devant le cinéma?
d) On se voit à dix-neuf heures trente/ sept heures et demie?
e) Tu veux venir au match de foot samedi?

A2
a) Je veux bien, merci./D'accord.
b) Qu'est-ce qu'il y a comme film?
c) La séance commence à quelle heure?
d) Où est-ce qu'on se rencontre?
e) Je dois rentrer avant minuit.

TUTORIAL

T1
a) *Remember to make* policiers *plural, to agree with* films.
b) Devoir *is followed immediately by the infinitive.*
c) *'Outside' a place is usually expressed by* devant.
d) *You can use either the 24-hour clock or the 12-hour clock, but be consistent. The 24-hour clock is always just a number of hours followed by a number of minutes. It never uses expressions like half-past.*
e) Vouloir *is followed immediately by the infinitive.*

T2
a) D'accord *shows a little less enthusiasm.*
b) *This expression using* comme *is very useful for finding out what sort of thing is available, as also in* Qu'est-ce que tu aimes comme films?
c) *It's best to find out what time the programme* (la séance) *begins.*
d) On *is very often used instead of* nous *in everyday conversation.*
e) Rentrer *often means 'to return' in the sense of 'to go home'.*

GOING FURTHER

On pourrait aller en boîte si tu préfères.	We could go to a night-club if you prefer.
Tu veux m'accompagner au bal, ou peut-être au concert?	Do you want to go with me to the dance, or maybe to the concert?
Je regrette, mais vraiment je ne peux pas ce soir.	I'm sorry, but I really can't tonight.
Dis, demain c'est la boum de Joël. On y va?	Listen, tomorrow it's Joël's party. Shall we go?
Il y aura un monde fou.	There'll be a real crowd there.
Oh, je n'aime pas tellement les foules, tu sais.	Oh, I don't like crowds you know.
Tu es libre après-demain?	Are you free the day after tomorrow?
Non, disons plutôt huit heures.	No, let's say 8 o'clock instead.
La pièce était vraiment passionnante.	The play was really exciting.
C'est l'histoire de deux jeunes qui s'aiment, mais qui ne peuvent pas se marier à cause de leurs familles.	It's the story of two young people who love each other, but who can't get married because of their families.
C'est très triste.	It's very sad.

Many Higher Level tasks require you to offer alternatives, or to negotiate with other people to reach a satisfactory conclusion.

You don't have simply to accept or reject a suggestion, you can make alternative proposals of your own:

> *Tu veux venir au cirque avec moi?*
> *Non merci, je n'aime pas les cirques. On pourrait aller au concert si tu veux.*

OR

> *Je préférerais aller en disco.*

When you are making the invitation, you can offer alternatives:

> *Tu préfères aller au théâtre ou au cinéma?*

HOW THE GRAMMAR WORKS

SUBJECT PRONOUNS

The most common pronouns are the subject pronouns which tell us who is doing the action of the verb:

je	I	*nous*	we
tu	you	*vous*	you
il	he/it (masculine)	*ils*	they (masc or masc + fem)
elle	she/it (feminine)	*elles*	they (feminine)
on	one /we		

The French do not distinguish between pronouns which refer to people and those which refer to things. What matters is whether the noun referred to is masculine or feminine.

– *Où est mon père?*	Where is my father?
Il *est dans le salon.*	**He** is in the living-room.
– *Où est mon sac?*	Where is my bag?
Il *est dans le salon.*	**It** is in the living room.
– *Où est ma mère?*	Where is my mother?
Elle *est dans le salon.*	**She** is in the living room.
– *Où est ma veste?*	Where is my jacket?
Elle *est dans le salon.*	**It** is in the living room.

In the plural, *ils* is used to refer to a group of people/objects of which one or more are masculine:

> *Où sont mes frères et sœurs?* – Where are my brothers and sisters?
> **Ils** *sont dans le salon.* **They** are in the living-room.

Note that there are two pronouns which are the equivalent of 'you' in English. The French use *tu* to a person they know well, to a relative or to a small child (or to an animal!), but *vous* to strangers or adults outside the family. So you would address your French penfriend or exchange partner, and his/her friends, as *tu*, but you would say *vous* to his/her parents and other adult relatives, as well as shop assistants etc. Remember that *vous* is always used if you are speaking to more than one person.

OBJECT PRONOUNS

These are used to refer to the person/thing on the receiving end of the action of the verb. Like the subject pronouns above, they change according to whether the person/thing they refer to is masculine, feminine or plural.

The most common object pronouns are:

Referring to people		Referring to people or things	
me	me	*le*	him/it
te	you	*la*	her/it
nous	us	*l'*	(before vowel)
vous	you	*les*	them

Unlike in English, these pronouns come before the verb:
> *Il m'a vu en ville.* – He saw me in town.
> *Je t'ai envoyé une carte.* – I sent you a card.
> *Elle nous invite à une boum.* – She's inviting us to a party.
> *Je vous écoute.* – I'm listening to you.
> *Où est ton stylo? Je le cherche.* – Where is your pen? I'm looking for it.
> *Où est ta montre? Je la cherche.* – Where is your watch? I'm looking for it.

When *la* (or *l'* referring to a feminine noun) is used in the perfect tense, the past participle should agree, by adding an *-e*:
> *Où est la limonade? Je l'ai bue.* – Where is the lemonade? I've drunk it.

When *les* is used in the perfect tense, the past participle should agree by adding *-s* (if it refers to a masculine noun) or *-es* (if it refers to a feminine noun):
> *Où sont les bonbons?* – Where are the sweets?
> *Je les ai mangés.* I've eaten them.
> *Où sont les pommes?* – Where are the apples?
> *Je les ai mangées.* I've eaten them.

There is a special pronoun meaning 'to him' or 'to her'.
> *Ta mère sait que tu vas être en retard?* – Does your mother know you are going to be late?
> *Je lui ai téléphoné.* I've phoned her.

Lui becomes *leur* in the plural:
> *Tes parents savent que tu vas être en retard? Je leur ai téléphoné.*

Y/EN

The two pronouns *y* and *en*, which are not used in English, are never omitted in French.

Reference to a place is made with *y*:
> *Qui va au cinéma?* – Who's going to the cinema?
> *J'y vais ce soir.* – I'm going (there) tonight.

Reference to a quantity is made with *en*:
> *Tu as des crayons?* – Do you have any pencils?
> *Oui, j'en ai deux.* – Yes, I have two (of them).

QUI/QUE

Both these pronouns can be translated into English as 'who' when referring to a person, or 'which'/'that' when referring to a thing. It can seem hard to know which to use, unless you remember the following little rule:

- Use *qui* when the verb comes immediately after:
  L'homme qui a volé l'argent. – The man who stole the money.
  L'argent qui est sur la table. – The money which is on the table.

- Use *que* when the next word is a noun or a subject pronoun (see above):
  L'homme que j'ai vu. – The man (who) I saw.
  L'argent que l'homme a volé. – The money (that) the man stole.

Note that in English we often don't translate *que*, and simply leave it out.

This is a very rough guide, but almost aways works.

CE QUI/CE QUE

When connected to one verb which comes before, and another which comes after, we use *ce qui* or *ce que* instead of *qui* and *que*. However, the above rule still operates:
  Mangez ce que vous désirez. – Eat what you want.
  Mangez ce qui est bon pour la santé. – Eat what is good for your health.

ORDER OF PRONOUNS

If you use more than one object pronoun with the same verb, they must go in the following order:

| me | te | nous | vous |

followed by

| le | la | les |

followed by

| lui | leur |

followed by

y

followed by

en

Demande de l'argent à ton père.
Ask your father for some money.
Il m'en a déjà donné.
He's already given me some.

EMPHATIC PRONOUNS

These pronouns always refer to a person or people:

moi	me/I	*nous*	us/we
toi	you	*vous*	you
lui	him/he	*eux*	them/they (masc)
elle	her/she	*elles*	them/they (fem)

Most pronouns are linked with a verb, but emphatic pronouns are used in a number of different ways:

1 With a preposition:
  avec elle – with her
  chez vous – at your house
2 As a one-word answer:
  Qui veut une glace? – Who wants an ice-cream?
  Moi. – Me.
3 In a comparison:
  Je suis plus âgé(e) que lui. – I'm older than him.
4 To emphasise a subject pronoun:
  Moi, je préfère les films de science-fiction. – I prefer SF films.
  Il n'est pas gentil, lui. – He's not very nice.
5 After *à*, to indicate to whom something belongs:
  A qui est cet argent? – Whose is this money?
  Il est à moi. – It's mine.
6 After a verb in the imperative:
  Donne-moi ton cahier. – Give me your exercise-book.

Check yourself

QUESTIONS

Q1 *Answer the following questions in French, using the appropriate pronoun(s).*

a) Tu veux voir un western?
(You don't like them.)
b) Il va chez le médecin?
(He's going tomorrow.)
c) Elle va écrire à sa mère?
(She wrote to her yesterday.)
d) Tu as des frères?
(You have three.)
e) Où sont les cerises?
(Pierre has eaten them.)

Q2 *Respond to these invitations, but check your diary first.*

| **lundi après-midi:** *chez Isabelle* |
| **mardi matin:** *courses en ville* |
| **mercredi:** *cinéma — 'Le Héros'* |
| **jeudi soir:** |
| **samedi:** *pique-nique avec Marion* |

a) Tu viens à la piscine lundi après-midi?
b) Tu veux aller à la mer mardi?
c) Mercredi, tu veux jouer au tennis?
d) Il y a un bon film au cinéma cette semaine – c'est 'Le Héros'. On y va vendredi?
e) Tu viens au match de football jeudi soir?

REMEMBER! Cover the answers if you want to.

ANSWERS

A1
a) Je ne les aime pas.
b) Il y va demain.
c) Elle lui a écrit hier.
d) J'en ai trois.
e) Pierre les a mangées.

A2
a) Non, je ne peux pas. Je vais chez Isabelle.
b) Non, je ne peux pas. Je vais en ville pour faire des courses.
c) Non, je regrette. Mercredi je vais au cinéma.
d) Je m'excuse. Je l'ai déjà vu.
e) Oui, je veux bien. J'adore le foot.

TUTORIAL

T1
a) *Remember to use* les *(or* le/la*) for generalisations.*
b) *You need the word* y *even though there's no word in English.*
c) *Use* lui *for 'to him' or 'to her'.*
d) *You need* en *even though there's no word in English.*
e) *Add* -es *to the past participle, because* cerises *are feminine plural.*

T2
a) - d) *It doesn't matter which of the forms of apology you use, but make it polite!*
b) *Remember* pour *with the infinitive – 'in order to'.*
c) *No need for a word for 'on' with days of week.*
d) *Remember that the object pronoun comes before* avoir *in the perfect tense.*
e) *When accepting an invitation, sound enthusiastic!*

EXAM PRACTICE

F H LISTENING

1 Find Chapter 6 – Exam Practice Listening on the CD. Listen to the French (Track 11) twice, then answer these questions.

Choisis la bonne phrase, et écris la lettre dans la case.

1 Pierre invite Marie:
   A au concert   **B** au bal   **C** au cinéma   **D** au théâtre   ☐

2 Ils décident de se retrouver:
   A devant le théatre   **B** à la salle des fêtes
   C au café   **D** en ville   ☐

3 Ça commence à:
   A 8h00   **B** 8h30   **C** 9h00   **D** 9h30   ☐

4 Marie doit:
   A faire ses devoirs   **B** surveiller son frère
   C surveiller sa sœur   **D** attendre ses frères   ☐

5 Pierre va:
   A venir à la maison de Marie   **B** voir Marie au concert
   C attendre Marie chez lui   **D** voir Marie au bar   ☐

You will find the transcript and answers, with examiner's comments, on page 204.

H SPEAKING

2 Look at the situation below, and think what you might say.

Find Chapter 6 – Exam Practice Speaking on the CD and listen to the role-play (Track 12). Remember, Higher Level role-plays will involve some sort of problem or negotiation; they will not be straightforward.

—— da Gianni ——

cuisine italienne traditionnelle

ouvert de 19h30 à 23h30

fermé le dimanche et le lundi

You will find the transcript on page 205.

You phone a friend to invite her out for dinner. You want to go to this Italian restaurant. You work until 9 pm on Thursdays and Fridays.

F H READING

3 Choose a letter to match each of the notes.

Pour chaque invitation, choisis la bonne image, et écris la lettre dans la case.

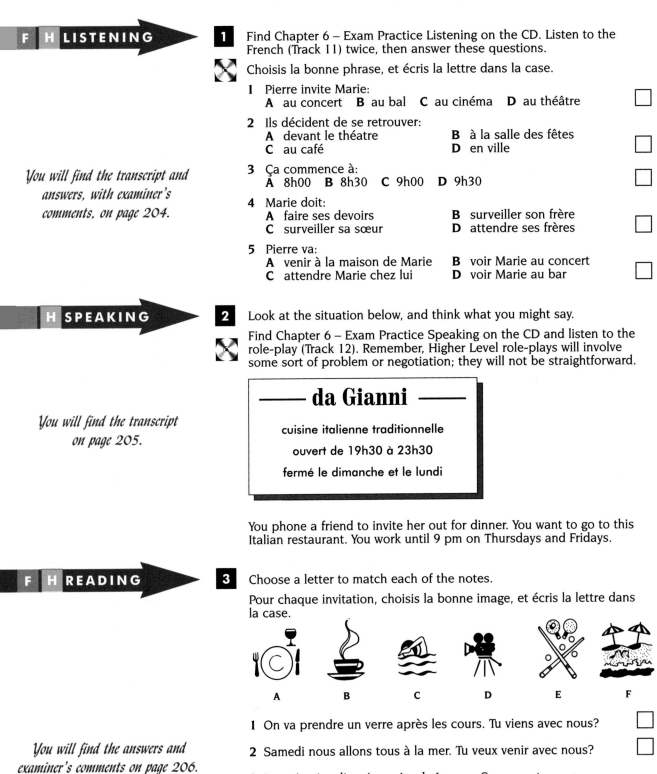

A   B   C   D   E   F

1 On va prendre un verre après les cours. Tu viens avec nous?   ☐

2 Samedi nous allons tous à la mer. Tu veux venir avec nous?   ☐

3 Demain c'est l'anniversaire de Jeanne. Ses parents nous invitent à dîner.   ☐

4 Si tu es libre cet après-midi, on va nager.   ☐

You will find the answers and examiner's comments on page 206.

4 Write a letter to your French friend inviting him/her to spend Saturday with you.

Ecris une lettre à ton ami(e).
– Commence et termine ta lettre avec les formules nécessaires.
– Dis ce que tu vas faire samedi. (3 activités)
– Demande s'il/si elle aime ces activités.
– Invite-le/la à t'accompagner.
– Fixe un rendez-vous. (Où? Quand?)
– Dis-lui l'heure de retour.
– Demande-lui de t'écrire ou de te téléphoner.

Sample Student's Answer

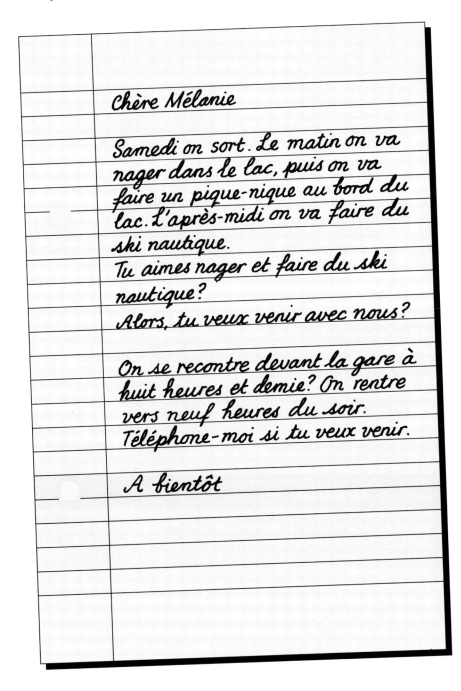

Chère Mélanie

Samedi on sort. Le matin on va nager dans le lac, puis on va faire un pique-nique au bord du lac. L'après-midi on va faire du ski nautique.
Tu aimes nager et faire du ski nautique?
Alors, tu veux venir avec nous?

On se rencontre devant la gare à huit heures et demie? On rentre vers neuf heures du soir.
Téléphone-moi si tu veux venir.

A bientôt

EXAMINER'S COMMENTS

● First, the good things. This fulfils all the tasks set out in the question. It is very accurate, and there are one or two good phrases (on sort; vers neuf heures; téléphone-moi; si tu veux venir). There are clear references to present and future. All of this makes this letter worth a Grade C.

● However, the tasks are all fulfilled at a fairly minimal level, with no real development or description, and no personal opinions. At 69 words it is rather short. There is also some repetition (on; nager; ski nautique).

● Without changing any of the detail, it could have been improved by:
1 Putting some extra detail in the first sentence: Samedi prochain je sors avec ma famille.
2 Instead of nager, se baigner would be more colloquial in the second sentence.
3 Adding an extra sentence or two: Nous y sommes déjà allés il y a trois mois. C'était vraiment super. This brings in a perfect and an imperfect tense, and a personal opinion, as well as a past participle agreement and a couple of adverbs.
4 Changing the subject of the next sentence to nous allons. Again, this gives more variety.
5 Changing the vocabulary in the following sentence, to avoid repetition: Tu aimes la natation et les sports nautiques?
6 Adding Si tu peux nous accompagner at the beginning of the second paragraph. This adds a more complex structure.
7 Instead of on rentre, use the more colloquial on sera de retour.

● These changes add some 25 words to the total, and would move the Grade up to at least a B.

CHAPTER 7

LA VILLE, LES REGIONS ET LE TEMPS

HOME TOWN, LOCAL ENVIRONMENT AND WEATHER

WHAT YOU NEED TO KNOW

J'aime bien habiter à	I like living in ....
C'est une ville industrielle dans le nord de l'Angleterre.	It's an industrial town in the north of England.
J'habite à ... depuis cinq ans.	I've lived in ... for five years.
A ... il y a un musée.	In ... there is a museum.
Je préfère habiter en ville.	I prefer living in town.
Il y a toujours quelque chose à faire.	There's always something to do.
C'est très bruyant.	It's very noisy.
C'est toujours animé.	It's always lively.
J'aime mieux habiter à la campagne.	I'd rather live in the country.
C'est un village typique.	It's a typical village.
On y est très tranquille.	You are very quiet there.
Il n'y a rien à faire.	There's nothing to do.
On devrait construire un complexe sportif.	They ought to build a sports centre.
Il manque une bibliothèque.	It needs a library.
Il n'y a pas de distractions.	There aren't any entertainments.
Demain, c'est la fête du village.	Tomorrow, it's the village festival.
Il y aura un bal, une foire, un concours de boules.	There will be a dance, a fair, a bowls competition.
On va en ville en car.	We go into town by bus.
Le trajet dure quarante minutes.	The trip takes 40 minutes.
Au printemps, on voit les petits agneaux.	In the spring, you can see the little lambs.
En été, le soleil brille.	In summer the sun shines.
En automne, il fait mauvais temps.	In autumn, the weather is miserable.
En hiver, il fait très froid.	In winter, it's very cold.
Quel temps fait-il en France?	What's the weather like in France?
En Angleterre il pleut toujours.	In England, it's always raining.
Il pleut/neige/gèle.	It's raining/snowing/freezing.
Il fait froid/mauvais/du soleil/ du vent/du brouillard.	It's cold/miserable/sunny/ windy/foggy.
Il ne fait pas très chaud aujourd'hui.	It's not very warm today.
Voici la météo pour ce week-end.	Here's the weather forecast for this weekend.
Dans le nord-ouest, il y aura des averses.	In the north-west, there will be showers.
Demain, il pleuvra.	Tomorrow, it will rain.
Cet après-midi, il fera plus froid.	This afternoon, it will be colder.

A LA CAMPAGNE

un bois	a wood
un champ	a field
un château	a castle
une colline	a hill
une ferme	a farm
une forêt	a forest

EN VILLE

une boutique	a small shop
un hypermarché	a hypermarket
un magasin	a shop

LA METEO

dans l'ouest	in the west	il y aura	there will be	des nuages	clouds
dans l'est	in the east	du soleil	sunshine	Le ciel sera couvert.	The sky will be grey.
dans le sud	in the south	de la neige	snow		
il fera	it will be	du vent	wind	La température maximale/ minimale sera de dix degrés.	The maximum/ minimum temperature will be 10°.
beau	nice	du brouillard	fog		
chaud	warm/hot	du verglas	black ice		
		des éclaircies	sunny periods		

A LA FERME

un canard

un cochon

une dinde

un mouton

un taureau

une vache

QUESTIONS/PROMPTS

Vous habitez en ville ou
à la campagne?

Vous allez souvent en
centre-ville?

Parlez-moi de votre ville/village.

Qu'est-ce qu'il y a à faire?

Que faites-vous s'il fait beau?

Check yourself

QUESTIONS

Q1 *Look at the map, then complete the forecasts.*

LA MÉTÉO POUR DEMAIN

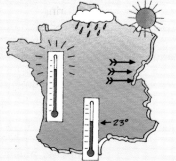

←23°

a) _____ il y aura du vent.

b) Dans le nord _____.

c) Il fera très chaud _____.

d) Dans le sud _____.

e) Il y aura du soleil _____.

Q2 *Do the people speaking live in the town
or the country?*

a) "Il y a beaucoup de distractions."

b) "En ville, il y a trop de bruit. Je préfère
ne pas y aller."

c) "Pour aller au cinéma, c'est un trajet
d'une heure."

d) "Le week-end, j'adore aller
à la campagne."

e) "Il n'y a pas grand-chose à faire."

REMEMBER! Cover the answers if you want to.

ANSWERS

A1
a) Dans l'est
b) il pleuvra
c) dans l'ouest
d) la température maximale sera de
vingt-trois degrés
e) dans le nord-est

TUTORIAL

T1
a/c) To understand weather forecasts, the region can
be as important as the weather itself.

b) In forecasts, the normal tense is the future.

d) Numbers can be important in weather forecasts.

e) The points of the compass combine in French
just as they do in English.

51

ANSWERS

A2 a) town
b) country
c) country
d) town
e) country

TUTORIAL

T2 a) Words like beaucoup *can reveal a lot about attitudes.*
b) Trop *reveals the attitude, but you need the second sentence to make it clear that the speaker doesn't live in the town.*
c/d) *Here, you need to understand the gist. There is no specific word which gives you the answer.*
e) *The negative makes all the difference.*

GOING FURTHER

En France, il y a moins de grandes villes qu'en Grande-Bretagne.

In France, there are fewer large towns than in Great Britain.

La vie à la campagne est beaucoup plus agréable – en ville les gens sont toujours pressés.

Life in the country is much more pleasant – in town people are always in a hurry.

A ... il y a à peu près cinquante mille habitants.

In ... there are about 50,000 inhabitants.

La population de la France est pareille à celle de la Grande-Bretagne.

The population of France is the same as that of Great Britain.

La France est deux fois plus grande que la Grande-Bretagne.

France is twice as big as Great Britain.

Les paysages de France sont très variés: il y a des lacs, des montagnes et des plaines.

The scenery in France is very varied: there are lakes, mountains and plains.

A l'ouest, il y a la côte Atlantique, et au sud, il y a la Méditerranée.

To the west, there is the Atlantic coast, and to the south, there is the Mediterranean.

Le climat est plus doux qu'en Grande-Bretagne.

The climate is milder than in Great Britain.

En Corse, il fait très chaud, mais en montagne, il fait souvent moins cinq.

In Corsica, it is very hot, but in the mountains, it's often minus five.

One way of developing what you say is to use comparisons. This will make your sentences more varied and interesting, and also probably more accurate.

- Avoid stating absolutes (*Il fait chaud en France*) by making a comparison (*Il fait plus chaud qu'en Grande-Bretagne*).

- Adjectives of comparison can make your opinions clearer: *plus agréable, moins bruyant.*

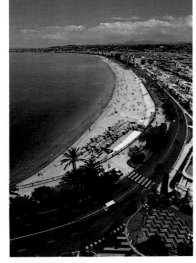

Nice

HOW THE GRAMMAR WORKS

COMPARISON

To use an adjective to compare one thing or person with another, put *plus* in front of the adjective and *que* after it:

Marie est plus âgée que Pierre.	– Marie is older than Pierre.
Les boîtes sont plus lourdes que les paquets.	– The boxes are heavier than the packets.

Exception:

bon – good   *meilleur* – better

That is the most common form of comparison, but the following are also used:

Louise est aussi grande que Claire.	– Louise is as tall as Claire.
Le car est moins rapide que le train.	– The bus is less fast than the train.

Note that the adjective agrees with the noun as usual.

Adverbs can be used for comparison in the same way:

L'avion va plus vite que la voiture.	– The plane goes more quickly than the car.
Parlez plus lentement, s'il vous plaît.	– Speak more slowly, please.

Exception:

bien – well   *mieux* – better

THE FUTURE TENSE

The future tense in French is used in just the same circumstances in which we use the future tense (shall/will) in English.

Like the present tense, it works through a system of endings. The endings are the same for all verbs:

je	*-ai*	*nous*	*-ons*
tu	*-as*	*vous*	*-ez*
il/elle/on	*-a*	*ils/elles*	*-ont*

For *er* and *ir* verbs, these endings are simply added to the infinitive:

Je mangerai une banane.	– I will eat a banana.
Tu finiras les pommes de terre?	– Will you finish the potatoes?

For *re* verbs, the final *-e* is removed before adding the ending:

Elle attendra le prochain car.	– She will wait for the next bus.

The following verbs are irregular in the way they form the future, though the endings are the same:

ACHETER	*j'achèterai* – I will buy		FAIRE	*je ferai* – I will do
ALLER	*j'irai* – I will go		POUVOIR	*je pourrai* – I will be able
AVOIR	*j'aurai* – I will have		VENIR	*je viendrai* – I will come
DEVOIR	*je devrai* – I will have to		VOIR	*je verrai* – I will see
ENVOYER	*j'enverrai* – I will send		VOULOIR	*je voudrai* – I will want
ETRE	*je serai* – I will be			

THE CONDITIONAL TENSE

This tense is used to refer to what **would** happen (if something else happened). It is formed in the same way as the future tense, but the endings are as follows:

je	*-ais*	nous	*-ions*
tu	*-ais*	vous	*-iez*
il/elle/on	*-ait*	ils/elles	*-aient*

Tu *voudrais habiter à la campagne?* — Would you like to live in the country?

Il *vendrait sa maison.* — He would sell his house.

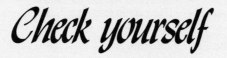

Check yourself

QUESTIONS

Q1 **How would you say in French?**

a) Tomorrow, I will go to town.
b) We will have dinner at seven o'clock.
c) Will you watch TV tonight?
d) They will buy some CDs.
e) On Saturday she will be seventeen.

Q2 **Write sentences in French, using these notes.**

Exemple: intéressant; télé; –; radio
La télé est moins intéressante que la radio.

a) passionnant; voile; +; tennis
b) âgé; Paul; +; son frère
c) intelligent; les filles; =; les garçons
d) court; les cheveux d'Anne; +; les cheveux de Marie
e) amusant; les films d'amour; –; les westerns

REMEMBER! Cover the answers if you want to.

ANSWERS

A1
a) Demain, j'irai en ville.
b) Nous prendrons le dîner à sept heures.
c) Tu regarderas la télé ce soir?
d) Ils achèteront des CDs.
e) Samedi elle aura dix-sept ans.

A2
a) La voile est plus passionnante que le tennis.
b) Paul est plus âgé que son frère.
c) Les filles sont aussi intelligentes que les garçons.
d) Les cheveux d'Anne sont plus courts que les cheveux de Marie.
e) Les films d'amour sont moins amusants que les westerns.

TUTORIAL

T1
a) Aller *is irregular in the future.*
b) Prendre *is more common than both* avoir *and* manger *when used with meals.*
d) Acheter *is slightly irregular* (achèteront).
e) *Remember: age is expressed by using* avoir – *and you always include* ans.

T2
This sort of activity, building up an account from notes, is used by some exam boards. Also, making notes like this in preparation for a written question is much more useful than doing the answer in rough and then writing it out in neat. It gives you a pattern for sentences, and will help you to avoid the common error of thinking a sentence out in English and then translating it into French. That would almost certainly result in producing sentences with grammatical mistakes, and which don't read like French.
a) Passionnante *agrees with* voile.
c) Intelligentes *agrees with* les filles.
d) *Remember:* cheveux *is plural, so* courts *must agree.*
e) *Again,* amusants *agrees with* les films.

EXAM PRACTICE

1 Find Chapter 7 – Exam Practice Listening on the CD. Listen to the French (Track 13) twice, then choose the most suitable activity for each weather forecast.

Ecoutez ces extraits de météo. Après chaque extrait, choisissez la bonne activité et notez la lettre.

A Bon, je vais bronzer sur la plage.

B Génial! Je pourrai faire de la planche à voile.

C Alors, je vais rester à la maison.

D Je devrai conduire très lentement.

E Je vais me promener à la campagne.

You will find the transcript and answers,
with examiner's comments, on page 206.

2 Find Chapter 7 – Exam Practice Speaking on the CD and listen to the conversation (Track 14). Think for a moment about what you have heard. Then read the examiner's comments. Did any of these points occur to you?

You will find the transcript and
examiner's comments on page 207.

Now think about some of the things you might want to say in French about your own home town or village. The following questions and prompts will help you to plan your answers:

- *Où habitez-vous?*

- *X se trouve où en Grande-Bretagne?*

- *Parlez-moi un peu de votre ville/village.*

---

3 Answer the following request in French, then compare your version with the sample answer on page 208.

Votre classe-partenaire vous demande de décrire votre ville. Voici leurs questions:

- Où est située votre ville exactement?
- C'est quelle sorte de ville?
- Comment est le climat de votre région?
- Qu'est-ce qu'il y a à faire dans la ville?
- Est-ce que ça vous plaît d'habiter là?

Ecrivez environ 150 mots.

You will find the sample answer and
examiner's comments on page 208.

4 Read the following newspaper article, then do the activity which follows it.

Lisez cet article.

Notre climat change-t-il?

Nous sommes au mois d'avril. En Dordogne, l'été est arrivé avec un mois d'avance. A midi, il fait presque aussi chaud qu'au mois de juillet. Pas une goutte de pluie depuis à peu près deux mois – et pourtant au mois de mars on s'attend habituellement à plusieurs dizaines de centimètres. Les agriculteurs devront limiter l'utilisation de l'eau – il leur sera défendu d'arroser leurs terres avec de l'eau du robinet. Ça, ce n'est pas si grave. Dans cette région bénie, il y a des milliers de sources, de fontaines, de rivières souterraines, alors on n'a pas vraiment besoin de l'eau du robinet pour arroser ses vignes. Mais ils ont surtout peur de la gelée. C'est vrai que c'est bientôt l'été, mais on se souvient du 21 avril 1996 – la température est tombée à -5°. Résultat: perte de 90% de la production!

On parle donc de changement de climat, de l'effet de serre, du réchauffement de la terre. Mais est-ce bien vrai? Les statistiques nous montrent qu'il y a toujours eu des variations climatiques, des pluies ou des froidures records, sans entraîner une nouvelle période glaciaire. On devra attendre encore quelques siècles pour décider s'il y a un vrai changement climatique, ou s'il est simplement question de variations normales.

Maintenant, remplissez les blancs dans ce résumé, en choisissant les mots dans la liste qui suit.

D'après l'article, il fait beaucoup plus ___1___ que d'habitude, et il ne pleut pas depuis ___2___ semaines. Mais la plupart des fermiers peuvent trouver sans difficulté de ___3___ sur leur propriété. Ce qui leur fait peur, c'est une baisse soudaine de ___4___, car s'il gèle, ils risquent de ___5___ presque toute leur production. Mais tout cela ne ___6___ pas que le climat est en train de ___7___. On a eu des périodes semblables dans le passé, sans catastrophe.

a) température	**b)** changer	**c)** pluie	**d)** perdre
e) prouve	**f)** chaud	**g)** humidité	**h)** plusieurs
i) quatre	**j)** l'eau		

You will find the answers and examiner's comments on page 208.

WHAT YOU NEED TO KNOW

Il y a une boîte aux lettres près d'ici?	Is there a post box nearby?
Où se trouve la banque la plus proche?	Where is the nearest bank?
Où est la poste?	Where is the post office?
Il y a une boulangerie à cinq cents mètres.	There is a baker's 500 metres away.
La boucherie est à côté de l'hôtel.	The butcher's is next to the hotel.
La charcuterie se trouve au coin, en face du supermarché.	The delicatessen is on the corner, opposite the supermarket.
Le magasin est ouvert de huit heures à vingt heures, sans interruption.	The shop is open non-stop from 8am to 8pm.
Nous sommes fermés le lundi.	We are closed on Mondays.
Je cherche un cadeau pour ma mère.	I'm looking for a present for my mother.
Quelle taille?	What size?
Quelle pointure?	What size? (shoes only)
Vous avez un pull vert, en trente-huit?	Do you have a green jumper, size 12?
Je peux l'essayer?	Can I try it on?
Je le prends.	I'll take it.
Il est trop long/court/cher.	It is too long/short/expensive.
Cette jupe ne me va pas.	This skirt doesn't suit me.
Vous l'avez dans d'autres couleurs?	Do you have it in other colours?
Non, je regrette, nous l'avons en gris seulement.	No, I'm sorry, we only have it in grey.
Vous pouvez me faire un paquet-cadeau?	Can you gift-wrap it for me?
Je ne m'intéresse pas à la mode.	I'm not interested in fashion.
Je voudrais un kilo de fraises.	I'd like a kilo of strawberries.
Et avec ça?	Would you like anything else?
C'est tout, merci.	That's all, thank you.
Je n'ai pas de pêches.	I haven't any peaches.
Je voudrais envoyer une lettre en Angleterre.	I'd like to send a letter to England.
C'est combien pour envoyer une carte postale?	How much is it to send a postcard?
Donnez-moi quatre timbres à deux francs soixante.	Give me four two-franc-sixty stamps.
Je voudrais changer un chèque de voyages.	I'd like to change a traveller's cheque.
La livre sterling est à combien?	How much is the pound sterling?
Allez à la caisse, s'il vous plaît.	Go to the cash desk, please.
Vous voulez signer ici?	Will you sign here?
On peut téléphoner d'ici?	Can you telephone from here?

AU ROYAUME-UNI

en Grande-Bretagne	to Great Britain
en Ecosse	to Scotland
en Irlande	to Ireland
au pays de Galles	to Wales

LES MAGASINS

l'épicerie	grocer's
la pâtisserie	cake shop
la pharmacie	chemist's
la librairie	bookshop
le magasin (de vêtements)	(clothes) shop
le bureau de tabac	tobacconist's (also sells stamps)

QUESTIONS/PROMPTS

Tu aimes faire des courses?

Quels sont tes magasins préférés?

Tu achètes beaucoup de vêtements?

Qu'est-ce que tu as acheté récemment?

LES VETEMENTS

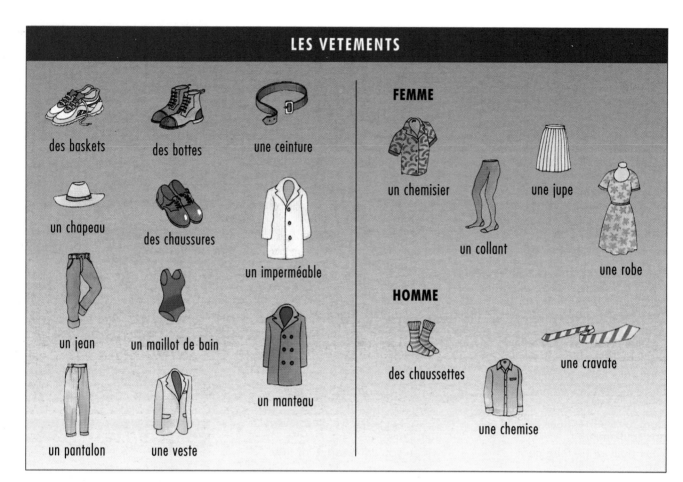

des baskets

des bottes

une ceinture

un chapeau

des chaussures

un imperméable

un jean

un maillot de bain

un manteau

un pantalon

une veste

FEMME

un chemisier

un collant

une jupe

une robe

HOMME

des chaussettes

une cravate

une chemise

Check yourself

QUESTIONS

Q1 *In a French shop, how would you:*

a) ask for a grey jacket?
b) say it's too small?
c) ask for a bigger one?
d) ask how much it is?
e) say you will take it?

Q2 *Match the correct shop with each item.*

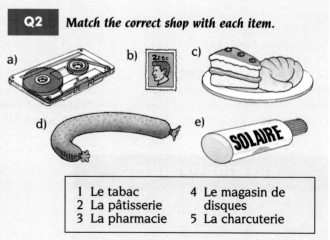

a)

b)

c)

d)

e) SOLAIRE

1 Le tabac	4 Le magasin de
2 La pâtisserie	disques
3 La pharmacie	5 La charcuterie

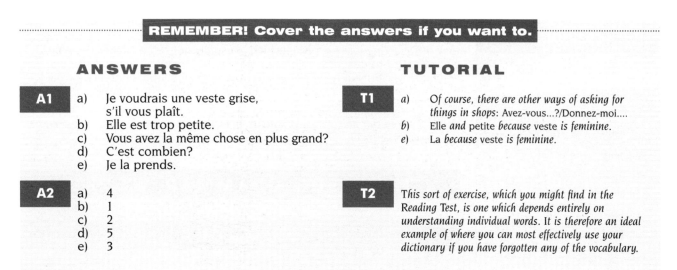

ANSWERS

A1
a) Je voudrais une veste grise,
s'il vous plaît.
b) Elle est trop petite.
c) Vous avez la même chose en plus grand?
d) C'est combien?
e) Je la prends.

A2
a) 4
b) 1
c) 2
d) 5
e) 3

TUTORIAL

T1
a) *Of course, there are other ways of asking for things in shops:* Avez-vous...?/Donnez-moi....
b) Elle *and* petite *because* veste *is feminine.*
e) La *because* veste *is feminine.*

T2
This sort of exercise, which you might find in the Reading Test, is one which depends entirely on understanding individual words. It is therefore an ideal example of where you can most effectively use your dictionary if you have forgotten any of the vocabulary.

GOING FURTHER

Où est le rayon des disques?
Where is the record department?

L'alimentation est au sous-sol.
The food department is in the basement.

Vous trouverez les surgelés là-bas, à côté de la crémerie.
You'll find frozen foods over there, next to the dairy produce.

Tous les samedis, je vais en ville pour acheter des vêtements.
Every Saturday, I go to town to buy clothes.

J'ai acheté ce baladeur ici la semaine dernière.
I bought this walkman here last week.

Malheureusement il ne marche pas.
Unfortunately, it doesn't work.

Vous pouvez me le rembourser?
Can you give me back my money?

Mon ami m'a acheté ce T-shirt, mais il y a un trou. Je peux l'échanger?
My friend bought me this T-shirt, but there's a hole in it. Can I change it?

La poche est déchirée.
The pocket is torn.

Ce n'est pas la bonne couleur/taille.
It's not the right colour/size.

Je voudrais envoyer ce colis aux Etats-Unis le plus rapidement possible.
I'd like to send this parcel to the USA as quickly as possible.

Quand est-ce qu'il arrivera?
When will it arrive?

Ça coûte combien pour envoyer cette carte en Allemagne?
How much will it cost to send this card to Germany?

Je n'ai qu'un billet de cinq cents francs.
I only have a five hundred franc note.

Vous pouvez me donner des pièces de dix francs?
Can you give me some ten franc coins?

J'ai perdu mon sac à main hier.
I lost my handbag yesterday.

Il est en cuir noir, avec mes initiales en or.
It's made of black leather, with my initials in gold.

Dedans il y avait mes cartes de crédit, mes clés et de l'argent.
Inside, there were my credit cards, my keys and some money.

Je crois que je l'ai laissé dans le car.
I think I left it on the coach.

On m'a volé ma montre Rolex il y a une heure à la gare.
My Rolex watch was stolen an hour ago at the railway station.

LE GRAND MAGASIN

au deuxième étage	on the 2nd floor
au premier étage	on the 1st floor
au rez-de-chaussée	on the ground floor

LES REDUCTIONS

soldes	sale
moins 15%	15% off
offre spéciale	special offer
trois pour le prix de deux	three for the price of two
gratuit	free
bon marché	cheap
prix imbattable	unbeatable price

EN QUOI?

	(made of)
en argent	silver
en bois	wood
en coton	cotton
en laine	wool
en nylon	nylon
en plastique	plastic
en soie	silk
en verre	glass

Clearly, the more details you can give when you are describing something, the higher will be the level of what you say or write. Also, if you are to fulfil the task of reporting lost property (which is usually in itself a Higher Level task) you will need to describe objects in more detail than just general size and colour. However, you need not restrict your use of shape, contents, or the material something is made of, just to that situation. For example:

Pour mon anniversaire, mon frère m'a donné un portefeuille vraiment super. Il est en cuir noir, avec mes initiales en or. Dedans, il y a de la place pour mes cartes de crédit.

HOW THE GRAMMAR WORKS

NUMBERS

1	un	6	six	11	onze	16	seize
2	deux	7	sept	12	douze	17	dix-sept
3	trois	8	huit	13	treize	18	dix-huit
4	quatre	9	neuf	14	quatorze	19	dix-neuf
5	cinq	10	dix	15	quinze	20	vingt

21	vingt et un	30	trente
22	vingt-deux	34	trente-quatre
23	vingt-trois	35	trente-cinq
		36	trente-six

40	quarante	80	quatre-vingts
50	cinquante	81	quatre-vingt-un
60	soixante	82	quatre-vingt-deux
70	soixante-dix	90	quatre-vingt-dix
71	soixante et onze	91	quatre-vingt-onze
72	soixante-douze	92	quatre-vingt-douze

100 cent
200 deux cents
201 deux cent un
999 neuf cent quatre-vingt-dix-neuf
1 000 mille (no word for 'a')
5 000 cinq mille
1998 mille neuf cent quatre-vingt-dix-huit
1 000 000 un million
1 000 000 000 un milliard (a billion)

U*n milliardaire* is the equivalent of 'a millionaire' (because you need more francs than pounds to be really rich!).

Percentages are written with a comma where we use a decimal point in English:
2,5% *(deux virgule cinq pour cent)* – 2.5% (two point 5 per cent)

1st – *premier* (fem. *première*)
2nd – *deuxième* (sometimes *second* as in *seconde classe*)
3rd – *troisième*
4th – *quatrième* (the final *-e* of *quatre* is dropped)
5th – *cinquième* (notice the extra *u*)
6th – *sixième*
7th – *septième*
8th – *huitième*
9th – *neuvième* (notice the *f* becomes *v*)
10th – *dixième*

Remember to use the simple number in dates (*le deux mars*; *le dix-huit février*).
The 1st is an exception:

> *le premier mai* – the 1st of May

If you want to be less precise, you can use round numbers:

> *une dizaine* – about 10   *une trentaine* – about 30
> *une vingtaine* – about 20   *une centaine* – about 100

QUANTITY

To refer to a specific quantity of something you can use:

a) a weight or liquid measurement:

> *un kilo* – 1kg   *un litre* – a litre
> *une livre* – 1lb/$\frac{1}{2}$kg (500g)   *un demi-litre* – $\frac{1}{2}$ litre
> *cent grammes* – 100g

b) the container

> *une boîte* – a box or a tin   *un paquet* – a packet
> *une bouteille* – a bottle   *un pot* – a jar
> *une cuillerée* – a spoonful   *une tasse* – a cup
> *un flacon* – a small bottle   *un verre* – a glass
>   (perfume, etc.)

Use the following to refer to quantities in a more general way:

> *assez* – enough   *un peu* – a little
> *beaucoup* – a lot   *un tas* – a heap
> *un morceau* – a piece

Note: All these quantities are followed by *de* before the name of the item,
whether that item is masculine or feminine, singular or plural:

> *une cuillerée de sirop* – a spoonful of syrup
> *un pot de confiture* – a jar of jam
> *un kilo de fraises* – a kilo of strawberries
> *Ce soir j'ai un tas de devoirs.* – I've got heaps of homework tonight.

ADVERBS

In English, we can turn many adjectives into adverbs by adding '-ly':

> happy → happily   quick → quickly

In French, you can often do the same by adding *-ment* to the feminine form:

> *lent* (slow) → *lentement* (slowly)
> *heureux* (happy) → *heureusement* (usually in the sense of 'fortunately')
> *malheureux* (unhappy) → *malheureusement* (unfortunately)

Adjectives ending in *-ent* or *-ant* become adverbs in a rather different way:

> *évident* (obvious) → *évidemment* (obviously)
> *récent* (recent) → *récemment* (recently)
> *bruyant* (noisy) → *bruyamment* (noisily)

There are some common adverbs to which the above does not apply:

> *bien* – well   *trop* – too much
> *mal* – badly   *vite* – quickly
> *souvent* – often

The adverb always comes after the verb:

> *Je vais rarement au cinéma.*   – I rarely go to the cinema.
> *Je le voyais souvent au*   – I often used to see him at the
> *centre sportif.*   sports centre.

Just like adjectives, adverbs can be used to make comparisons:

> *Les Français parlent plus*   – The French speak more quickly
> *rapidement que les Anglais.*   than the English.

QUESTIONS

Q1 *What would you say when returning the following items to a shop?*

a) the radio you bought yesterday which doesn't work.

b) the blouse you bought on Saturday which is torn.

c) the jumper your mother bought you which is much too big.

Q2 *You are reporting the loss of your jacket. Give the following details.*

a) I left my jacket on the train.
b) It's blue, made of cotton.
c) In the pocket, there was a 100F note ...
d) ... and a gold watch.

REMEMBER! Cover the answers if you want to.

ANSWERS

A1
a) J'ai acheté cette radio hier.
   Elle ne marche pas.
b) J'ai acheté ce chemisier samedi.
   Il est déchiré.
c) Ma mère m'a acheté ce pull.
   Il est beaucoup trop grand.

A2
a) J'ai laissé ma veste dans le train.
b) Elle est bleue, en coton.
c) Dans la poche, il y avait un billet de cent francs ...
d) ... et une montre en or.

TUTORIAL

T1
a/b) *Remember to use* il *or* elle *according to the gender of the noun being referred to.*
b) *Remember there is no word for 'on' with days of the week.*
c) Me *(here* m'*) in front of the verb can often mean 'for me'. Remember to give all the details – don't leave out* beaucoup.

T2
a) *With public transport, the French say* dans *for 'on'.*
b/d) *When saying what something is made of, always put* en *in front of the material. The material is a noun, so don't add* -e, *even if the item is feminine.*
c) *A 100F note is* un billet **de** cent francs *(but a 3F stamp is* un timbre **à** trois francs*).*

EXAM PRACTICE

1 Find Chapter 8 – Exam Practice Listening on the CD. Listen to the French (Track 15) twice, then complete the grid.

Des enfants discutent du cadeau à offrir à leur mère pour son anniversaire.

Complète la grille en français.

		cadeau	parce que
Ils décident de ne pas acheter	1		
	2		
	3		
Enfin ils décident d'acheter			

You will find the transcript and answers, with examiner's comments, on page 209.

2 Match the attitudes below with the correct person.

Pour chaque personne, choisis la bonne phrase.

Amir: Ce n'est pas souvent que je vais en ville, mais ce n'est pas que je ne trouve rien à acheter. Tout au contraire, je pourrais dépenser tout mon argent d'un seul coup – c'est pour ça que j'essaie de résister à la tentation. L'année prochaine, j'irai en faculté, alors j'aurai besoin de pas mal d'argent.

Pascale: Tous les samedis, ma mère insiste pour que je l'accompagne en ville. Elle met des heures à se décider, puis souvent elle n'achète rien du tout. Alors maintenant, même avec mes amies, je ne trouve plus aucun plaisir à faire les magasins.

Elodie: J'ai la folie des courses. Vraiment, c'est comme une maladie. Je finis le travail à midi le vendredi – c'est le jour où je suis payée. Quand je rentre le soir, il ne me reste plus rien. Et je n'achète que des bêtises, des trucs sans valeur. Alors, j'ai demandé à mon patron de travailler le vendredi après-midi. Comme ça, j'aurai moins l'occasion de faire des achats.

A J'ai horreur de faire des courses.

B Je dépense mon argent le jour-même où je le reçois.

C J'aime bien chercher des cadeaux.

D Je préfère faire des économies.

You will find the answers and examiner's comments on page 210.

H SPEAKING ➤

3 Look at the situation below, and think what you might say.
Then find Chapter 8 – Exam Practice Speaking on the CD and listen to the role-play (Track 16).

You have bought a sweater. When you get back to your penfriend's house, you realise there is something wrong with it. The following day, you take it back to the shop.

- **Quand?**
- **Problème**
- **Solution**

★ MODE DE ★
★ PRINTEMPS ★
———————————
- rue Lafayette -
- 8h30 à 19h00 -
- Fermé le lundi -
- Tél: 02 35 86 92 22 -

You will find the transcript and examiner's comments on page 210.

F H WRITING ➤

4 Answer the following question in French, then compare your version with the sample answer on page 211.

Imagine que tu es en vacances en France, et que tu as perdu ton sac, comme sur ces images. Raconte ce qui s'est passé. Ecris au moins 120 mots.

You will find the sample answer, with examiner's comments, on page 211.

WHAT YOU NEED TO KNOW

Pardon, monsieur/madame.	Excuse me (to a man/woman).
Pour aller à la gare, s'il vous plaît?	How do I get to the station please?
Où est la station de métro?	Where is the underground station?
C'est loin?	Is it far?
Non, c'est à cinq minutes à pied.	No, it's five minutes walk.
Oui, il faut prendre le bus.	Yes, you have to get the bus.
C'est la ligne huit.	It's a number eight (bus).
Vous continuez tout droit.	You go straight on.
Aux feux, vous tournez à gauche.	At the lights, you turn left.
Prenez la première à droite.	Take the first on the right.
Je me suis égaré(e).	I'm lost.
Je cherche l'hôtel Ibis.	I'm looking for the Ibis hotel.
Je suis allé(e) en ville à pied.	I walked to town.
Je voudrais un aller-retour pour Paris.	I'd like a return ticket to Paris.
Donnez-moi un aller simple, deuxième classe.	Give me a second class single.
Je voudrais un carnet (de tickets).	I'd like a book of (ten) tickets.
A quelle heure part/arrive le train?	What time does the train leave/arrive?
Le train pour Lyon part du quai numéro sept.	The train to Lyon leaves from platform 7.
Je peux réserver une place?	Can I book a seat?
Le train est direct?	Is it a through train?
Non, il faut changer à Lille.	No, you have to change at Lille.
Le train 1234 à destination de Calais part du quai numéro trois.	Train No 1234 to Calais is leaving from platform 3.
Le train 1157 en provenance de Marseille entre en gare, quai numéro cinq.	Train No 1157 from Marseille is arriving at platform 5.
C'est bien le train pour Caen?	Is this the right train for Caen?
Cette place est libre?	Is this seat free?
Vos billets/passeports, s'il vous plaît.	Tickets/passports, please.
Le plein de super/Trente litres de sans-plomb/Cent francs de gazole.	Fill it up with super/30 litres of lead-free/100F worth of diesel.
Vous acceptez les cartes de crédit?	Do you accept credit cards?
Vous vendez des cartes routières?	Do you sell road maps?
Où sont les toilettes?	Where are the toilets?
Vous voulez vérifier l'eau/l'huile/ la pression des pneus?	Will you check the water/oil/ tyre pressure?

LES PANNEAUX

Accès aux quais	To the platforms
Consigne	Left luggage
Douane	Customs
Passage souterrain	Subway

QUESTIONS/PROMPTS

Parlez-moi d'un voyage que vous avez fait.

Vous avez voyagé comment?

Quel est votre moyen de transport préféré? Pourquoi?

Comment venez-vous au collège?

LES INDICATIONS

à droite	right
à gauche	left
tout droit	straight on
la première à gauche	1st left
la deuxième à droite	2nd right
au carrefour	at the crossroads
au rond-point	at the roundabout

LES TRANSPORTS

un aéroglisseur	hovercraft
un car-ferry	car ferry
un taxi	taxi
un TGV (train à grande vitesse)	high-speed train
l'aéroport	airport
la gare routière	bus station
la gare SNCF	railway station
le port	port

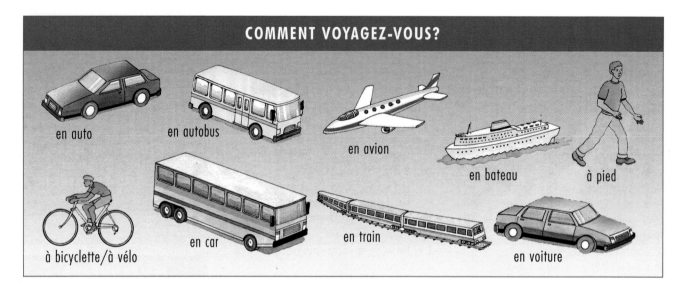

COMMENT VOYAGEZ-VOUS?

en auto

en autobus

en avion

en bateau

à pied

à bicyclette/à vélo

en car

en train

en voiture

Check yourself

QUESTIONS

Q1 **A French passer-by asks you for directions. What do you tell her/him?**

a)

b)

c)

d)

Q2 **You are at the station. What do you say to the clerk?**

a) DIEPPE

b) DIJON 1

c) **?** DEPART

d) LE HAVRE 13h00 ↓ 16h00 **?**

REMEMBER! Cover the answers if you want to.

ANSWERS

A1
a) Au carrefour, tournez à droite.
b) Aux feux, continuez tout droit.
c) Après l'église, prenez la troisième à gauche.
d) Continuez jusqu'au rond-point, et tournez à droite.

TUTORIAL

T1
a) Don't confuse *droit* (*straight on*) *and* droite (*right*).
b) *In* droite *the final -t is pronounced; in* droit *it is silent.*
c) *Landmarks like churches are often used in directions. Here, you need* après: *it wouldn't make sense to say* à l'église.
d) *You often link two separate instructions with* et.

ANSWERS

Q2
a) Je voudrais un aller simple pour Dieppe, s'il vous plaît.
b) Je voudrais un aller-retour, première classe, pour Dijon, s'il vous plaît.
c) A quelle heure part le train?
d) Il y a un train pour Le Havre cet après-midi?

TUTORIAL

T2
a/b) In role-plays, you are often expected to ask a question, and to do so politely. You may lose marks if you don't. It is also important to get in all the information you are given.
c) Apart from *C'est combien?* (*How much is it?*), *A quelle heure?* is one of the most likely questions you will be asked to produce.
d) You often need to combine language from different topics to carry out a task. Here, *cet après-midi* has not been covered specifically within this chapter.

GOING FURTHER

Pour aller en ville, il y a un bus toutes les vingt minutes. | To get to town, there is a bus every 20 minutes.
Je préfère voyager en train – c'est assez rapide, et c'est très confortable. | I prefer to travel by train – it's quite fast, and it's very comfortable.
Hier, mon train est arrivé avec une heure de retard. | Yesterday, my train arrived an hour late.
Moi, je prends toujours l'avion. C'est beaucoup plus rapide. | I always go by plane. It's much faster.
D'accord, mais j'ai horreur d'attendre des heures à l'aéroport. | Fine, but I hate waiting hours at the airport.
La semaine dernière, je devais aller à Berlin, mais mon vol a été annulé. | Last week, I was going to Berlin, but my flight was cancelled.
Moi, j'ai peur de prendre l'avion, alors je suis allé(e) en Belgique en bateau, malgré le mal de mer. | I'm frightened of flying, so I went to Belgium by boat, in spite of my sea-sickness.
Si on prend la voiture, on part quand on veut – il n'y a pas d'horaires. | If you go by car, you leave when you like – there are no timetables.
Mais ça coûte cher, et c'est polluant. | But it's expensive, and it causes pollution.

Et en plus, il y a des embouteillages. | And what's more, there are traffic jams.
Je suis tombé(e) en panne sur la RN13, entre X et Y. | I've broken down on the RN13, between X and Y.
Ma voiture est une Renault anglaise. Elle est blanche. | My car is an English Renault. It's white.
Le numéro d'immatriculation est K570 TVA. | Its registration number is K570 TVA.
Vous pouvez m'aider? | Can you help me?
Il y a eu un accident. | There's been an accident.
Un camion a heurté une moto. | A lorry has hit a motor-bike.
Il n'y a pas de blessés. | No-one has been injured.

EN ROUTE

une autoroute (à péage)	motorway (for which you have to pay)
le péage	the pay-station
la sortie	exit
une route nationale (RN)	main road
une route de campagne	country road
le périphérique	ring road

EN PANNE

J'ai un problème avec:	I have a problem with:
la batterie	the battery
les freins	the brakes
le moteur	the engine
les phares	the lights
Je suis en panne d'essence.	I've run out of petrol.
J'ai un pneu crevé.	I've got a puncture.

LES PANNEAUX

Autres directions	All other routes
Toutes directions	All routes
Déviation	Diversion

HOW THE GRAMMAR WORKS

ASKING QUESTIONS

There are three different ways of asking questions in French:

1 Putting the subject pronoun after the verb:
> *Tu as un chien.* – You have a dog.
> *As-tu un chien?* – Do you have a dog?
> *Vous aimez le chocolat.* – You like chocolate.
> *Aimez-vous le chocolat?* – Do you like chocolate?

Note: In this form of question, a hyphen links the pronoun and the verb.

This form is most commonly used in writing, though it is also used quite often in conversation with question words (see below):
> *Quel âge a-t-il?* – How old is he?

Note: If the verb before *il/elle* ends in a vowel, an extra '*t*' must be put in.

2 Putting *est-ce que* in front of the verb:
> *Est-ce que tu parles bien le français?* – Do you speak French well?
> *Est-ce qu'elle arrive en train?* – Is she arriving by train?

This form is common in both writing and speech.

3 By ending the sentence on a rising tone:
> *Elle est anglaise.* (ending on a level or falling tone) – She's English.
> *Elle est anglaise?* (ending on a rising tone) – Is she English?

This form can only be used in conversation.

All these methods of forming questions can be used in any tense:
> *Est-ce qu'elles sont allées au cinéma?* – Have they gone to the cinema?
> *Vous prendrez un café?* – Will you have a coffee?

However, a little extra care needs to be taken in the perfect tense when inverting the pronoun and the verb:
> *Il a fini ses devoirs.* – He has finished his homework.
> *A-t-il fini ses devoirs?* – Has he finished his homework?

Although it's not very complicated, asking questions is an area where GCSE candidates tend not to do very well. One reason for this may be that in class students have less practice in asking questions than in answering them. It may also be that the fact that there are three different ways of asking questions puts candidates off – they have difficulty choosing. Whatever the reason, it is very important to be able to ask questions competently. In real life, a large part of most conversation is asking questions – it is one way you can show you are interested. In the exam, the role-plays will always expect you to ask at least some questions, and in many cases in the writing paper you will need to ask some questions as part of a letter.

If you are not very confident about your accent and intonation, it is probably better for you not to try the 'tone of voice' method. It is in fact possible to keep to just one method of asking questions. If you decide to do this, you should use *est-ce que*, although for the sake of a bit of variety, it might be a good idea to try to use the 'inversion' method in a few very familiar questions, for example:
> *Comment t'appelles-tu?*
> *Où habites-tu?*

QUESTION WORDS

There are a number of question words which it is very important to know. You will need them in order to be able to ask questions, but they are also vital in order for you to understand the questions you will be asked in the conversation part of your exam. The question words – especially since they often (though not always) come at the beginning of the question – will often make the difference between understanding and not.

Où – Where   Quand – When   Qui – Who

Où es-tu allé(e) en vacances l'année dernière?	– Where did you go on holiday last year?
Quand es-tu allé(e) en vacances?	– When did you go on holiday?
Qui est allé en vacances avec toi?	– Who went on holiday with you?

Quel/Quelle/Quels/Quelles – What/Which

Quel âge as-tu?	– How old are you?
Quelle est la date aujourd'hui?	– What's the date today?
Quelles sont tes matières préférées?	– What are your favourite subjects?
A quelle heure arrive l'avion?	– What time does the plane arrive?
De quel quai part le train?	– Which platform does the train leave from?

Comment – How (sometimes)   Combien – How much/many

Comment viens-tu au collège?	– How do you come to school?
BUT *Comment est ta sœur?*	– What is your sister like?

(To ask 'How is your sister?' you need to say: *Comment va ta sœur?*)

Tu reçois combien d'argent de poche?	– How much pocket money do you get?
Tu as combien de frères?	– How many brothers have you got?

Pourquoi – Why

Pourquoi aimes-tu les maths?	– Why do you like maths?

This is a very popular question in the conversation part of the exam, because it encourages you to give a detailed explanation, and it certainly almost forces you to answer in a sentence. The answer should usually contain *parce que*.

Qu'est-ce que – What

Another very popular question, again because you can't just answer *Oui* or *Non*! You really ought to answer in a sentence if possible.

Qu'est ce que tu aimes manger?	– What do you like to eat?

Finally, there is a very simple way in conversation of turning a question back to the person you are talking to:

Et toi? – How about you?

(It could be *Et vous?* if you were talking to an adult or a stranger.)

– *Tu aimes le sport?*	– Do you like sport?
– *Oui, j'adore le tennis et la natation. Et toi?*	– Yes, I love tennis and swimming. How about you?

Check yourself

QUESTIONS

Q1 Last week, you went to Rome. Describe your journey.

a)

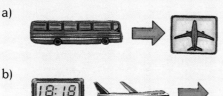

b)

c)

d)

e)

Q2 Match the following statements with the appropriate means of transport below.

a) Il y a toujours quelque chose à faire – un film, un repas – mais ce n'est pas très rapide.

b) On arrive très vite, c'est vrai, mais je n'aime pas l'idée de voyager sous la mer.

c) C'est mon transport idéal. C'est assez rapide et très confortable.

d) C'est pratique, ce n'est pas cher, on est indépendant, et ça ne pollue pas. Mais c'est fatigant!

e) Ça ne coûte pas très cher, mais c'est moins rapide que le train, et il y a quelquefois des embouteillages.

avion	train	car
voiture	vélo	bateau
tunnel sous la Manche		

REMEMBER! Cover the answers if you want to.

ANSWERS

A1
a) Je suis allé(e) à l'aéroport en car.
b) L'avion est parti à dix-huit heures dix.
c) Je suis arrivé(e) à vingt heures trente.
d) J'ai pris un taxi pour aller à l'hôtel.
e) C'était à vingt minutes de l'aéroport.

A2
a) bateau
b) tunnel sous la Manche
c) train
d) vélo
e) car

TUTORIAL

T1 If you are asked to describe an event in the past, make sure you use the appropriate tenses (see Chapter 12).
b/c) Remember the use of the 24-hour clock in timetables.
The prompts would probably lead you to begin both sentences with L'avion, but it is always a good idea to introduce variety when you can.
d) If you say J'ai pris un taxi à l'hôtel it means you got in the taxi at the hotel. You need to add pour aller to make your meaning clear.

T2 Don't be tempted to jump in too quickly; you may need the gist of the whole utterance before you can answer. There is sometimes a key phrase, such as voyager sous la mer in b), but sometimes you may simply have to put all the information together.
a) The key here is ce n'est pas très rapide.
c) It's really assez that tells you this isn't about the plane.
d) Perhaps the real clue here is C'est fatigant.
e) Here it really is a question of putting the whole thing together.

EXAM PRACTICE

LISTENING F H

Find Chapter 9 – Exam Practice Listening on the CD. Listen to the French (Track 17) twice, then complete the grid.

 En voiture, vous écoutez la radio. Indiquez le numéro de la route (par exemple A10, RN123, D254) et le problème en français.

ROUTE	PROBLEME
1	
2	
3	
4	

You will find the transcript and answers, with examiner's comments, on page 212.

Look at the situation outlined below, and think what you might say. Then find Chapter 9 – Exam Practice Speaking on the CD and listen to the account (Track 18). Your version will certainly not be exactly the same, but you may hear things that you did not think of.

SPEAKING H

A se lever — beau — le petit déjeuner — Céline — une promenade

B pique-nique — chercher — partir

C la campagne — regarder — tomber

D avoir mal? — TELEPHONE — AMBULANCE

E l'hôpital

You will find the transcript and examiner's comments on page 212.

H READING ▶ **3** Read this article, then answer the questions in French.

50 000 km en 3 mois pour un tour du monde en hélico

JENNIFER MURRAY, une Britannique de 56 ans, a quitté l'Angleterre ce week-end accompagnée d'un coéquipier. Elle est la première femme à tenter un tour du monde en hélicoptère. Impressions avant son départ.

"Les passages les plus difficiles seront la traversée des mers. Car, en cas de problème technique ou de très mauvais temps, nous pourrions tomber à l'eau!" annonce Jennifer Murray. Cette femme de 56 ans est la première femme et la première grand-mère à tenter le tour du monde en hélicoptère. Elle a quitté l'Angleterre ce week-end avec son coéquipier Quentin Smith. Tous deux espèrent boucler leur périple en 90 jours. "J'ai déjà volé sur cet appareil 600h. Il est très maniable," lance-t-elle enthousiaste. Et le Robinson 44 est un appareil léger. "Avec un plein, nous avons une autonomie maximale de 6h de vol. Soit environ 1 000km. Nous devrons donc faire 80 escales de ravitaillement."

26 pays traversés
Les deux pilotes voleront à une altitude moyenne de 3 000m. Ils parcourront 50 000km et traverseront 26 pays. "Nous avons choisi un itinéraire varié qui nous permet de survoler tous les types de paysage. Des déserts d'Arabie aux glaciers de Grœnland en passant par les forêts tropicales de Brunëi, en Asie." L'engin sera relié au monde grâce à des caméras, un téléphone par satellite. Il emporte aussi une balise de détresse et un canot pneumatique, au cas où.

Une aventure au profit des enfants
Grâce à son voyage, Jennifer espère récolter 4 millions de francs pour l'association caritative Sauvons les Enfants. Lors des escales, Jennifer rencontrera des enfants.

1 En quoi Jennifer Murray sera-t-elle unique? [2]
2 Quand est-ce que le voyage sera le plus dangereux? [1]
3 Pourquoi? [2]
4 Combien de temps faudra-t-il pour faire le tour du monde? [1]
5 Combien de kilomètres l'hélicoptère peut-il faire avant d'atterrir pour faire le plein? [1]
6 Quels genres de terrain est-ce que les pilotes vont survoler? [3]
7 Pourquoi est-ce que Jennifer fait ce vol? [2]

You will find the answers and examiner's comments on page 213.

4 Answer the following question in French.

Votre excursion s'est mal passée. Ecrivez un article de 150 mots environ sur votre voyage. Utilisez ces notes que vous avez prises pendant le voyage pour écrire l'article.

```
samedi
6h00    Départ de la maison
8h00    Petit déjeuner au café
9h30    Le sac de maman??
10h30   Retour au café
14h00   Pique-nique
14h35   Tombé en panne
        Téléphoné au garage
20h40   Retour à la maison
```

Sample Student's Answer

Samedi dernier nous nous sommes levés de très bonne heure pour aller à la mer. Nous n'avons rien mangé, et à six heures nous sommes partis. Après deux heures de route, nous nous sommes arrêtés pour prendre le petit déjeuner dans un café au bord de la route. Après avoir mangé, nous sommes repartis.

Une heure plus tard, maman a crié "Mon sac! Où est mon sac?" Elle l'avait laissé au café. Alors, nous avons dû faire demi-tour. Nous avons trouvé le sac de maman, et nous avons quitté le café pour la deuxième fois vers onze heures.

A cause de ce retard, il était déjà deux heures quand nous avons pris notre pique-nique. "Nous sommes en retard," a dit papa. "Il faut manger vite."

Nous sommes repartis à deux heures et demie, mais cinq minutes plus tard, papa a arrêté la voiture. "Qu'est-ce qu'il y a?" a demandé maman. "Je ne sais pas," a répondu mon père, fâché. "Je ne suis pas mécanicien, moi!" Il a téléphoné au garage, mais ils n'ont pas pu réparer la voiture, alors ils nous ont ramenés à la maison. Quelle journée!

EXAMINER'S COMMENTS

- There are many good points in this account.

- There is a wide variety of tenses, with at least one example of the present, imperfect, perfect, and pluperfect.

- The verbs used include both regular and irregular, as well as verbs with avoir and with être in the perfect tense.

- There are some uses of the infinitive (after pour, devoir, pouvoir and il faut).

- There are several examples of impressive expressions:
  – après avoir
  – à cause de
  – faire demi-tour

- There is good use of object pronouns, including an agreement (ils nous ont ramenés).

- There is some dialogue, which adds variety.

- There is an attempt at humour (Je ne suis pas mécanicien, moi!) – but don't overdo this!

- This is a clear Grade A performance.

CHAPTER 10

L'ENSEIGNEMENT SUPERIEUR, LA FORMATION ET L'EMPLOI

FURTHER EDUCATION, TRAINING AND JOBS

LES LIEUX DE TRAVAIL

une bibliothèque	library
un bureau	office
un laboratoire	laboratory
un magasin	shop
une usine	factory

QUESTIONS/PROMPTS

Qu'est-ce que tu vas faire après les examens?

Tu espères continuer tes études?

Qu'est-ce que tu as l'intention d'étudier? Pourquoi?

Qu'est-ce que tu voudrais faire comme métier?

Tes parents, que font-ils dans la vie?

WHAT YOU NEED TO KNOW

Je vais quitter l'école.	I'm going to leave school.
Je voudrais rester à l'école.	I'd like to stay at school.
Après le bac, j'espère aller à l'université.	After the bac (*see Chapter* 1), I hope to go to university.
Si je réussis à mes examens, je vais aller en faculté.	If I pass my exams, I want to go to university.
J'ai étudié les langues.	I have studied languages.
Je veux étudier la géographie.	I want to study geography.
Je vais continuer mes études.	I'm going to continue my education.
Je voudrais être mécanicien.	I'd like to be a mechanic.
Je ne voudrais pas être facteur.	I wouldn't like to be a postman.
Il faut se lever trop tôt le matin.	You have to get up too early in the morning.
Ce n'est pas très bien payé.	It's not very well paid.
Je veux devenir professeur.	I want to become a teacher.
Je voudrais travailler en plein air.	I'd like to work outdoors.
Ma sœur est au chômage.	My sister is unemployed.
Elle cherche un emploi dans l'informatique.	She's looking for a job in computers.
J'ai un petit job le soir/le week-end.	I have a little job in the evening/ at weekends.
Je fais du baby-sitting.	I baby-sit.
Je travaille dans un restaurant.	I work in a restaurant.
Je livre le lait/les journaux.	I deliver milk/newspapers.
J'ai fait un stage dans un complexe sportif.	I did work experience in a sports centre.
J'aide les touristes.	I help tourists.
Je réponds au téléphone.	I answer the phone.
Je travaille le samedi, de huit heures à six heures.	I work on Saturday, from eight till six.
Je gagne deux livres de l'heure.	I earn two pounds an hour.
Je fais des économies.	I put some money away.
C'est un métier intéressant.	It's an interesting job.
Mon père est électricien.	My father is an electrician.
Mon frère travaille dans une boutique.	My brother works in a small shop.
Ma mère est femme au foyer.	My mother is a housewife.

LES METIERS

un agent de police	policeman	un dentiste	dentist
un chauffeur (de taxi)	(taxi) driver	un ingénieur	engineer
un(e) coiffeur/se	hairdresser	un médecin	doctor
un garçon de café	waiter	un(e) serveur/se	waiter/ress
une hôtesse de l'air	air hostess	un(e) vendeur/se	shop assistant
un(e) informaticien(ne)	computer specialist	un vétérinaire	vet

une secrétaire

une caissière

un fermier

une infirmière

(Most of these jobs can be used to refer to a man or a woman, simply by changing *un* to *une*, or vice versa.)

Check yourself

QUESTIONS

Q1 *Tell your friend about your part-time job.*

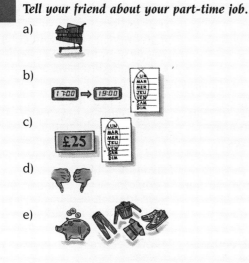

a)

b)

c)

d)

e)

Q2 *Que font ces personnes?*

a) J'écris des lettres sur l'ordinateur, et je réponds au téléphone.
b) Les clients me donnent de l'argent, et je les aide à mettre leurs achats dans les sacs.
c) Je me lève de bonne heure pour distribuer le courrier.
d) Je travaille souvent avec les animaux.
e) Je donne des renseignements aux touristes.

... est facteur.
... travaille au syndicat d'initiative.
... est caissier.
... est fermier.
... travaille dans un bureau.

REMEMBER! Cover the answers if you want to.

ANSWERS

A1
a) Je travaille au supermarché.
b) Je travaille de dix-sept heures à dix-neuf heures du lundi au vendredi.
c) Je gagne vingt-cinq livres par semaine.
d) Je n'aime pas le travail.
e) Je fais des économies pour acheter des vêtements.

A2
a) travaille dans un bureau.
b) est caissier.
c) est facteur.
d) est fermier.
e) travaille au syndicat d'initiative.

TUTORIAL

T1
a) *Your exam board will have a set of icons, like these, to represent common objects and ideas. You should make sure you are familiar with them.*
b) *Make sure you give both bits of information – failure to do so could well cost you more than half the marks.*
c) *Here, par semaine is again an important part of the message, which you mustn't leave out.*
d) *There are lots of other things you could say here. C'est ennuyeux/fatigant/mal payé would fit equally well.*
e) *If you couldn't remember faire des économies, you could say instead J'achète des vêtements avec l'argent, which would be almost as good.*

T2
This sort of question is often a matter of vocabulary. If you try to understand the gist, and then use the dictionary to fill in any gaps if you need to to answer the question, you will save yourself time.
a) *You may have forgotten ordinateur, but do you **really** need it?*
b) *You really need to understand the gist here. Why not do the others first, and come back to this? If you are sure of the other answers, this must be the one that's left.*
c) *Courrier is probably the word you need to check – and that gives you the answer.*
d) *There's only one of these jobs that could possibly involve animals.*
e) *If you looked up syndicat d'initiative and noticed the word touristes, you must have got this one!*

GOING FURTHER

Je voudrais apprendre à taper à la machine.	I'd like to learn keyboarding.
J'ai l'intention de devenir médecin, alors j'ai besoin d'aller à l'université.	I intend to become a doctor, so I need to go to university.
Pour être professeur de langues, il faut faire un stage à l'étranger.	To be a language teacher, you need to do work experience abroad.
Si on veut être informaticien, il faut être bon en maths.	If you want to work with computers, you have to be good at maths.
J'ai décidé de quitter l'école.	I've decided to leave school.
Je voudrais travailler dans un restaurant – je veux être chef de cuisine.	I'd like to work in a restaurant – I want to be a chef.
Mon ambition, c'est de ne pas travailler. Je vais gagner à la loterie nationale.	My ambition is not to work. I'm going to win the national lottery.
J'ai choisi d'étudier les sciences et les maths – ce sont mes matières préférées.	I've chosen to study science and maths – they are my favourite subjects.
Je ne sais pas encore ce que je vais faire dans la vie. Ça dépend des résultats.	I don't know yet what sort of job I want to do. It depends on my results.
Je ne voudrais pas travailler dans un bureau.	I wouldn't like to work in an office.
J'ai horreur de rester enfermé(e) toute la journée.	I hate being shut up indoors all day.
Je préférerais travailler avec le grand public.	I'd rather work with the general public.
J'aimerais travailler avec les enfants handicapés.	I'd like to work with handicapped children.
Je voudrais être journaliste, mais il y a très peu d'emplois.	I'd like to be a journalist, but there are very few jobs.
Mon père est au chômage depuis deux ans.	My father has been unemployed for two years.

QUELLE SORTE DE TRAVAIL?

dans un groupe	in a group
seul	alone
avec d'autres gens	with other people
avec les enfants	with children
avec les animaux	with animals

For this topic, you may well need to use past, present and future tenses – and probably the conditional too: what subjects you've done and what subjects you are going to do; a part-time job you've had, one that you do now, and the job you would like to do. The topic also gives you many opportunities to give reasons for what you say, and if you've applied for a job, you will probably be asked about your experience, your qualifications (such as any foreign languages you speak) and your reasons for wanting this particular job.

HOW THE GRAMMAR WORKS

NEGATIVES

ne ... pas	not
ne ... jamais	never
ne ... rien	nothing
ne ... personne	no-one/nobody
ne ... plus	no more/no longer
ne ... que	only
ne ... guère	hardly
ne ... ni ... ni	neither ... nor

Remember to put *ne* between the personal pronoun and the verb, and *pas* after the verb:

Je n'aime pas le chou-fleur. – I don't like cauliflower.
Il ne va jamais aux boums. – He never goes to parties.
Nous ne voulons rien. – We don't want anything. (We want nothing.)
Il n'y a personne dans la salle. – There is no-one in the room.
Tu n'aimes plus danser? – Don't you like dancing any more?
Elle n'a plus d'argent. – She has no more money.
Je n'ai que dix francs. – I only have ten francs.
Il ne vient guère me voir. – He hardly comes to see me.
Elle n'a ni frères ni sœurs. – She has neither brothers nor sisters.

When the verb is in the perfect tense, the second part of the negative comes before the past participle:

Je n'ai rien mangé ce matin. – I didn't eat anything this morning.

An exception to this is:

Elle n'a vu personne. – She didn't see anyone.

Personne, and occasionally *rien,* can be used as the subject of the verb, but remember that you still need the *ne*:

Personne n'est venu me voir. – Nobody came to see me.

Personne, jamais and *rien* can be used as one-word answers:

– *Qui as-tu vu au club?* – Who did you see at the club?
– *Personne!* – No-one!
– *Jacques! Qu'est-ce que tu as dit?* – Jacques! What did you say?
– *Rien!* – Nothing!
– *Vous êtes allée à l'étranger, Marie?* – Have you been abroad, Marie?
– *Jamais.* – Never.

Pas can also sometimes be used without *ne*:

Pas ce soir. – Not tonight.

In conversation, the French often leave out the *ne*:

C'est pas vrai! – It's not true!
J'ai jamais vu un tel film. – I've never seen such a film.

You need to listen out for this in the Listening Test, though you should probably not do it yourself, and certainly not in writing.

THE PASSIVE

This is a structure which it is probably better not to try to use yourself, as it can lead to a lot of unnecessary errors. You may well come across it, however, especially in newspaper extracts:

Trois voitures ont été détruites – Three cars were destroyed by a
par un incendie sur l'autoroute A6. fire on the A6 motorway.

However, you rarely need to use it, and the French often avoid it, especially in speech, by using *on*:

On m'a volé mon sac dans le métro. – My bag was stolen in the metro.

Check yourself

QUESTIONS

Q1 *Choose a suitable job for these people.*

a) Je pense que la forme est très importante pour les adolescents.

b) A l'école, je ne suis pas très forte, mais on me dit que je suis très sympa, surtout quand les gens sont malades.

c) Au collège, je suis assez bon en sciences, mais ce que j'aime le mieux, c'est m'occuper de la vieille voiture de mon père.

d) Je ne suis pas bon élève, mais j'aime voyager et rencontrer des gens.

e) J'adore la mode et la beauté. Je ne veux pas travailler seule.

informaticien	médecin
moniteur de ski	coiffeuse
chauffeur de camion	mécanicien
réceptionniste dans un cabinet de médecin	
professeur de gymnastique	

Q2 *Match up these halves of sentences.*

a) Je suis très fort en anglais et allemand,

b) Je vais travailler dans le magasin de mon oncle,

c) Avant d'aller à l'université

d) L'année dernière, j'étais faible en sciences,

e) Pourquoi est-ce qu'on travaillerait à l'école,

1 je vais passer une année en Belgique.

2 quand il y a tant de chômage?

3 alors je vais faire une licence de langues.

4 donc je n'ai pas besoin d'aller en faculté.

5 mais maintenant je vais travailler dur.

REMEMBER! Cover the answers if you want to.

ANSWERS

A1
a) professeur de gymnastique
b) réceptionniste dans un cabinet de médecin
c) mécanicien
d) chauffeur de camion
e) coiffeuse

A2
a) 3
b) 4
c) 1
d) 5
e) 2

TUTORIAL

T1
a) *The mention of* adolescents *rules out* moniteur de ski.
b) *You need to understand the first half of the sentence to eliminate* médecin.
c) *Here, what is said about school is not really relevant, because it is outweighed by* ce que j'aime le mieux.
d) Voyager *is the real clue, though you could have been misled by* voiture *in* c).
e) *You need to understand the gist, and then draw a conclusion.*

T2
For this exercise, you really need quite a detailed understanding of both the vocabulary and the structures to work out the answers.
a) *The specific languages should make the link with* langues (*and not with* Belgique – *they are the wrong languages!*)
b) *In this sort of exercise, you need to keep an eye on the whole exercise. If you choose 2 as your answer here (it's just about logical), you are left with nothing for e).*
c) *This is the only beginning which can be followed without a linking word, as it's already there in* avant de.
d) *A sentence with an imperfect tense can easily be followed by a contrast (*mais*).*
e) *The conditional tense is important here ('Why would one work').*

EXAM PRACTICE

1 Find Chapter 10 – Exam Practice Listening on the CD. Listen to the French (Track 19) twice, then decide which person would say each of the sentences below.

Choisis la bonne personne pour chaque phrase. Ecris **L** (Léo), **M** (Marika) ou **V** (Vestine).

1 Je sais exactement le métier que je voudrais faire.
2 Je vais faire un bac scientifique.
3 Je voudrais devenir médecin.
4 Je ne suis pas fort en sciences.
5 Je veux être photographe. [4 marks]

You will find the transcript and answers, with examiner's comments, on page 214.

2 Find Chapter 10 – Exam Practice Speaking on the CD. Listen to the conversation (Track 20). Think for a moment about what you have heard. Then read the examiner's comments. Did any of these points occur to you?

> *Now think about some of the things you might want to say about your education and future plans. These questions will help you to plan your answers:*
> * *Quelles sont tes matières préférées?*
> * *Tu vas continuer tes études?*
> * *Qu'est-ce que tu vas faire dans la vie?*

You will find the transcript and examiner's comments on page 215.

3 Read this article, then choose the right word from the list below to fill each gap.

Pour chaque blanc dans cet article, choisis le mot approprié dans la liste qui suit.

Les enfants au travail
Une enquête sur le travail des enfants au Bangladesh

"Ça m'a vraiment ouvert ___1___ sur ce problème de l'exploitation des enfants," a dit un des jeunes américains qui ont visité l'Asie. Les jeunes 'reporters' (âgés de 14 à 17 ans) ont parlé avec plusieurs enfants qui avaient été esclaves. Ils ont visité des ateliers de confection où les enfants travaillent jusqu'à 12 heures par jour pour des salaires ___2___ . Les enfants ont parlé plus facilement aux jeunes journalistes qu'avec des ___3___ . "Nous avons parlé avec des enfants de 12 ans qui avaient été insultés et battus, et qui travaillaient dans des conditions d'hygiène ___4___ ," a dit un autre reporter. Mais comment peut-on distinguer entre le travail et ___5___ des enfants? Car beaucoup de ces enfants veulent travailler – sans leur salaire, même très petit, leur ___6___ n'aurait pas de quoi manger, et ils sont fiers d'apporter quelque chose au budget familial. Mais le travail empêche leur développement ___7___ (car ils ne vont pas souvent à l'école) et physique – c'est à dire qu'ils sont exploités. A long terme, la solution serait d'assurer un salaire ___8___ aux adultes – mais ce n'est pas pour demain.

You will find the answers and examiner's comments on page 216.

l'encouragement	minimes	intellectuel	employeurs
les yeux	épouvantables	adultes	l'exploitation
enfants	la porte	famille	suffisant

H WRITING

4 Write a reply to the following letter in French, then compare your version with the sample answer on page 216.

Tu as reçu cette lettre d'un ami français. Réponds à la lettre. Réponds à toutes ses questions.

You will find the sample answer, with examiner's comments, on page 216.

Lille, le 23 juin

Cher ...

Ouf! Enfin, les examens sont finis. Maintenant, il faut attendre les résultats. Tu as passé des examens, toi aussi? Ils étaient durs? Tu crois que tu vas avoir de bonnes notes? Moi, non. Je suis nul en langues, alors j'aurai de très mauvaises notes, et mes parents vont me gronder – comme d'habitude. Ils ne comprennent pas, les parents, pas vrai?

Et puis, il faudra bientôt décider ce que je vais faire plus tard. Tu veux aller à l'université, toi? Pour étudier quoi? Ou peut-être préfères-tu trouver un emploi tout de suite? Mais quel genre d'emploi? Moi, j'aimerais être comptable, comme mon père, mais je ne sais pas si je suis assez fort en maths. Qu'est-ce que tu en penses? Tu as déjà décidé d'un travail?

Ecris-moi bientôt.

WHAT YOU NEED TO KNOW

French telephone numbers are now all ten digits long, and all begin 01, 02, 03, 04 or 05 depending on the area. The French put the numbers together in pairs, so 0153569620 is printed as 01 53 56 96 20 and said as: *le zéro un, cinquante-trois, cinquante-six, quatre-vingt-seize, vingt.*

Quel est votre numéro de téléphone?	What's your telephone number?
Mon numéro de téléphone est le deux cent cinquante-trois, trente-neuf, quatre-vingt-quinze.	My telephone number is two five three, three nine, nine five (253 39 95).
Allô, M. Lenormand à l'appareil.	Hello, Mr Lenormand speaking.
Ici Jean-Luc.	Jean-Luc here.
Qui est à l'appareil?	Who's speaking?
Je peux parler au directeur?	May I speak to the manager?
Pourriez-vous me passer M. Martin?	Could you put me through to Mr Martin?
Je vous le/la passe.	I'm putting you through to him/her.
Ne quittez pas.	Hold the line.
Elle n'est pas là en ce moment.	She's not in at the moment.
Il est occupé.	He's busy.
Il peut vous rappeler?	Can he call you back?
Vous pouvez me contacter au ...	You can contact me on ....
Vous voulez laisser un message?	Do you want to leave a message?
Il y a un répondeur.	There is an answering machine.
Je rappellerai plus tard.	I'll call back later.
Il y a une cabine téléphonique près d'ici?	Is there a phone box nearby?
Il faut de la monnaie.	You need change.
Vous vendez des télécartes?	Do you sell phone cards?
Je voudrais téléphoner en Angleterre.	I'd like to phone England.
L'indicatif, c'est le zéro-zéro, quarante-quatre.	The code is 00 44.
Ce soir, sur la place du village, il y aura un grand bal.	This evening, in the village square, there will be a big dance.
Venez voir le cirque.	Come and see the circus.
Achetez vos billets à l'entrée, ou au syndicat d'initiative.	Buy your tickets at the entrance, or at the tourist office.
Je n'aime pas les publicités.	I don't like adverts.
Les pubs sont plus amusantes que les émissions.	The ads are more fun than the programmes.
J'ai vu l'annonce dans le journal.	I saw the notice in the newspaper.

LES FETES

le championnat	the championship
un concert	a concert
un concours de boules	a bowls competition
une foire	a fair
les gagnants	the winners
le gros lot	the big prize
les jours fériés	public holidays
un spectacle	a show
la musique folklorique	folk music

LES PETITES ANNONCES

cherche	wanted
à louer	for hire/to let
neuf/ve	new
d'occasion	second-hand
à vendre	for sale

DANS UNE CABINE TELEPHONIQUE

Décrochez le combiné.	Lift the receiver.
Attendez la tonalité.	Wait for the tone.
Introduisez les pièces.	Put in the coins.
Composez le numéro.	Dial the number.
Raccrochez le combiné.	Hang up.

QUESTIONS/PROMPTS

Vous aimez les publicités?

Quelle est votre publicité préférée? Pourquoi?

Qu'est-ce que vous aimez comme spectacle?

Vous avez déjà travaillé? Où ça?

Check yourself

QUESTIONS

Q1 **What is being advertised here?**

a) Miami – au vrai jus de fruits.
b) Dop – pour la santé de vos cheveux.
c) La bonne musique moins chère.
d) Chaque semaine, un poster géant.
e) En vrai coton.

> de la nourriture pour chiens
> un yaourt   un magasin de disques
> une machine à laver
> un magazine pour les jeunes   un pull
> des pommes   un shampooing

Q2 **Fill in the missing words in these telephone messages.**

a) M. Dupont rappellera _____.
b) _____ à Mme Leblanc ce matin.
c) Mme Borie a _____ à six heures.
d) Jeanne arrivera _____.
e) Appelez M. Lucas au _____.

> en retard   rendez-vous   téléphonez
> plus tard   bureau   urgent
> vous   arrivé

REMEMBER! Cover the answers if you want to.

ANSWERS

A1
a) un yaourt
b) un shampooing
c) un magasin de disques
d) un magazine pour les jeunes
e) un pull

ANSWERS

A2
a) plus tard
b) téléphonez
c) rendez-vous
d) en retard
e) bureau

TUTORIAL

T1
a) You always need to be careful with the first answer in this sort of question. It's true that yaourt *might* fit, but is there anything else which might fit better? Here, there isn't!
b) Be careful not to answer on the basis of just one word. For example, santé could be appropriate for yoghourt. It's only when you get to cheveux that you have enough information.
c) Don't confuse magazine and magasin (shop).
d) Try to be aware of French words which look like English words. There are a lot of them, and it can save you time.
e) Coton *might have made you think about* une machine à laver, *but the* en *should give you the correct answer.*

T2
a/d) The difference between plus tard (later) and en retard (late) is crucial in these.
b) Rendez-vous *would only fit here if the next word was* avec, *not* à.
c) Téléphoné *would fit here, but not* téléphonez, *so the only possibility is* rendez-vous.
e) Again, téléphone *would fit, but not* téléphonez.

GOING FURTHER

Vous pouvez m'envoyer un fax?	Can you send me a fax?
Marquez votre fax "à l'attention de Mme Valadié".	Mark your fax "for the attention of Mrs Valadié".
Vous pouvez me contacter par courrier électronique. Voici mon adresse.	You can contact me via e-mail. Here is my address.
Je dois écouter les messages sur le répondeur, et écrire des notes.	I have to listen to the messages on the answering machine, and write memos.
Je suis aussi responsable des photocopies.	I'm also in charge of photocopies.
Pour faire une demande d'emploi, il faut remplir un formulaire.	To apply for a job, you have to fill in an application form.
On m'a demandé de me présenter pour un entretien.	I've been asked to go for an interview.
Pourquoi est-ce que ce poste vous intéresse?	Why are you interested in this job?
Vous avez de l'expérience de ce genre de travail?	Do you have any experience of this sort of job?
Vous avez déjà travaillé dans l'hôtellerie/la restauration?	Have you any experience of hotel work/catering?
Parlez-moi de vos qualités personnelles.	Tell me about your personal qualities.
Je suis consciencieux/se, mais un peu timide.	I'm conscientious, but a bit shy.
Je m'entends très bien avec les autres/les enfants/les animaux.	I get on very well with other people/children/animals.
Quelles sont les heures de travail?	What are the working hours?
Quel est le salaire?	What is the salary?
Vous travaillerez du mardi au samedi, de seize heures à vingt-trois heures, et un dimanche sur deux.	You will work from Tuesday to Saturday, from 4pm to 11pm, and every other Sunday.
Le lundi, vous êtes libre.	You are free on Mondays.
Les publicités présentent toujours des idées stéréotypées.	Advertisements always show stereotyped ideas.
Le but de la publicité, c'est d'encourager les gens à dépenser plus d'argent, et à acheter des choses dont ils n'ont pas besoin.	The aim of advertising is to encourage people to spend more money, and to buy things they don't need.
Est-ce qu'on doit interdire certaines publicités?	Should certain advertisements be banned?

HOW THE GRAMMAR WORKS

THE SUPERLATIVE

We have already seen in Chapter 7 how adjectives can be used to compare things or people, by using *plus* (more), *aussi* (as) or *moins* (less).

> *L'histoire est plus intéressante que la géographie.* — History is more interesting than geography.

A similar structure is used to identify someone or something as the most (or the least). Simply put the definite article before *plus* (or *moins*). This is known as the superlative form.

> *La matière la plus intéressante, c'est la biologie.* — The most interesting subject is biology.

AU BUREAU

un(e) client(e)	customer
la direction	management
l'expédition	despatch
la photocopieuse	photocopier
le président	chairman
une réunion	a meeting

LA PUBLICITE

l'alcool	alcohol
les jouets	toys
la lessive	washing powder
la marque	brand
la nourriture	food
les produits (de ménage)	(household) products
le racisme	racism
la sécurité	safety
le sexisme	sexism
le tabac	tobacco
la vitesse	speed

LES QUALITES PERSONNELLES

aimable	pleasant, polite
de bonne humeur	cheerful
distrait(e)	absent-minded
élégant(e)	smart (in dress)
ouvert(e)	outgoing
ponctuel(le)	punctual
pratique	practical
sérieux	serious-minded
travailleur/se	hard-working

Note that the adjective (and the article) agree with the noun:

Jean est le garçon le plus travailleur.	– John is the most hard-working boy.
Ce sont les élèves les plus intelligents.	– They are the most intelligent pupils.

The adjective keeps its usual position. In the case of most adjectives, the adjective follows the noun. However, if it is an adjective which comes before the noun (see Chapter 4), the superlative also comes before:

C'est la plus petite entreprise.	– It's the smallest firm.
On a vu les plus beaux animaux.	– We saw the most beautiful animals.

le mont Everest

While the superlative in English is often followed by 'in', in French it is followed by *de*:

C'est l'élève le moins intelligent de la classe.	– He's the least intelligent pupil in the class.
C'est la montagne la plus haute du monde.	– It's the highest mountain in the world.

Exceptions:

bon → *meilleur* (better) → *le meilleur* (the best)
mauvais → *pire* (worse) → *le pire* (the worst)

The superlative of adverbs is formed in the same way as the superlative of adjectives:

C'est Hélène qui court le plus vite.	– It's Hélène who runs most quickly.

Note that, since adverbs do not agree, there are no feminine or plural forms.

DEMONSTRATIVE ADJECTIVES

In French, the same words are usually used for both 'this' and 'that':

ce message (masculine) – this/that message
cette lettre (feminine) – this/that letter
ces publicités (plural) – these/those advertisements

There is another form – *cet* – which is used only before a masculine singular noun beginning with a vowel or with the letter *h*:

cet emploi – this/that job
cet homme – this/that man

If it is really important to distinguish between 'this' and 'that', you can add *-ci* or *-là* respectively to the end of the noun:

Donnez-moi cette liste, s'il vous plaît.	– Give me that list please.
Non, cette liste-là.	No, that list.
Je n'ai jamais lu ce roman-ci.	– I've never read this novel.

DEMONSTRATIVE PRONOUNS

celui (masculine)	*celle* (feminine)
ceux (masculine plural)	*celles* (feminine plural)

Like demonstrative adjectives, these are usually used to distinguish between two similar objects or people:

Je trouve que Nathalie est vraiment adorable. Tu sais, celle aux cheveux blonds.	– I think Nathalie is really lovely. You know, the one with the blond hair.
J'ai vu ce film. Tu sais, celui avec Gérard Depardieu.	– I've seen that film. You know, the one with Gérard Depardieu.
Tu n'aimes pas les documentaires? Même pas ceux avec les animaux?	– Don't you like documentaries? Not even the ones with animals?
J'adore les pâtisseries, surtout celles avec de la crème.	– I love pastries, especially the ones with cream.

When no specific thing is referred to, use *ceci* or *cela* (often shortened to *ça*).

Marc m'a donné ceci.	– Marc gave me this.
Je n'ai jamais vu ça.	– I've never seen that.

Gérard Depardieu

Check yourself

QUESTIONS

Q1

You are applying for a job in France.

a) Say you are free in July and August.
b) Say you have already worked in a restaurant.
c) Say you get on well with customers.
d) Say you would like to work evenings, but not weekends.
e) Find out how much you will be paid.

Q2

You are telling your friend about your new job.

a) You have to answer the telephone – it's difficult in French.
b) You have to help English customers.
c) You get on very well with the manager.
d) You have to work every other weekend, but you are free on Fridays and Mondays.
e) The salary isn't enormous, but it's not bad.

REMEMBER! Cover the answers if you want to.

ANSWERS

A1

a) Je suis libre aux mois de juillet et août.
b) J'ai déjà travaillé dans un restaurant.
c) Je m'entends bien avec les clients.
d) Je voudrais travailler le soir, mais pas le week-end.
e) Je gagnerai combien?

A2

a) Je dois répondre au téléphone – c'est difficile en français.
b) Je dois aider les clients anglais.
c) Je m'entends très bien avec le directeur.
d) Je dois travailler un week-end sur deux, mais je suis libre le vendredi et le lundi.
e) Le salaire n'est pas énorme, mais ce n'est pas mal.

TUTORIAL

T1

a) *'In' with a month is* en (*not* dans), *but* au mois de *is also very common. Here,* aux *has to be plural since it refers to both July and August.*
b) *In the past,* déjà *comes before the past participle.*
c) *You need to be able to create new sentences by substituting fresh elements: you know* je m'entends bien avec, *and you can add all sorts of new endings.*
d) *Remember this use of* pas *without* ne.
e) *There is often another way of expressing an idea, if you're not sure of a word. For example, here you could say:* Le salaire, c'est combien? *or even* Ça paie combien?

T2

a) *To answer the phone =* répondre au téléphone.
a/b) *Remember:* devoir *is followed by the infinitive.*
c) *Don't leave out the little words –* très *is an important part of the message.*
d) *'Every other' is easily expressed in French by* un ... sur deux. *In the same way,* un ... sur trois/quatre *means 'one in three/four'.*
e) *You could use* formidable (*great*) *here, but when referring to size, and particularly money, the French often use* énorme. Ce n'est pas (*or* c'est pas) mal *is very commonly used for 'It's not bad'.*

EXAM PRACTICE

H LISTENING

You will find the transcript and answers, with examiner's comments, on page 217.

1 Find Chapter 11 – Exam Practice Listening on the CD. Listen to the French (Track 21) twice, then answer the question.

Quelle est l'attitude de ces jeunes? Ecrivez **C** (Caroline), **M** (Matthieu), **E** (Elise) ou **L** (Luc).

1 ____ est tout à fait contre la publicité.

2 ____ n'aime pas que les publicités interrompent les émissions.

3 ____ trouve que les publicités sont souvent mauvaises, mais les aime quand même.

4 ____ a toujours faim quand elle regarde les publicités.

F H READING

2 Read this article, then answer the questions in French.

La pub contre le racisme?

Pour profiter de la journée contre le racisme, que l'on célèbre aujourd'hui, l'entreprise italienne Benetton, spécialiste depuis quelques années de la publicité "choc", vient de sortir une nouvelle affiche. Celle-ci montre trois cœurs humains qui portent les mots (en anglais) BLANC, NOIR, JAUNE.

Est-il vraiment acceptable de profiter d'un mouvement comme l'anti-racisme pour faire de la publicité pour les vêtements?

Est-ce que les gens seront choqués – ou même offensés – par une telle image au coin de la rue?

Les 40 à 60 ans ont souvent été choqués par l'image (64%). Parmi les 25 à 40 ans, 40% se disent offensés par "l'exploitation de l'anti-racisme pour des fins commerciales", mais très peu ont été choqués. Mais chez les moins de 15 ans, le choc est totalement absent, et ils approuvent à cent pour cent le message: "Je suis pour cette pub, car on a tous le même cœur" (Raphaëlle, 13 ans); "Ce ne sont pas les jeunes qui seront choqués, mais plutôt les personnes âgées" (Jérôme, 11 ans); "Cette pub n'est pas choquante si c'est pour lutter contre le racisme" (Céline, 12 ans).

1 La réaction à cette publicité a été la plus favorable chez
   a) les enfants **b)** les moins de 25 ans
   c) les plus de 40 ans.

2 La publicité a choqué
   a) les enfants **b)** les jeunes adultes
   c) les personnes plus âgées

3 L'image a été choisie pour montrer que
   a) la couleur de la peau n'a pas d'importance
   b) tous les cœurs sont différents
   c) Benetton produit de jolies couleurs

You will find the answers and examiner's comments on page 217.

4 Qui a prévu les résultats du sondage?
   a) Raphaëlle **b)** Jérôme
   c) Céline

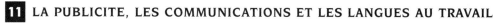

3 First, look at the situation below and think what you might say. Then find Chapter 11 – Exam Practice Speaking on the CD and listen to the role-play (Track 22).

SPEAKING F H

You are on work experience in a French estate agency. You answer the telephone.

The manager is not in. Answer the caller's question. Ask if you can help. Find out the caller's phone number.

- absent
- !
- aider?
- numéro?

You will find the transcript and
examiner's comments on page 218.

4 Answer the following question in French, then compare your answer with the sample on page 218.

WRITING H

Vous voulez trouver un emploi en France. Vous avez vu cette annonce dans le journal. Ecrivez une lettre pour demander l'emploi.

Ecrivez 100 à 120 mots.

LE FAST

Restaurant fast-food

hamburgers, saucisses, pizza

CHERCHE
serveur/serveuse

Ecrire à M. Dupont
3 rue Lafayette, Dijon

Donnez vos détails personnels.
Parlez:
– de pourquoi ce travail vous intéresse
– des emplois que vous avez eus
– de vos qualités personnelles
– de vos études de français

Demandez:
– les heures de travail
– le salaire

Dites:
– quand vous pouvez travailler

You will find the sample answer and
examiner's comments on page 218.

CHAPTER 12

LA VIE A L'ETRANGER, LE TOURISME, LES COUTUMES ET LE LOGEMENT

LIFE ABROAD, TOURISM, CUSTOMS AND ACCOMMODATION

WHAT YOU NEED TO KNOW

Pendant les grandes vacances, j'ai passé une semaine sur la côte d'Azur.	During the summer holidays, I spent a week on the Mediterranean coast.
Je me suis très bien amusé(e).	I had a very good time.
C'était une jolie région.	It was a pretty area.
Il a fait beau.	The weather was good.
L'hôtel était excellent.	The hotel was excellent.
Nous avons très bien mangé.	We ate very well.
Nous sommes allés dans beaucoup de musées.	We went to a lot of museums.
C'était ennuyeux.	It was boring.
Vous avez une chambre pour deux personnes pour ce soir?	Do you have a double room for tonight?
avec douche/salle de bains/WC?	with shower/bathroom/toilet?
avec un grand lit/deux lits?	with a double bed/two single beds?
C'est pour deux nuits.	It's for two nights.
Je voudrais réserver une chambre.	I'd like to book a room.
La chambre est cent quarante-neuf francs la nuit.	The room is 149F per night.
Le petit déjeuner coûte trente-huit francs par personne.	Breakfast costs 38F per person.
Le petit déjeuner est de sept heures à huit heures trente.	Breakfast is from 7 to 8.30.
Je peux voir la chambre?	Can I see the room?
Il n'y a pas d'oreillers/de couvertures/de serviettes.	There are no pillows/blankets/towels.
Il y a une salle de bains à chaque étage.	There is a bathroom on each floor.
Le garage est derrière l'hôtel.	The garage is behind the hotel.
Il y a une auberge de jeunesse près de la gare.	There is a youth hostel near the station.
Il est interdit de faire la cuisine dans les dortoirs.	Cooking in the dormitories is forbidden.
Je regrette, le camping est complet.	I'm sorry, the campsite is full.
Votre emplacement est tout près des bacs à vaisselle.	Your pitch is right next to the washing-up sinks.
Vous pouvez louer des draps/des sacs de couchage.	You can hire sheets/sleeping bags.

AU CAMPING

par personne	per person
par tente	per tent
par nuit	per night
par emplacement	per pitch
par caravane	per caravan
les sanitaires	the shower/lavatory blocks
les poubelles	the dustbins
l'aire de jeux	the play area

LE REGLEMENT DE L'AUBERGE

Il est interdit de:	You must not:
faire du bruit	make a noise
préparer les repas	prepare meals
faire la lessive	do your washing

Il faut:	You must:
rentrer avant onze heures	be back before 11
nettoyer la cuisine	clean the kitchen

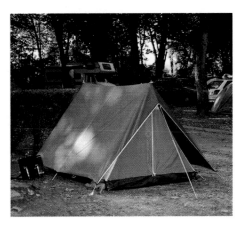

QUESTIONS/PROMPTS

Tu as déjà fait du camping?

Tu préfères passer les vacances à l'hôtel ou au camping? Pourquoi?

Tu aimes la cuisine étrangère? Laquelle?

Où passes-tu tes vacances d'habitude?

Parle-moi de tes vacances l'année dernière.

Check yourself

QUESTIONS

Q1 *You are at a hotel. What do you say?*

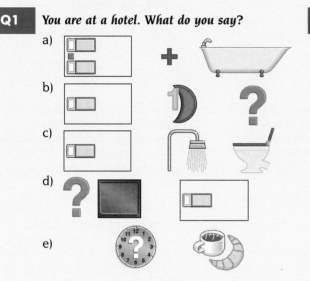

a)

b)

c)

d)

e)

Q2 *Fill in the gaps in the following sentences.*

a) Vous avez un _____ pour une tente et une caravane?

b) Vous êtes priés de ne pas faire de bruit _____ dix heures du soir.

c) L'auberge est _____ entre dix heures et demie et sept heures.

d) Vous êtes priés de faire la vaisselle _____ de partir.

e) Le _____ des filles est au premier étage, à droite.

fermée	ouverte	dortoir
restaurant	après	avant
garage	emplacement	vers

REMEMBER! Cover the answers if you want to.

ANSWERS

A1
a) Je voudrais une chambre pour deux personnes, avec salle de bain.
b) Avez-vous une chambre pour une personne pour une nuit?
c) Je voudrais une chambre pour une personne avec douche et WC.
d) Il y a une télévision dans la chambre?
e) A quelle heure est le petit déjeuner?

A2
a) emplacement
b) après
c) fermée
d) avant
e) dortoir

TUTORIAL

T1
a) *Your exam board will use icons of this sort to represent various kinds of room. Make sure you can recognise them easily.*
b) *The question mark tells you to ask a question.*
c) *Make sure you give all the required details.*
d) *The phrase il y a is very useful when you want to find out if something is available. In speech, don't forget to use a rising tone to make it a question.*
e) *Finding out what time something is, is one of the most likely questions you will need to ask. Make sure you can do it.*

T2
a) *After un, there must be a noun. There are four nouns in the list, but do you really want a restaurant, a garage or a dormitory for your tent and caravan? Emplacement is a hard word to translate, but it just means the bit of land (pitch) on which you put your tent.*
b) *Avant (before) would fit here grammatically, but logically it makes no sense.*
c) *Again, ouverte would fit grammatically, but not logically.*
d) *As in b), you need to use your common sense as well as your knowledge of French.*
e) *The youth hostel is not likely to have a restaurant especially for girls, so the answer must be dortoir.*

LES RECETTES

ajoutez	add
battez	beat
faites bouillir	boil
faites chauffer	heat
faites frire	fry
au four	in the oven
dans une poêle	in a frying-pan
mélangez	mix
versez	pour

L'HOTEL

les arrhes	deposit
un ascenseur	a lift
confirmer (par écrit)	to confirm (in writing)
pension complète	full board (room, with breakfast, lunch & evening meal)
demi-pension	half board (room, with breakfast & evening meal)
une réservation	a reservation
une salle de jeux	a games room

GOING FURTHER

La bouillabaisse est une sorte de soupe de poisson.

Pour faire une crème caramel pour quatre personnes, il vous faut un litre de lait, 250 grammes de sucre, et six œufs.

En France, on mange généralement assez tard le soir.

Dis, on se tutoie maintenant?

J'ai l'intention de visiter votre région au mois de juillet prochain.

Pourriez-vous m'envoyer un plan de la région et une liste des hôtels?

Avez-vous des brochures sur les excursions et les sites touristiques?

L'année prochaine, j'irai au Kenya faire un safari.

Ce sera passionnant de voir tous les animaux sauvages.

Je préfère les vacances actives – cette année, par exemple, je vais faire du canoë-kayak.

Moi, par contre, je vais en vacances pour me détendre: quinze jours sur une plage avec un bon livre, voilà l'idéal.

Ah non! Ça m'ennuierait énormément.

Vraiment, ça ne va pas. Il n'y a pas d'eau chaude, et la chambre est sale.

Je n'arrive pas à dormir. Il y a du bruit au bar jusqu'à deux heures du matin.

Il y a un robinet qui goutte. Vous pouvez envoyer quelqu'un?

Il y a de la circulation toute la nuit.

Vous pouvez me trouver une autre chambre?

Bouillabaisse is a sort of fish soup.

To make a creme caramel for four people, you need a litre of milk, 250 grams of sugar and six eggs.

In France, they usually eat quite late in the evening.

Shall we call each other "tu" now?

I intend to visit your area next July.

Could you send me a map of the region and a list of hotels?

Do you have any brochures about excursions and tourist attractions?

Next year, I'm going on a safari in Kenya.

It will be exciting to see all the wild animals.

I prefer active holidays – this year, for example, I'm going canoeing.

For me, it's the opposite. I go on holiday to relax: a fortnight on a beach with a good book, that's my ideal.

Oh no. I'd be terribly bored.

Really, this won't do. There's no hot water, and the room is dirty.

I can't get to sleep. There's noise in the bar until two in the morning.

There's a dripping tap. Can you send someone?

There's traffic all night.

Can you find me another room?

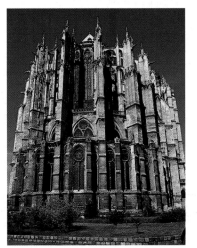

LES EXCURSIONS

la cathédrale	the cathedral
une cité médiévale	a medieval walled town
l'église	the church
les îles	the islands
un lac	a lake
un monument historique	a historical monument
le paysage	the scenery
la vieille ville	the old town
une demi-journée	half a day
une journée	a day
une soirée	an evening
à cheval	on horse-back

HOW THE GRAMMAR WORKS

THE IMPERFECT TENSE

As with other tenses, the imperfect tense works with a system of endings.
There is only one set of endings, which are used for all verbs:

je	**-ais**	nous	**-ions**
tu	**-ais**	vous	**-iez**
il/elle/on	**-ait**	ils/elles	**-aient**

These endings are added to the *nous* form of the present tense, minus the *-ons*:

Nous regardons → regard → je regardais	I was watching
Nous choisissons → choisiss → je choisissais	I was choosing
Nous descendons → descend → je descendais	I was going down
Nous allons → all → j'allais	I was going

The only exception to this is the verb *être*, though it uses the same endings:

j'étais	nous étions
tu étais	vous étiez
il/elle/on était	ils/elles étaient

The imperfect tense is used for description in the past, and to describe
repeated or interrupted actions in the past. In English, these are often
expressed by 'was/were ...ing' or 'used to ...', but this is only a rough guide,
and there are many exceptions. The only way to get to grips with the
imperfect tense is by seeing it in action. Here are some examples:

Elle prenait le petit déjeuner quand le téléphone a sonné.	–	She was having breakfast when the phone rang. (interrupted action)
Quand nous étions jeunes nous passions toujours les vacances au bord de la mer.	–	When we were young (description) we always spent (repeated action) our holidays at the sea-side.
Je suis allé en France pour la première fois quand j'avais douze ans.	–	I went to France for the first time when I was twelve. (description)
Il fumait beaucoup, mais il a arrêté l'année dernière.	–	He used to smoke a lot (repeated action), but he stopped last year.

THE PLUPERFECT TENSE

This tense is used when the main action is in the past, and you need to refer
to something which had happened even earlier. It is formed like the perfect
tense, by using part of *avoir* or *être* and the past participle, but using the
imperfect tense.

j'avais préparé – I had prepared
tu avais fini – you had finished
il/elle/on avait vu – he/she/one had seen
nous avions fait – we had done
vous aviez dit – you had said
ils/elles avaient eu – they had had

j'étais entré(e) – I had gone in
tu étais parti(e) – you had left
il/on était allé – he/one had gone
elle était venue – she had come
nous étions retourné(e)s – we had returned
vous étiez arrivé(e)s – you had arrived
ils étaient sortis – they had gone out
elles étaient tombées – they had fallen

Reflexive verbs also use *être*:

>*je m'étais levé(e)* – I had got up
>*nous nous étions couché(e)s* – We had gone to bed

Remember the agreement of the past participle with verbs using *être*.

VENIR DE + INFINITIVE

To express the idea of having just done something, use the verb *venir* in the present tense, followed by *de* then an infinitive:

>*Je viens de parler à Marie.* – I have just spoken to Marie.
>*Ils viennent d'arriver.* – They have just arrived.

This construction can also be used in the imperfect:

>*Je venais de quitter la maison.* – I had just left the house.
>*Nous venions de dîner.* – We had just had dinner.

IL Y A

As well as meaning 'there is/are', *il y a* can also be used with expressions of time to mean 'ago':

>*Je l'ai vu il y a dix minutes.* – I saw him 10 minutes ago.
>*Elle est partie il y a une semaine.* – She left a week ago.

Note that *il y a* always comes before the time expression.

OTHER TENSES

You may (especially in the Reading Test) meet other tenses than the ones mentioned in these chapters. Your syllabus may, for example, mention the Subjunctive or the Past Historic (see Grammar Summary). You will not be expected to use these tenses, but you should be able to recognise the verb. If you simply remove the ending you may well find that you know the verb. If not, you can check in your dictionary.

Check yourself

QUESTIONS

Q1 *You are writing to a French hotel. What do you write?*

a) You want to book a room for two weeks ...

b) ... from the 23rd July to the 5th August.

c) You want a room for two people, with shower and toilet, with breakfast and evening meal.

d) You want them to send you some brochures about the region.

e) You want them to confirm your booking.

Q2 *Your friends are telling you about their holidays. Match each sentence with the appropriate person.*

a) Ma chambre donnait sur la route nationale. Le bruit de la circulation était affreux.

b) L'hôtel était impeccable, à cent mètres d'une belle plage. La cuisine était très bonne aussi, mais le soir ce n'était pas très animé.

c) On était quatre, alors on s'est bien amusé. Mais les chambres étaient sales, et les lits n'étaient pas du tout confortables.

d) Il a fait un temps splendide, on a passé toute la journée à la plage, et je me suis beaucoup ennuyée.

e) C'était vraiment super. J'ai déjà réservé au même camping pour l'année prochaine.

Maryse, qui a passé de bonnes vacances malgré l'hôtel
Marc, qui s'est fait beaucoup d'amis
Samir, qui était content de l'hôtel, mais qui s'est un peu ennuyé
Rachelle, qui a passé d'excellentes vacances
Annie, qui est rentrée très fatiguée
Chloé, qui aurait préféré des vacances plus actives

REMEMBER! Cover the answers if you want to.

ANSWERS

A1
a) Je voudrais réserver une chambre pour deux semaines ...

b) ... du vingt-trois juillet au cinq août.

c) Je voudrais une chambre pour deux personnes, avec douche et WC, en demi-pension.

d) Pourriez-vous m'envoyer des brochures sur la région?

e) Pourriez-vous confirmer ma réservation?

A2
a) Annie
b) Samir
c) Maryse
d) Chloé
e) Rachelle

TUTORIAL

T1
a) Quinze jours is more common than deux semaines to mean 'a fortnight'.

b) Remember du and au with dates: 'from ... to'.

c) Instead of en demi-pension you could equally correctly say avec petit déjeuner et dîner.

d/e) Pourriez-vous is a very polite way of asking someone to do something for you, the equivalent of 'Could you' or 'Would you' in English.

d) Here, 'about' would usually be sur.

e) It probably wouldn't matter if you said la réservation instead of ma.

T2
a) You have to deduce that the traffic noise kept her awake, so that she came home tired.

b) In the first 1½ sentences, you can work out that he is being complimentary about the hotel, even if you don't understand impeccable (faultless). However, to understand the 'but', you probably need to look up animé (lively), as that is the link with 'bored'.

c) Malgré means 'in spite of', so you are clearly looking for someone who had a poor hotel, but still had a good time.

d) This is hard – everything she says about the holiday is good except that she was bored.

e) You have to deduce that, since she has already booked again, she had a really good time.

EXAM PRACTICE

H LISTENING

1 Find Chapter 12 – Exam Practice Listening on the CD. Listen to the French (Track 23) twice, then complete the grid.

Pour chaque personne, choisis la destination idéale, et explique pourquoi.

A SAFARI EN AFRIQUE

B PETIT STUDIO – COTE MEDITERRANEENNE

C ANCIENNE FERME ISOLEE

D VIVRE EN FAMILLE AU CANADA

You will find the transcript and answers, with examiner's comments, on page 219.

	Destination	**Raison**
Nathalie		
Antoine		
Sophie		

H WRITING

2 Answer the following question in French, then compare your answer with the sample on page 220.

Ecris un article sur ta visite en France l'année dernière. Développe ces notes que tu as prises pendant ton séjour.

You will find the sample answer and examiner's comments on page 220.

	samedi 18h	arrivée à l'hôtel
		réservation perdue
	samedi 20h	arrivée 2ème hôtel
	dimanche	repos
●	lundi	excursion – château
	mardi – vendredi	plage

3 First, look at the situation below and think what you might say. Then find Chapter 12 – Exam Practice Speaking on the CD and listen to the role-play (Track 24).

When you get to your hotel room, after a long, hot journey, you discover there is a problem with the shower. You need to try to solve this problem with the receptionist.

SPEAKING **H**

You will find the transcript and examiner's comments on page 221.

Hôtel de la Plage ★★★	
tout confort	
chambre	**249F**
chambre avec douche	**309F**
chambre avec salle de bains	**329F**

4 Read this article, then answer the questions in French.

READING **H**

Disneyland Paris fête ses cinq ans

EN AVRIL 1992 les Français ont pour la première fois pu rendre visite à Mickey et à ses amis sans le long et coûteux vol à destination des Etats-Unis.

Pour fêter son anniversaire, le parc d'attractions a lancé quelques nouveautés: un nouveau spectacle à Vidéopolis et l'entrée gratuite pour les moins de 12 ans. La chaîne de télé Disney est arrivée en France au mois de mars. En mai, on a vu l'ouverture de huit salles de cinéma à l'entrée du parc, dont une possède le plus grand écran de cinéma de France. En juillet, l'avant-dernière étape du Tour de France est partie de Disneyland pour gagner les Champs-Elysées.

Est-ce que tout ça a réussi à encourager de nouveaux clients? Nous avons posé la question à plusieurs jeunes. "C'est toujours très cher, vous savez, à 150F par enfant. Les parents avec deux/trois enfants ne pourront pas y aller." (Fabienne, 13 ans). "Oh oui, c'est génial, j'y suis allée il y a deux ans; mais mon père est au chômage maintenant, alors je ne pourrai pas y aller cette année." (Isabelle, 14 ans). "Moi, je préfère le Parc Astérix. Ils viennent d'introduire la toute nouvelle montagne russe – 'Tonnerre de Zeus' – ça m'a fait vraiment peur. Et puis c'est moins cher. Et c'est plus français." (Christophe, 13 ans).

You will find the answers and examiner's comments on page 221.

1 Avant l'ouverture de Disneyland Paris, pourquoi était-il difficile d'aller à Disneyland?

2 Comment est-ce qu'on essaie d'encourager les petits enfants à venir à Disneyland Paris?

3 Qu'y a-t-il de spécial dans l'une des nouvelles salles de cinéma?

4 Quelle était l'intention de toutes ces nouveautés?

5 Parmi les jeunes, quelle est la critique la plus fréquente concernant Disneyland Paris?

6 A part sa nouvelle attraction, quels sont les avantages du Parc Astérix, d'après Christophe? [2 marks]

QUELQUES PAYS

l'Afrique	Africa
l'Allemagne	Germany
l'Amérique	America
la Belgique	Belgium
le Canada*	Canada
le Danemark*	Denmark
l'Espagne	Spain
les Etats-Unis**	United States
la Grèce	Greece
l'Italie	Italy
les Pays-Bas**	Netherlands
le Portugal*	Portugal
la Suisse	Switzerland

to/in = en
BUT
* to/in = au   ** to/in = aux

LES LANGUES

le danois	Danish
le flamand	Flemish
le grec	Greek
le hollandais	Dutch
le portugais	Portuguese

QUESTIONS/PROMPTS

Vous avez visité les autres pays de l'Europe?

Vous voudriez aller aux Etats-Unis? Pourquoi?

Parlez-moi de votre chanteur préféré.

Que faites-vous pour protéger l'environnement?

WHAT YOU NEED TO KNOW

Tu as visité beaucoup de pays?	Have you been to many countries?
Non, je connais seulement l'Europe.	No, I only know Europe.
Nous faisons tous partie de l'Union Européenne.	We are all part of the European Union.
Je ne suis jamais allé(e) en Grèce.	I've never been to Greece.
Je voudrais aller en Inde un jour.	I'd like to go to India one day.
Quelle est la capitale de l'Italie?	What is the capital of Italy?
La capitale du Royaume-Uni est Londres.	The capital of the UK is London.
Au Québec (au Canada) on parle français.	In Quebec (in Canada) they speak French.

Au Québec on parle français

En Suisse, il y a quatre langues – le français, l'allemand, l'italien et le romanche.	In Switzerland, there are four languages – French, German, Italian and Romansh.
C'est un tennisman français très célèbre.	He's a famous French tennis player.
C'est le meilleur footballeur du monde.	He's the best footballer in the world.
Elle a gagné la médaille d'or aux jeux Olympiques.	She won the gold medal at the Olympic Games.
Elle a battu le record mondial.	She beat the world record.
Ils sont champions du monde.	They are the world champions.
Il est vedette de cinéma.	He is a film star.
Elle a eu un succès fou en Suède.	She was a wild success in Sweden.
La France va gagner la coupe du monde.	France is going to win the World Cup.
Il a perdu en demi-finale.	He lost in the semi-finals.
L'Italie a battu l'Irlande.	Italy beat Ireland.
Il y a beaucoup de problèmes.	There are lots of problems.
Le problème le plus grave, c'est la pollution.	The most serious problem is pollution.
Il faut conserver l'énergie.	We have to save energy.
J'essaie de ne pas consommer d'essence.	I try not to use petrol.
Je vais au collège à pied.	I walk to school.
Les voitures émettent des gaz toxiques.	Cars give off poisonous fumes.
Je suis écologiste.	I am an ecologist.
Au collège, il y a des papiers partout.	At school, there is paper everywhere.
C'est affreux.	It's disgusting.
Il faut protéger les animaux sauvages.	We have to protect wild animals.

LES STARS

un acteur/une actrice	actor/actress
un(e) chanteur/se	singer
l'équipe (de France)	the (French) team
un groupe	group
un(e) guitariste	guitarist
un(e) joueur/se	player
un présentateur/une présentatrice	presenter/announcer

QUESTIONS

Q1 **How would you say in French?**
a) I went to the Netherlands last year.
b) The most important city is Amsterdam.
c) All the Dutch can speak English.
d) Next year I will go to Africa.
e) I'd like to go round the world.

Q2 **Which country is it?**
a) La capitale est Berne.
b) Elle se trouve au sud-ouest de la France.
c) Une des plus grandes villes est Edimbourg.
d) On y parle flamand et français.
e) Elle était divisée en deux parties, est et ouest.

REMEMBER! Cover the answers if you want to.

ANSWERS

A1
a) Je suis allé(e) aux Pays-Bas l'année dernière.
b) La ville la plus importante est Amsterdam.
c) Tous les Hollandais parlent anglais.
d) L'année prochaine j'irai en Afrique.
e) Je voudrais faire le tour du monde.

A2
a) C'est la Suisse.
b) C'est l'Espagne.
c) C'est l'Ecosse.
d) C'est la Belgique.
e) C'est l'Allemagne.

TUTORIAL

T1
a) *If you are female, make* allée *agree. Remember that* Pays-Bas *is masculine plural, so use* aux.
b) *To say 'the most ...', you have to repeat the definite article (*la ... la plus ...*).*
c) *When referring to the people of a country, use a capital letter (but not when it's an adjective, or a language).*
d) *'To' or 'in' with continents is* en.
e) Je voudrais *can be used for saying what you'd like to do, as well as asking for something (*Je voudrais un café.*). Notice* faire le tour de = *to go round.*

T2
a) *Note that the capital of Switzerland is not* Genève, *as many people think.*
b) *The combined compass points –* nord-est, sud-ouest, *etc. can be easy to miss.*
c) *Names of cities are almost always the same in French as in English – except for* Londres, Edimbourg *and* Douvres (Dover).
d) *Unlike in Switzerland, where many people speak at least two of the official languages, in Belgium most people speak either one or the other, not both.*
e) *In French, East Germany used to be referred to as* la RDA *and West Germany as* la RFA.

L'ENVIRONNEMENT

l'atmosphère	atmosphere
le climat	climate
l'eau	water
l'effet de serre	the greenhouse effect
la pluie (acide)	(acid) rain
la pollution des eaux	water pollution
le recyclage	recycling
le réchauffement de la planète	global warming
le trou dans la couche d'ozone	the hole in the ozone layer

LES SOURCES D'ENERGIE

l'énergie solaire	solar power
l'énergie nucléaire	nuclear power
l'énergie des vagues	wave power
l'hydro-électricité	hydro-electricity
le pétrole	oil

LES PROBLEMES

la drogue	drugs
la faim	hunger
la pauvreté	poverty
la sécheresse	drought
la soif	thirst

GOING FURTHER

On devrait utiliser l'énergie du vent.
We should use wind power.

Nous devons essayer de conserver les ressources naturelles.
We ought to try to save natural resources.

Dans cinquante ans, il n'y aura plus de pétrole.
In 50 years there will be no more oil.

Les gaz carboniques émis par les véhicules sont très dangereux.
The carbon gases produced by vehicles are very dangerous.

Il y a plus de maladies respiratoires.
There are more respiratory (breathing) illnesses.

Un autre problème, c'est les CFC émis par les bombes aérosol.
Another problem is the CFCs produced by aerosols.

L'atmosphère, les océans, les rivières, sont tous pollués.
The atmosphere, the oceans, the rivers, are all polluted.

Nous laissons des ordures partout – les papiers, les sacs en plastique, même les déchets nucléaires.
We leave our rubbish everywhere – paper, plastic bags, even nuclear waste.

Il faut essayer de sauver les espèces en danger.
We must try to save endangered species.

Il y a certains éléphants qui sont en voie de disparition.
Certain elephants are becoming extinct.

Les zoos protègent les animaux sauvages.
Zoos protect wild animals.

Si la population continue à augmenter, il y aura encore des famines.
If the population continues to grow, there will be more famines.

On peut facilement recycler le papier et le verre.
One can easily recycle paper and glass.

These are very wide topics, and you will not be expected to discuss them in the same detail as you might in English. However, at Higher Level, you will be expected to be able to say a couple of sentences about major world issues such as pollution, the environment and conservation, and to understand simple discussions or newspaper articles about them.

HOW THE GRAMMAR WORKS

RELATIVE PRONOUNS

The relative pronouns *qui/que* and *ce qui/ce que* have been dealt with in Chapter 6. There is, however, another set of relative pronouns which are usually used with prepositions.

Like most pronouns, they change according to the gender of the noun to which they refer:
lequel (masculine singular)   *laquelle* (feminine singular)
lesquels (masculine plural)   *lesquelles* (feminine plural)

J'ai un cahier dans lequel j'écris tous mes devoirs.	– I have a notebook in which I write all my homework.
Il y a de petites tables sur lesquelles elle a mis des plantes.	– There are some little tables on which she has put plants.

They can be used as one-word answers to questions:

Tu me passes un stylo, s'il te plaît?	– Will you pass me a pen please?
Lequel?	– Which one?

INDEFINITE ADJECTIVES, ADVERBS AND PRONOUNS

Autre is used in a number of different ways:

Tu as une autre jupe?	– Do you have another dress?
J'ai un disque de Vanessa Paradis. Je voudrais les autres.	– I have one record by Vanessa Paradis. I'd like the others.
C'était pas moi. C'était quelqu'un d'autre.	– It wasn't me. It was somebody else.
Entre autres.	– Among other things.

N'importe is used to stress impreciseness:

Tu l'as fait n'importe comment.	– You did it anyhow (haphazardly).
Moi, j'irai n'importe où.	– I'll go anywhere.
Il sort avec n'importe qui.	– He goes out with anybody.
Apporte-moi un livre. N'importe lequel.	– Bring me a book. Any one will do.

Quelqu'un/quelque chose mean 'someone' and 'something':

Je voudrais te présenter quelqu'un.	– I'd like to introduce you to someone.
J'ai quelque chose à te montrer	– I have something to show you.

Tout has a number of different uses:

J'ai mangé toute la glace.	– I've eaten all the ice-cream.
Il a vu tous les films de Depardieu.	– He's seen all Depardieu's films.
(Note the irregular masculine plural).	
Il les a vus tous.	– He's seen them all.
(Note that, when used in this way, the final -s is pronounced.)	

Tout is also used in a number of common expressions:
tout le monde – everybody (always singular in French)
tout de suite – straight away
tout à fait – completely
tous/toutes (les) deux – both

Check yourself

QUESTIONS

Q1 Fill in the missing word.

a) On peut utiliser l'_____ des vagues.
b) Il ne reste plus beaucoup de_____ .
c) Il faut essayer de _____ l'énergie.
d) On doit utiliser le vélo plutôt que la _____.
e) A la maison, nous recyclons toutes nos _____ .

bouteilles	sauver	conserver
énergie	papier	voiture
pétrole	vent	

Q2 What are they talking about?

a) On n'a pas eu une goutte de pluie depuis le mois de février. C'est un vrai problème.
b) Il y a trop de personnes au Tiers-Monde qui n'ont pas assez à manger. C'est une honte.
c) Si on continue à les tuer comme ça, ils vont disparaître.
d) Il faut interdire les bombes aérosols – sinon, on ne pourra plus sortir au soleil.
e) Les plages et les rivières deviennent de plus en plus dangereuses. On ne peut pas se baigner sans risques.

la pollution des eaux
la sécheresse
les espèces en danger
la pluie acide
la pollution de l'atmosphère
la surpopulation
la faim

REMEMBER! Cover the answers if you want to.

ANSWERS

A1
a) énergie
b) pétrole
c) conserver
d) voiture
e) bouteilles

A2
a) la sécheresse
b) la faim
c) les espèces en danger
d) la pollution de l'atmosphère
e) la pollution des eaux

TUTORIAL

T1
a) *An easy one to start: it's the only word which begins with a vowel.*
b) *Bouteilles, vent and papier would also fit grammatically, but none makes sense.*
c) *After essayer de, the next word must be an infinitive.*
d) *This is the only answer which fits with vélo.*
e) *It could be papier, except that toutes is feminine plural.*

T2
a) *Pluie could link with pollution des eaux or pluie acide but this is clearly about drought.*
b) *Trop de personnes might lead you to surpopulation, but the gist obviously refers to lack of food.*
c) *Put tuer and disparaître together and this is the only possible answer.*
d) *You have to understand the whole sentence to pick out the right answer here. There is no word-to-word link.*
e) *The connection between rivières, plages and eaux should be fairly clear.*

EXAM PRACTICE

1 Find Chapter 13 – Exam Practice Listening on the CD. Listen to the French (Track 25) twice, then choose the right person to complete each sentence.

 LISTENING H

Choisissez la bonne personne pour chaque phrase. Ecrivez **J** (Julien), **K** (Karine), **S** (Salim) ou **V** (Véronique).

1 _____ pense que nous devons nous débarrasser de nos déchets avec soin.

2 _____ s'inquiète sur le manque possible d'eau douce.

3 _____ croit qu'il y aura tant de gens sur la terre qu'ils n'auront pas assez à manger.

4 _____ a peur de la pollution atmosphérique.

5 _____ dit que l'eau douce se trouve souvent dans les régions où il n'y a pas beaucoup de gens.

6 _____ pense qu'on doit se servir de l'eau des océans.

7 _____ croit que la surpopulation amènera bien d'autres problèmes que la faim.

[6 marks]

You will find the transcript and answers, with examiner's comments, on page 222.

2 Find Chapter 13 – Exam Practice Speaking on the CD and listen to the presentation (Track 26). Think about what you have heard. Then read the examiner's comments.

 SPEAKING H

You will find the transcript and examiner's comments on page 223.

> *You might then like to prepare your own presentation on a foreign country, or on your favourite singer or sports personality. When you are practising your presentation, it's a good idea to record it on cassette, so you can listen to it and spot errors, and areas for improvement.*

3 Read this article, then tick the sentences below which are correct.

Des animaux marins tués par des sacs en plastique

Les débris que l'on trouve dans l'eau au large des côtes françaises inquiètent les chercheurs. Il est souvent question de matières plastiques qui risquent d'étouffer des animaux.

"Un des problèmes," a expliqué Louise Dubosc, qui travaille à l'Institut de Recherche pour la Protection de la Mer, "c'est que les sacs en plastique peuvent mettre des centaines d'années à s'autodétruire."

En ce qui concerne les autres formes de pollution, comme par exemple le pétrole, la situation s'améliore, mais pour les débris, surtout en plastique, ce n'est malheureusement pas le cas. Rien que dans la Méditerranée, au large du delta du Rhône, on a compté plus de dix millions d'objets jetés à la mer.

Le résultat: des tortues et des dauphins qui s'approchent des plages à cause des bonnes conditions climatiques sont étouffés après avoir avalé des sacs en plastique. On a trouvé une trentaine de tortues mortes sur la côte Atlantique le mois dernier – normalement, on en trouve cinq ou six.

D'après cet article, cochez les phrases qui sont vraies.

1 Les chercheurs trouvent que le problème des débris en plastique s'améliore. ☐

2 Le problème est plus grave dans le sud de la France. ☐

3 Il y a moins de pollution chimique aujourd'hui. ☐

4 Les sacs en plastique ne sont pas facilement biodégradables. ☐

5 Les débris ont tué au moins une centaine de tortues. ☐

6 Les animaux marins mangent les sacs en plastique. ☐

7 Les tortues s'approchent de la terre quand il fait mauvais temps. ☐

[4 marks]

You will find the answers and examiner's comments on page 223.

4 Answer the following question in French.

Votre ami(e) français(e) vous a demandé de lui parler de la pollution et de la défense de l'environnement. Ecrivez-lui une lettre.

Parlez:
- de ce que vous faites à la maison pour conserver l'énergie.
- de ce qu'on fait dans votre école.
- des problèmes de pollution dans votre ville.
- de votre attitude en ce qui concerne la pollution.

Posez-lui deux questions sur la pollution ou la défense de l'environnement.

Sample Student's Answer

> Chez nous, on fait beaucoup de choses pour conserver l'énergie. On sépare toujours les bouteilles, les journaux et les boîtes de conserve avant de les jeter à la poubelle. Puis, chaque semaine, on les emmène pour être recyclés.
>
> Aussi, mon frère et moi, nous allons à l'école à vélo. Comme ça, ma mère n'a pas besoin de sortir la voiture. Enfin, si on a un peu froid le soir, on met un pull, au lieu de mettre le chauffage.
>
> Au collège, on ne fait pas grand-chose, mais on essaie toujours d'éteindre les lumières.
>
> J'habite une grande ville, donc il y a un problème de circulation, qui cause beaucoup de pollution.
>
> Moi, la pollution m'inquiète beaucoup, car mon petit frère est asthmatique, et il souffre beaucoup.
>
> Et toi, que fais-tu pour combattre la pollution? Tu habites à la campagne, n'est-ce pas? Est-ce qu'il y a beaucoup de pollution chez toi?

EXAMINER'S COMMENTS

- This is clearly the work of a very good candidate who has acquired a lot of vocabulary within this topic, and can use it to good effect.

- There are a number of good phrases: mon frère et moi, nous allons; au lieu de; qui cause; and the whole thing reads very well.

- However, for a candidate who is aiming for a Grade C or better – as this candidate obviously is – there is a serious problem. To get the higher grades, candidates must refer to past, present and future events. It is possible that this was taken care of in the other written question, but it really is important to make sure, by getting in different tenses in every answer.

- Here, it would have been quite easy to say mon frère et moi, nous avons décidé d'aller à l'école à vélo. Later, the candidate could add: La semaine prochaine, j'écrirai un article dans le magazine de mon collège pour parler de ses problèmes. With a little thought, it is possible to fit at least one past and one future into almost any piece of written work.

- As it stands, therefore, in spite of the excellent language, this piece of work would only earn a Grade D.

CHAPTER 14

LISTENING AND RESPONDING

In some ways, it is impossible to separate the four skills. To understand and use French, you need to know the vocabulary, and to know how the structures work. This is as true when you are reading French as when you are listening to it. However, there are some ways in which listening is different. Listed below are some of the general problems associated with listening. You can help yourself to overcome them mainly by practising.

Problem 1

When you are listening, the French is gone after the second hearing, and you can do nothing to bring it back (whereas when you are reading, you can simply look back at the previous paragraph).

Solution 1

The Listening Test in the French exam isn't like most of the listening you do. Most of your everyday listening (music on the radio, the conversation of your friends, even sometimes school assembly!) is no more than a background to some other activity. In your Listening Test, you really need to concentrate on what you hear. You can practise concentrating on listening in very short bursts – even a TV soap can be useful. Listen for five minutes (time yourself), then try to write down as much detail as you can of what you heard. If you can record it, then play it back to check, so much the better. Obviously, you need to practise listening to French as well, so ask to borrow a cassette from your teacher – almost anything will do. What you are trying to do is to build up your power to concentrate on what you hear.

Problem 2

Distractions can be much more important when you are listening. There isn't much you can do about low-flying aircraft, but it is all too easy to drift off into a day-dream, and completely miss a sentence or two.

Solution 2

This is clearly linked to (1). If you don't often listen to anything in a concentrated way, you probably never concentrate on listening for a long period, which you need to do in your Test. Again, you need to practise, but this time it's easier with your teacher's help. Ask him/her to make sure you do some practice on past papers, so that you have an idea of how long you will need to concentrate for. Also, perhaps even more than for any other sort of test, you need to be fresh. Everyone will tell you this is true for all your exams (and so it is) but if you are in any danger of nodding off, the Listening Test will surely encourage you to do so – and of course it's absolutely fatal!

Problem 3

The speakers in the Test may have regional accents, and would therefore sound very different from your teacher. There will also be both male and female voices, which you may not be used to in French.

Solution 3

If your school has a French assistant(e), or any native-speaker teachers, take advantage of them to get used to different voices and accents. Similarly, if there are any French exchange students in your school/area, listen to them.

Problem 4

It's more difficult listening to someone you can't see, as you don't have the benefit of gestures, lip movements and so on.

Solution 4

Get as much practice as you can in listening to tapes, to get used to having no visual clues. Even try closing your eyes sometimes in French lessons – as long as the teacher won't think you've fallen asleep!

Problem 5

There may well be sound effects recorded (from traffic noises to echo effects like the telephone) which come between you and the meaning of what you hear.

Solution 5

The sound effects in Listening Tests shouldn't be too off-putting – in fact they are usually meant to help you, to put what you hear in some sort of context. Try to make use of them.

Problem 6

Even if your exam board allows the use of a dictionary in the Listening Test, you can only use it for five minutes reading time at the beginning of the Test, and five minutes checking time at the end.

Solution 6

The dictionary will be most useful for you to check unfamiliar words which are printed on the question paper. It is hard to check a word you have heard, as you are probably not sure exactly how to spell it.

GENERAL STRATEGIES

Use the question to help you

- When the question is a simple factual one. The question will often tell you exactly what information you are listening for, for example:

    Une glace coûte: 7F50   75F   7F45   7F15   ?

    You know that you are listening for a number, and you can ignore any other information you hear.

- If the question is less simple, but still factual, for example:

    Une glace à la vanille coûte: 7F50   75F   7F45   7F15   ?

    Here, you have to put the price and the flavour together, but once you have got the cost of a vanilla ice-cream, that's all you need.

- If the question is about an emotion or an attitude. In that case, there are certain kinds of word you should listen for, for example:

    Myriam aime l'anglais: VRAI   FAUX   ?

    You might listen for words like *ennuyeux/difficile/préférée/intéressant/ passionnant*, or phrases like *le prof est sympa/je ne suis pas forte*.

    What you probably **won't** hear is *j'aime* or *j'adore* – that would be too easy!

Use the context to help you

- For example, you might hear the following:

    Derrière la maison, il y avait un vieux chêne. Quand il était petit, il s'installait dans les branches pour regarder les voisins dans le jardin d'à côté.

    You may not know that *un chêne* is an oak tree, but the context should make it fairly clear that it's a tree of some sort.

Use your common sense

- If you know that someone is in a hotel, he/she is more likely to say:

    Vous avez une chambre pour une nuit?

    than:

    Vous avez des oignons?

● You have acquired some knowledge of France and the French way of life, so make use of it. You should know that an ice-cream is more likely to cost 10F than 100F.

Check yourself 1

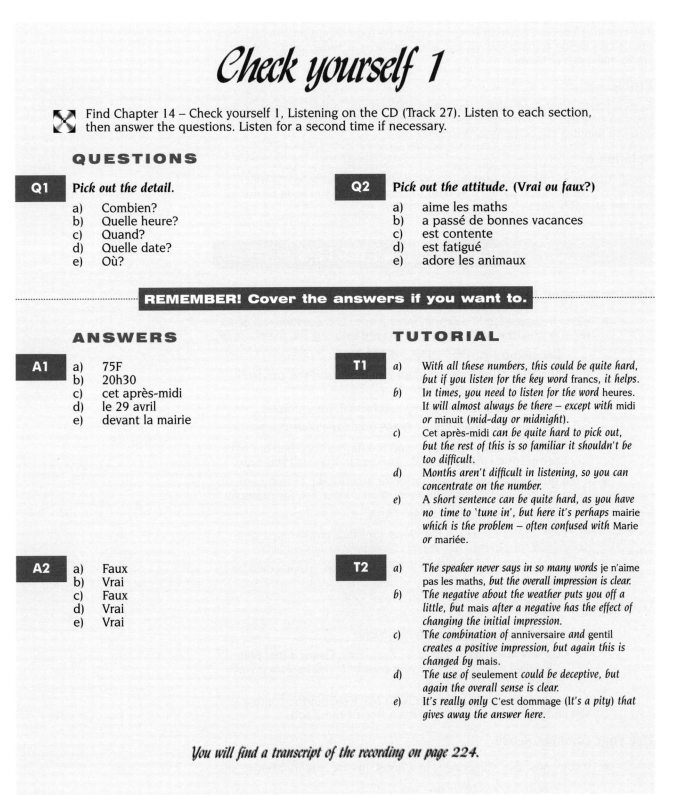

Find Chapter 14 – Check yourself 1, Listening on the CD (Track 27). Listen to each section, then answer the questions. Listen for a second time if necessary.

QUESTIONS

Q1 Pick out the detail.

a) Combien?
b) Quelle heure?
c) Quand?
d) Quelle date?
e) Où?

Q2 Pick out the attitude. (Vrai ou faux?)

a) aime les maths
b) a passé de bonnes vacances
c) est contente
d) est fatigué
e) adore les animaux

REMEMBER! Cover the answers if you want to.

ANSWERS

A1
a) 75F
b) 20h30
c) cet après-midi
d) le 29 avril
e) devant la mairie

A2
a) Faux
b) Vrai
c) Faux
d) Vrai
e) Vrai

TUTORIAL

T1
a) *With all these numbers, this could be quite hard, but if you listen for the key word* francs, *it helps.*
b) *In times, you need to listen for the word* heures. *It will almost always be there – except with* midi *or* minuit *(mid-day or midnight).*
c) *Cet après-midi can be quite hard to pick out, but the rest of this is so familiar it shouldn't be too difficult.*
d) *Months aren't difficult in listening, so you can concentrate on the number.*
e) *A short sentence can be quite hard, as you have no time to 'tune in', but here it's perhaps* mairie *which is the problem – often confused with* Marie *or* mariée.

T2
a) *The speaker never says in so many words* je n'aime pas les maths, *but the overall impression is clear.*
b) *The negative about the weather puts you off a little, but* mais *after a negative has the effect of changing the initial impression.*
c) *The combination of* anniversaire *and* gentil *creates a positive impression, but again this is changed by* mais.
d) *The use of* seulement *could be deceptive, but again the overall sense is clear.*
e) *It's really only* C'est dommage *(It's a pity) that gives away the answer here.*

You will find a transcript of the recording on page 224.

SPECIFIC POINTS TO PRACTISE

Numbers

- These are often tested at Foundation Level (in times, prices and so on) and even at Higher Level they can form an important element of a number of answers. Ask your teacher, or the French assistant(e), or a friendly 6th form French student, to record some numbers for you to practise listening to.

- Remember that the numbers in context often sound different from the numbers you practised when you were in Year 7. *Deux* on its own has one sound (*deuh*) but it can sound very different before a word beginning with a vowel (*deuz enfants*). This can be a real comprehension problem – try comparing *deux enfants* and *douze enfants*. The only sound difference is the vowel sound (*eu* and *ou*). Similar problems occur with *trois/treize*, and *six/seize*.

- The other difficulty with French numbers comes in the numbers between 70 and 99. Again, lots of specific practice in listening to numbers is the answer. Try practising particular times and telephone numbers, where you are likely to hear a combination of several numbers: *quinze heures cinquante-trois* (15.53); *le zéro-quatre, soixante-sept, quatre-vingt-huit, onze, quatre-vingt-quatorze* (04, 67, 88, 11, 94).

The alphabet

- Spelling out of certain words, especially names and places, is quite common over the telephone.

- Particular problems can be caused by:

  E (euh – as in the word *deux*) and I (ee – as in the English word 'peep')
  B (bé) and P (pé)
  D (dé) and T (té)
  G (jé) and J (jee) (both with a soft *j* as in the French word *je*)
  H (ash)
  M (emm) and N (enn)
  Y (ee grec)

  See also Chapter 15 Speaking, page 120.

Consonants

- Any pronunciation practice you have done has probably been mainly concerned with vowel sounds. While it is true that French vowel sounds can be quite difficult for an English speaker to produce, they don't often lead to confusion in listening, except in some numbers and some letters of the alphabet (see above).

- It can be much harder to hear the difference between some consonant sounds, and the problem is greater because either way can result in real French words. Try to get a recording of some odd-one-out exercises based on consonant differences, for example:

  bain   pain   bain   bain

  Other easily confused consonants are *m/n; d/t; f/v.*

Negatives

- These are very easy to miss, and yet are vitally important to understanding. Indeed, their whole purpose is to change the meaning of a sentence.

- In colloquial speech, the problem is even greater, since the *ne* is quite often omitted. Again, try some odd-one-out listening exercises:

  je l'ai vu   je l'ai vu   je l'ai pas vu   je l'ai vu

Language patterns

- These are much easier to make use of in reading, but it is worth noting the different ways the French can spell the same or a similar sound, so that you can try various alternatives for a sound you don't recognise:

  -ant, -ent, -end, -and, -an, -en, -amp, -anc at the end of words all have the same sound.

  -ez, -é, -ait, -aient all sound the same or similar, and are all verb endings.

- Do some listening practice where you try to distinguish between these spellings simply on the basis of grammar:

  a) *Il regardait le journal.*
  b) *Vous regardez le journal.*
  c) *Elle a regardé le journal.*

  This is only partly a listening exercise, but it will help put together sounds and structures, which is a very important part of listening for meaning.

Word separation

- This is really what listening problems are all about. In reading, you can identify the words by the white space on each side. In listening, all the words are often run together. It can be hard to use your knowledge of vocabulary if you can't distinguish the words.

- The only solution is lots of listening practice, aided by a variation on an old-fashioned technique called dictation. Take a recording of almost any piece of French which is at, or a little below, your level – taken from your course-book, for example – and try to write down what you hear, using clues like intonation and natural pauses, to help you identify the words. Of course, one of the most important clues is the meaning: you will recognise lots of the words, and this will help you to pick out the unknown ones. If you have a transcript of the recording, you can check how well you did. Don't forget, the object of the exercise is to distinguish the individual words rather than to spell them right, but it's almost equally valuable without the check, since it's doing the exercise that matters.

Check yourself 2

 Find Chapter 14 – Check yourself 2, Listening on the CD (Track 28). Listen to each section, then answer the questions. Listen for a second time if necessary.

QUESTIONS

Q1 *Just write the number.*

a) ..... F
b) ..... F .....
c) ..... élèves
d) ..... heures .....
e) En .....

Q2 *Write what you hear – but think about the grammar. Which word is it?*

a) étais; était; étaient; été
b) en tant; entend; entends; en tente
c) attente; sa tante; attendent; attend

QUESTIONS

Q3 *Which is the odd-one-out? Write 1, 2, 3, or 4.*

a)
b)
c)
d)

Q4 *Try to write what you hear.*

a)
b)
c)
d)

REMEMBER! Cover the answers if you want to.

ANSWERS

A1
a) 89F
b) 34F60
c) 1300
d) 16h40
e) 1973

A2
a) étaient
b) entends
c) attente

A3
a) 3
b) 1
c) 4
d) 2

A4
a) Alors, qu'est-ce qu'il y a au cinéma ce soir?
b) Carole, c'est ma meilleure amie, tu sais.
c) Je vais aller en ville après le match.
d) Ma tante habite près de chez nous.

You will find a transcript of the recording on page 224.

TUTORIAL

T1
a) Don't confuse quatre-vingts *with* vingt-quatre.
c) Remember not to put un *in front of* mille.
e) The year can either be said dix-neuf cent soixante-treize *or* mille neuf cent, *etc.*

T2
a) There are two clues to the fact that it is plural: ils *and* tous.
b) En tente *would actually sound different, as you would hear the* t *before the final* e. Entends *must end in* -s *because of* tu.
c) It's quite easy to confuse salle d'attente *and* sa tante – *you need the meaning to help.*

T4
a) There are almost no pauses to help, but the vocabulary is quite familiar.
b) The pauses after Carole *and before* tu sais *should help.*
c) It's the running together of vais aller *which makes this hard.*
d) Especially in this sort of context, it's easy to hear chez nous *as a place name.*

HIGHER LEVEL PERFORMANCE

At Higher Level, you will be expected to be able to do a number of things which are not expected at Foundation Level.

Understanding French spoken at normal speed

At Foundation Level, especially for Grades E, F and G, the speakers will slow down a little – as a French person would, knowing he/she was speaking to a foreigner. At Higher Level, the speakers will speak more naturally – though not at the very rapid rate they might use to their friends. Speakers are also more likely to use colloquial expressions and even some slang (understanding of this will not be tested), and to use the contracted forms common in everyday speech, for example J'*sais pas, moi* instead of the more formal Je *ne sais pas, moi.*

Extracting information from longer utterances

Here, it's not that the information is more difficult, but that you have to pick out what is relevant from a longer item. For example, at Foundation Level, you might be asked to identify the weather from a sentence like:

Demain, il fera beau.

At Higher Level, you might hear an extract from a weather forecast:

Demain, dans le nord-est du pays, il fera assez froid. Dans le sud, il fera beau, et dans l'ouest, il y aura des orages.

You might then, for example, be asked to identify the weather in the south. In each case, the French targeted by the question is the same (*il fera beau*), but at Higher Level you have to understand more of the context in order to get there.

Picking out the main points from what you hear

You might listen to a discussion on going out, in which three people make a number of different points but all say how important the cost is – in different ways. One might say:

Ça doit coûter au maximum trente francs.

Another might say:

Le problème, c'est que les discothèques sont souvent trop chères.

The third might say:

Ça dépend du prix d'entrée.

You need to identify the fact that they are all concerned about the cost.

Identifying attitudes and opinions

This does not mean just understanding words like *heureux, content* or *ennuyé*, but understanding that when someone says *Franchement, pendant les cours d'histoire, je m'endors*, this implies that they are bored.

Making deductions from what you have heard

As a simple example, if you hear:

Il a plu tous les jours. La tente était toute mouillée.

you can deduce that the speaker has been camping.

Understanding the gist of what you hear

If you hear someone say:

Il y a tant de problèmes aujourd'hui. On manque d'eau potable dans plusieurs régions du monde. Puis il y a la pluie acide qui menace les arbres, et les gaz toxiques qui menacent notre santé.

you can put all that together and identify that they are concerned about the environment.

Answering questions using French which you have not heard

You may have to answer questions in phrases or sentences that are not simply repeating what you have heard. In the previous example, if you were given the question:

Quelle est l'attitude de Jean?

you would have to reply with (for example):

(Il pense qu') il y a des problèmes d'environnement.

Giving any of the individual details (lack of drinking water, acid rain, poisonous gases) would not score the mark.

Understanding vocabulary outside the minimum core vocabulary

Each board defines a minimum core vocabulary for Foundation Level. This would normally be the vocabulary which you need to carry out the tasks specified in the syllabus, though there will certainly be words in the Listening Test which you have not met. One of the Higher Level skills is to use your linguistic skills to fill in any blanks in vocabulary. Just as in English, if someone uses a word you don't know, you can still follow the gist of what they are saying. Obviously, the more words you know, the better your understanding will be, but understanding is not simply a matter of knowing the words.

Check yourself 3

Find Chapter 14 – Check yourself 3, Listening on the CD (Track 29). Listen to each section, then answer the questions. Listen for a second time if necessary.

QUESTIONS

Q1 *Pick out the detail.*

a) Tomorrow's weather.
b) What do the speakers have in common?
c) What is their problem?

Q2 *Identifying attitudes. Choose the appropriate word from the box for each speaker.*

travailleur/se	sérieux/se
inconscient(e)	paresseux/se
confiant(e)	timide

REMEMBER! Cover the answers if you want to.

ANSWERS

A1
a) nice
b) problems with brothers and sisters.
c) money

A2
a) travailleuse
b) timide
c) paresseuse

You will find a transcript of the recording on page 224.

TUTORIAL

T1
a) You need to pick out the key word demain to identify the right section.
b) Here, it's a question of trying to pick out a common theme. It's not enough to say 'brothers and sisters' – you need the idea of problem.
c) You need to work out the gist of what each person says, then again pick out the common factor – money.

T2 You may well need to check some of the words in your dictionary before you start.
a) The clues to 'hard-working' are Je ne trouve pas toujours ça facile *and* je fais des efforts.
b) Je voudrais *is looking to the future, so the answer is most likely to be* confiant *or* timide. *The second half of what is said leads you to* timide.
c) If you pick out aider à la maison you will notice that none of the appropriate vocabulary is there – which leads you straight to the correct conclusion.

DIFFERENT KINDS OF LISTENING

Listening for detail

Start from the question. Decide whether the word(s) you are listening for is, for example, a time, a price, a place or an object, etc., and concentrate on listening for that.

Listening for gist

If the question is more general, asking for someone's feelings or opinions, or asking 'what sort of ...?', individual words and phrases are less important. What matters is the whole message. In some ways this kind of question is more difficult, but at least it is less important if there is a word that you don't understand.

Dialogues

If the question asks you to link different views or opinions to different people, it is very important to keep track of who is speaking. The names of the speakers will be clearly recorded. In an interview, the interviewer may introduce each speaker by name:

Qu'est-ce que tu en penses, Joël?

In a conversation, the speakers will refer to each other frequently by name:

Moi, je préfère les maths. Et toi, Lucie?

In this sort of question, the name will always be printed on the question paper, so you don't need to worry about recognising unfamiliar names. Quite often, the question will ask you to write the name (or the initial) of the person who expresses a particular view:

..... pense qu'il va devenir professeur

or to complete a grid by putting the correct information next to each person's name.

Monologues

These are more likely to be factual. Possible examples include: radio news bulletins, weather forecasts, advertisements, guides to tourist attractions and recordings of pen-friends. The question will make it clear who is speaking, so keep this in mind when you are answering the questions.

Announcements

These are mainly at the lower levels, and may include: announcements in shops, stations, airports, etc.; public address announcements (on the beach, in town, on a boat, etc.). The questions will often target dates, times and prices.

Telephone calls and recorded messages

Again, these will often target dates and times, with perhaps the added complication of a change in arrangements. In this last case, you will have on the question paper details of, for example, an appointment. As you listen to the message, you need to compare what is written with what you hear, and note any differences.

DIFFERENT KINDS OF QUESTION

There are four basic question-types, but there are a number of possible variations within each.

Multiple-choice (in pictures)

In this kind of question, you simply have to choose the picture which best fits what you hear. There will usually be four pictures to choose from, lettered or numbered, and you write down the appropriate letter/number. Sometimes, there may be six or more pictures to accompany several questions. For example, you might see six pictures lettered A to F, each representing a job. You will then hear four recordings in which a person describes the job he/she wants to do. For each person, you choose a letter A to F.

1 The pictures may be symbols (icons), for example a stethoscope to represent a nurse, or a plane to represent an airport. Your exam board will have a published set of such symbols. Make sure you know them.

2 They may be numbers (clock faces, calendars, prices, etc.).

3 They may be more general pictures to represent a more complicated idea, for example a beach scene with the sun and people playing volleyball.

The first two types of picture will usually give a factual detail which you need to listen out for. The third will probably relate to the gist of what you hear. It may be important with this sort of picture to make sure that all the details fit with what you have heard – in other words that if the speaker talks of a beach

holiday playing volleyball, but spoilt by the weather, you do not choose the picture with the sun on it! However, the pictures will never be all that complicated, and any detail differences will be very clear.

Multiple-choice (in words)

There are a number of types, in increasing order of difficulty:

1   One-word answers. Typically, these will be filling in blanks, often at the end of a sentence:
   Marie est .... [contente/ennuyée/fâchée/triste]
   In simpler questions of this type, the missing word will be one that you hear; in more complicated questions, you will have to work out which of the words offered fits best.

2   Phrase answers. These are similar to one-word answers:
   Elle va vous rencontrer .... [à la gare/au café/à l'hôtel/au cinéma]

3   Sentence answers. These are usually more difficult, and can take two forms.
   Either:
   Pourquoi est-ce que Jacques est content?
   A *Il adore l'anglais.*
   B *Il a réussi à son examen d'anglais.*
   C *Il a passé son examen d'anglais.*
   D *Il aime le prof d'anglais.*
   Or:
   Choisissez la bonne personne pour chaque phrase:
   – est bon élève
   – travaille seulement quand il aime la matière
   – n'a pas fait grand-chose à l'école
   – espère devenir professeur

   In this type of question, it is important that you understand **exactly** the meaning of the sentences offered. Use your dictionary if you are allowed to.

Answers in French

Again, the answer can consist of one word, a phrase or a whole sentence.

1   One-word answers. These will often ask you to fill in a form or a grid. Spelling will usually only be taken into account if it gets in the way of communication, but you do need to take care. For example, *collage* (a very common error) is only one letter different from *collège*, but since the mistake creates a real French word, it is a big problem for communication. The word required for the answer will often be one you have heard on the recording.

2   Phrase answers. These are more complex than the multiple-choice phrase answers, since not only do you have to produce the correct key word, but the rest of the phrase will also need to be appropriate. For example, in answer to the question:
   Où vont-ils se rencontrer?
   the answer *café* is not clear enough. You would need *au café* (or maybe *devant le café*) to make yourself understood, and to score the mark.

3   Sentence answers. These will only appear in the most difficult questions (Grades B and A), as they require you not only to understand what you have heard, but to be able to manipulate the language in order to reply. This may simply be a question of adapting what you have heard on the recording. For example, you have heard someone say:
   Je suis forte en maths.
   In your answer you have to say:
   Elle est forte en maths.
   However, you may sometimes have to create a whole sentence for yourself. For example, the question is:
   Des jeunes parlent de leur ville. Quelle est l'attitude de Claire?
   You hear Claire say *Il y a pas mal de choses à faire – le cinéma, les discothèques, le théâtre.*
   You need to answer *La ville est intéressante* or *Il y a beaucoup de distractions*, etc.

Answers in English

Though these may seem to be the easiest, they will often be used to test the most difficult items, and the most difficult kinds of understanding. They will frequently be used to test your understanding of the gist of longer items, or your ability to draw conclusions from what you hear, or identify opinions and attitudes. Don't assume that you can simply pick out key items of vocabulary. The question is often looking for more than this. These questions will often contain the words 'How?' or 'Why?' or phrases such as 'What was X's reaction?'.

Check yourself 4

Find Chapter 14 – Check yourself 4, Listening on the CD (Track 30). Listen to each section, then answer the questions. Listen for a second time if necessary.

QUESTIONS

Q1 **Answer in French.**

a) Paul va travailler .....
b) Il voudrait .....
c) Louise va .....
d) Elle ne veut pas .....

Q2 **Answer in English.**

a) Where does Marc want to go on holiday?
b) Why?
c) What is his father's reaction?
d) Why does his mother disagree with both of them?

REMEMBER! Cover the answers if you want to.

ANSWERS

A1
a) dans le garage de son oncle
b) acheter une voiture
c) rester à l'école
d) être professeur

A2
a) sea-side (or lake/river)
b) had good time last year OR lots of friends thère.
c) wants to go somewhere different.
d) tired of housework OR wants hotel.

TUTORIAL

T1
a) Dans un garage *might be enough, but more detail is better.*
b) *There is nothing you can simply borrow from the recording which will answer the question. You have to supply* acheter *yourself.*
c) *You have to turn round* Je ne vais pas quitter l'école *to* rester à l'école.
d) *You have to supply the infinitive –* devenir *would be equally good.*

T2
a) *You have to deduce sea-side, lake or river from what Marc says.*
b) *The alternative answers are quite clearly stated, but they are quite long phrases.*
c) *You need to interpret what Marc's father says, and supply the word 'different' yourself. You could, of course, say that he doesn't want to go to the same place.*
d) *Of the alternative answers, 'hotel' is quite simple, but the other needs quite careful phrasing.*

You will find a transcript of the recording on page 225.

EXAM PRACTICE

Find Chapter 14 – Exam Practice Listening on the CD (Track 31). Listen to each item twice, then answer the questions.

1 A l'hôtel, vous avez demandé l'heure du dîner.

FOUNDATION/HIGHER

Le dîner est à quelle heure? Cochez la case appropriée.

A de 7h00 à 9h00 ☐   **C** de 7h00 à 9h30 ☐

B de 7h30 à 9h00 ☐   **D** de 7h30 à 9h30 ☐   [1]

2 Qu'est-ce que vous devez faire quand vous quittez l'hôtel? Cochez la case appropriée.

FOUNDATION/HIGHER

A prendre la clé à la réception ☐

B laisser la clé à la réception ☐

C le dire à la réception ☐

D emporter la clé ☐   [1]

3 Vous écoutez la météo. Indiquez le temps sur la carte. Ecrivez une lettre dans la case appropriée.

FOUNDATION/HIGHER

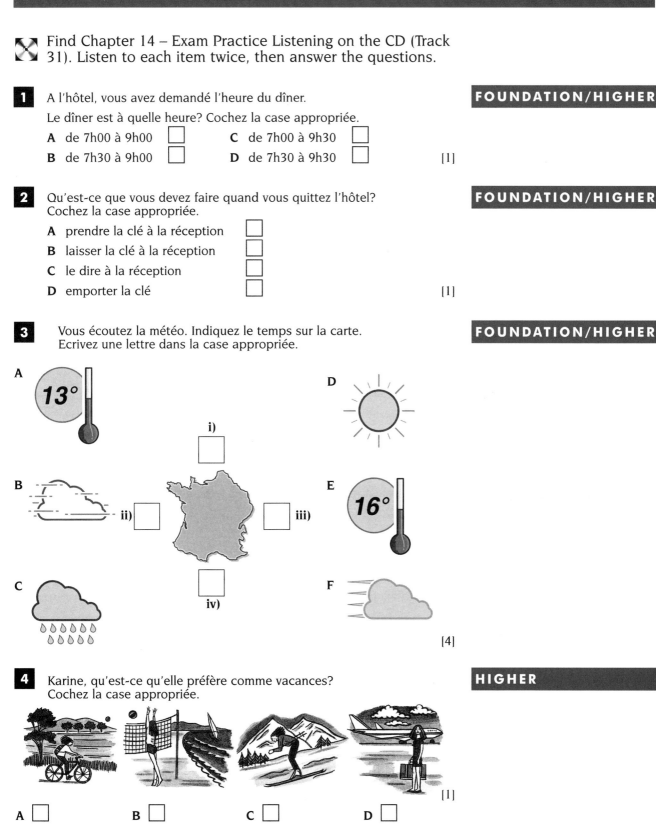

[4]

4 Karine, qu'est-ce qu'elle préfère comme vacances? Cochez la case appropriée.

HIGHER

A ☐   B ☐   C ☐   D ☐   [1]

HIGHER **5** Ecoutez l'annonce. Indiquez les phrases qui sont vraies.
Cochez **deux** cases.

A Si vous achetez vos billets au syndicat d'initiative,
ils sont moins chers. ☐

B Si vous achetez vos billets à l'entrée, ils sont moins chers. ☐

C L'annonce concerne un cirque étranger. ☐

D Le spectacle commence à neuf heures. ☐

E Il y a beaucoup d'animaux au cirque. ☐ [2]

HIGHER **6** Ecoutez ce message téléphonique. Corrigez les erreurs.

MESSAGE TELEPHONIQUE	
POUR:	Mme Lucas
DE LA PART DE:	M. Dupuis
MESSAGE:	Rendez-vous à l'hôtel de ville à 6h15

[3]

HIGHER **7** Ecoutez ces conversations, puis choisissez le mot qui convient pour
chaque personne.

Ecrivez **J** (Jeanne) ou **A** (Amélie) dans la case appropriée.

réservé(e) ☐   sérieuse ☐

enthousiaste ☐   timide ☐

égoïste ☐ [2]

HIGHER **8** Où était le camping? Complétez la phrase.

Le camping était .... [1]

HIGHER **9** Où étaient les parents? Complétez la phrase.

Les parents étaient .... [1]

HIGHER **10** Julien, pourquoi veut-il aller à l'université? [1]

HIGHER **11** Hélène, pourquoi a-t-elle décidé d'étudier les maths? [1]

HIGHER **12** ANSWER IN ENGLISH.

M. Blanchard is talking about his family's recent holiday.

a) Name two of the problems they had at the hotel. [2]
b) Why could M. Blanchard not solve the problems? [1]
c) What was the result of one of the problems? [1]
d) (i) How did they finally feel about the holiday? [1]
    (ii) Why? [2]

[**Total: 25 marks**]

*You will find the transcripts and answers,
with examiner's comments, on pages 225–227.*

CHAPTER 15

SPEAKING

INTRODUCTION

This chapter concentrates on the specific skills and techniques which will enable you to perform at your best in the Speaking Test. There are three possible parts to the Speaking Test. Role-plays and General Conversation are common to all the exam boards; the Presentation is used by MEG and NEAB only.

Unlike in listening, where you have no control over the language used – you simply respond to what other people say – in speaking you always have some room for manoeuvre.

In the role-plays, there are often slightly different ways of saying the same thing, and you need to choose the one which you are most comfortable with.

In the General Conversation, you have some freedom of expression in responding to what your teacher says, but you also have a great deal of choice about the content. You can choose how much to say in response to any question, and you can select the information that you decide to include.

Finally, if your exam board includes a Presentation in the Speaking Test, you have total choice about the topic and language you use.

Here are some general problems which are specific to speaking, with some possible strategies for overcoming the difficulty, or getting round it.

Problem 1

One of the major difficulties many candidates find in the Speaking Test is overcoming their nerves. Even the most outgoing personality can be reduced to a nervous wreck as soon as he/she is faced with a microphone. One reason for this is that, unlike in any other exam, your teacher is actually there with you – and will notice every silly mistake you make.

Solution 1

Before the Test – in fact from the beginning of the course – practise speaking French onto a cassette. When you are asked to prepare a role-play, or any other piece of oral work, don't just do it in your head, get out your cassette recorder. In this way, not only will you get used to being recorded, you will have a record of what you have done, and you'll be able to go back and listen again in the light of your teacher's comments. When it comes to the day itself, try to relax. A really deep breath as you go into the exam room will help, as will taking a few seconds to settle yourself comfortably and arranging your papers before you start.

Problem 2

The temptation is to rush the parts you have prepared, before you have time to forget! This can not only spoil your pronunciation and intonation, but it can also lead to your making errors that you wouldn't otherwise make.

Solution 2

When you are making your practice recordings, make sure you speak steadily and clearly. No-one will expect you to speak as quickly as a native French speaker at this level. You are still in the position of needing to think about intonation, and sometimes about some pronunciations, so don't let your desire to get it over with let you down.

Problem 3

However, speaking steadily does not mean hesitating after every other word. This will spoil your pronunciation just as much as rushing, and will also be taken into account in the marking.

Solution 3

There are two sorts of hesitation. The first, when you've been asked a question in the Conversation and need to think about the information you're going to give – your favourite film, for example – is perfectly natural, and nothing to worry about. The second sort of hesitation, which you should avoid if possible, is when you are searching for a word in French. It shouldn't happen in the Foundation or Foundation/Higher role-plays, which you should have prepared thoroughly in advance. If it happens in the Higher role-play, where you can't always predict exactly what's coming, or in the Conversation, you can try to conceal it – with 'noises' like *euh* .... , or phrases like *Je ne sais pas.*

Problem 4

Sometimes, however, there is no way of concealing either that you can't answer a question, or that you haven't understood the question. It is very easy, when this happens, to simply allow the conversation to grind to a halt, and it can then be quite hard for you and your teacher to get it going again.

Solution 4

The important thing here is to let the teacher know as precisely as possible what the problem is, so that he/she can take appropriate action to keep the conversation moving.

- If the problem is that you don't understand what you've been asked, say so as clearly as possible. If it's a general problem, you can say *Je ne comprends pas* or *Voulez-vous répéter, s'il vous plaît*. This should result in the teacher either repeating the question – probably a little more slowly – or re-phrasing it slightly in the hope that you will then understand it.

- If the problem is simply that you don't understand one of the words in the question, you could say *Je ne comprends pas* (French word) or *Que veut dire* (French word)?, in which case the teacher will try to explain, so that the conversation can continue in the same direction.

- If the problem is that you can't remember a word you need for your answer, you could say *J'ai oublié le mot pour* (English word), in which case the teacher will tell you, and the conversation will continue as above.

  These last two techniques will not gain you any credit for the words you didn't know, but they will allow the conversation to flow fairly naturally.

Don't just sit there in silence. This makes it hard for your teacher, who doesn't know whether you are just pausing for thought or whether you're really stuck, and will therefore hesitate to move on. This will make the conversation sound very stumbling, and will also waste time.

Problem 5

You may be allowed to make notes when you are preparing the role-plays. If a Presentation is part of the Speaking Test, you may be allowed to make notes or cue-cards. You will be able to take these with you into the exam room.

Solution 5

Whatever form these written notes take, try not to read them out. Reading aloud is a skill on its own, and most candidates are not very good at it – it affects their intonation and pronunciation very badly.

- For the role-plays, you should use the notes:
  a) to make sure that you know exactly what you are going to say (for the Foundation and Foundation/Higher role-play).
  b) in the exam room, as a back-up, in case your mind suddenly goes blank.

- For the Presentation, you should use the cue-cards simply to keep your ideas in order, as a guide to the sequence of what you are going to say. Some candidates make their cue-cards in visual form, just to avoid the danger of being tempted to read aloud.

Problem 6

You will only be able to use your dictionary during the preparation time for the role-plays. (If you have any vocabulary problems during the Conversation, see Solution 4 above.)

Solution 6

Don't waste time checking words you already know. Look at the instructions and visuals on the Foundation or Foundation/Higher role-plays, and make sure you have the vocabulary you need. Again, if you have a choice, for example of items to buy to take to a party, choose ones that you know in French and don't waste time looking up the others. For the Higher role-play, you should also try to predict what is going to happen, and make sure you have the vocabulary to cope. There is no guarantee that your prediction will be right, but it might be.

PRONUNCIATION

Without using a special alphabet, it is difficult to describe the sounds which are made by particular letters. One way is to compare the sounds with words which you certainly know – in English where there is a close match, otherwise in simple French words. The other way is to model your pronunciation on that of a native French speaker. The first part of the CD for Chapter 15 (Track 32) contains most of the French sounds you are likely to need. Listen to the CD while you follow this list of words. In the printed list, the sounds being practised are in bold.

A	**m**a		N	**n**oir	
B	**b**ar		O	m**o**t	p**o**rt
C	**c**ar	**c**ette	P	**p**ère	
D	**d**ix		Q	**q**ui	
E	l**e**	m**è**re fê**te** mang**é**	R	**r**este	
F	**f**aux		S	**s**a	
G	**g**ant	â**g**e	T	**t**a	
H	**h**abite		U	s**u**r	
I	s**i**	f**i**n	V	**v**in	
J	**j**e		W	**w**agon	
K	**k**ilo		X	fa**x**	
L	**l**a		Y	S**y**lvie	
M	**m**a		Z	**z**éro	

AI	m**ai**son		OI	s**oi**r
AU	**au**		OU	s**ou**s
EI	r**ei**ne		UI	h**ui**t
EU	h**eu**re d**eu**x			

AN/EN	d**an**s d**en**t		AIN	b**ain**
IN/IM	**in**stant* **im**pact*		EIN	h**ein**
ON	m**on**		OIN	c**oin**
UN	br**un**			

*BUT if the consonant is doubled, pronunciation is much more like the English: **imm**édiat; **inn**ocent.

Vowels

As you can see from the above, vowels have a number of different sounds, depending on which other letter(s) they are combined with, or, in the case of E, on the use of accents. When used on its own:

- **a** is pronounced as in the English word 'man'.

- **e** is pronounced as in *de*.
  é is pronounced as in *clé*.
  è and **ê** are pronounced as in *mère*.

- **i** is pronounced as in the English word 'peep'.

- **o** is not like any English sound.

- **u** is not like any English sound.

119

Consonants

Although French consonants are not pronounced in exactly the same way as English consonants, the differences are not usually enough to cause any real problems. However, here are a few tips:

- **c** is pronounced like 's' before *e* and *i*, but like 'k' before *a*, *o* and *u*.

- **g** is pronounced 'soft' (i.e. as in *je*) before *e* and *i*, but 'hard' (as in the English 'gun') before *a*, *o* and *u*.

- **h** is completely silent in French, though it can affect the sound of other letters, as in *château* and *pharmacie*.

- **q** sounds like 'k', as in *qui*.

- **r** is probably most easily produced by rolling the tip of the tongue against the roof of the mouth. Don't worry too much about it, as long as you make sure it can be clearly heard.

- **w** is pronounced like 'v'.

- **x** is usually pronounced like 'ks', as in *fax* (but is usually silent at the end of a word).

- **y** is pronounced like the French *i*.

- **z** is usually pronounced like 'z', as in *zéro* (but is usually silent at the end of a word).

Probably the most useful thing to remember about consonants in French is that, if they come at the end of a word, they are not usually pronounced, unless the next word begins with a vowel. For example:

- *Vert* is pronounced as if it did not have a *t* at the end, but in *verte* you can clearly hear the *t*.

- The sentence *Ils regardent la télé* sounds exactly the same as *Il regarde la télé*. (The *-ent* plural ending on verbs is always silent.)

- However, in the sentence *Ils entrent dans la cuisine* you can hear the *s* on *Ils* since it's followed by a vowel.

The alphabet

You are quite likely, in one of the role-plays, to be asked to spell out someone's name or the name of a place. Listen to the next section of Chapter 15 on the CD (Track 33) and learn the sounds of the French alphabet. Make sure that you can spell out your own name, and any family names (especially if they are very different from French names) and the place where you live. Practise recording these onto your own cassette.

An approximate guide to the pronunciation of the letters of the alphabet is given below, for quick revision.

A	**a** as in 'man'	O	**o** as in *mot* (no English equivalent)
B	**bé**	P	**pé**
C	**sé**	Q	**ku** (no English equivalent of *u* sound)
D	**dé**		
E	**eu** as in *deux*	R	**airr**
F	**eff**	S	**ess**
G	**jé**	T	**té**
H	**ash**	U	**u** (no English equivalent)
I	**ee** as in 'jeep'	V	**vé**
J	**ji** (almost) as in *jupe*	W	**dooble-vé**
K	**ka**	X	**eeks** as in 'peeks'
L	**ell**	Y	**ee-grek**
M	**emm**	Z	**zed**
N	**enn**		

If a word contains a double letter, say *deux* followed by the letter:

    ... ss ... = <u>**deux ess**</u>*

    ... pp ... = **deux pé**

    ... rr ... = <u>**deux airr**</u>*

* The *x* is heard but it sounds like a *z*.

Check yourself 1

Find Chapter 15 – Check yourself 1, Speaking on the CD (Track 34). Answer the questions, then compare your answers with the recording.

QUESTIONS

Q1 *Spell out these words.*

a) LONDRES
b) BRUXELLES
c) WASHINGTON
d) JERSEY
e) SHEILA

Q2 *Say these words out loud. Try not to read them – look, remember, then speak.*

a) beurre
b) intéressant
c) content
d) plaindre
e) soirée

REMEMBER! Cover the answers if you want to.

ANSWERS

A1 Listen to the CD. If you made any errors, try again.

A2 Compare your pronunciation with the CD, then try to imitate it as closely as you can.

TUTORIAL

T1
a) *Remember E is pronounced* eu, *as in* deux.
b) *Try to get the U sound right – listen to the CD. Remember how to say a double letter –* deux ell. *Here, the x of* deux *should sound like a* z.
c) *It is easy to mispronounce I, since in English it sounds like the wrong letter. The same is true of G.*
d) *J is also easy to get wrong. From an English point of view, G and J sound the wrong way round.*
e) *It's easy to get E and I wrong when they are together like this.*

T2
a) *The combination EU almost always has the same sound as in* heure *except for the past participle of* avoir, *which sounds just like the letter U.*
b/d) *These combinations all make the same sound:* in, im, ain, aim, ein, eim.
c) *If a word has the same spelling as an English word, it is a common mistake to pronounce it as if it was English. Remember, too, not to pronounce the final* t.
d) *Try not to pronounce* -dre *as if it was the English '-der'.*
e) *The combination OI is quite common, as in* moi, noir *and* fois, *but some people find it hard to pronounce. Remember that the accent on the first E makes a difference to the sound.*

Verbs

One of the most common mistakes in the Speaking Test is to pronounce all verbs, especially *er* verbs, as if they end in *é*. This makes it impossible for the person you are talking to, to work out whether you are speaking in the past (perfect or imperfect) or the present, since *je mangé* could be a mistake for *Je mange*, or *j'ai mangé*, or even *je mangeais*. This would lead to a lot of confusion, and possible misunderstanding, so would have a serious impact on your accuracy mark. Practise making it absolutely clear whether you are saying:

> *Je mange à la cantine.* (I have lunch in the canteen.)
> *J'ai mangé à midi.* (I ate at twelve o'clock.)

or even:

> *Je mangeais quand le professeur est entré.* (I was eating when the teacher came in.)

THE DIFFERENT PARTS OF THE SPEAKING TEST

ROLE-PLAYS

These are used by all exam boards. In most cases, candidates who are entered for Foundation Tier will do the Foundation role-play and the Foundation/Higher role-play, while candidates entered for Higher Tier will do the Foundation/Higher role-play and the Higher role-play.

The MEG Higher role-play is slightly different from the others, in that it asks the candidate to relate a series of events, rather than take part in a dialogue.

Candidates are given 10–12 minutes to prepare the role-plays, during which time they may use a dictionary.

The boards will use symbols, such as a question mark (**?**) to tell you that you should ask a question.

In the instructions for the role-plays you might meet the following phrases:

C'est à vous de commencer	You should begin	*Donnez*	Give
Choisissez	Choose	*Epelez*	Spell
Commandez	Order	*Expliquez*	Explain
Décrivez	Describe	*Payez*	Pay
Demandez	Ask for	*Proposez*	Suggest
Dites	Say	*Répondez*	Answer
		Saluez	Greet

Check your own syllabus to know exactly what you should expect.

Foundation

The tasks will be presented in English, either as a paragraph or as separate instructions, accompanied by visuals.

Preparation

- Check any vocabulary you need and rehearse in your mind what you will say for each of the four or five tasks.

- Remember that the instructions tell you what the task is. You do not have to translate them into French. For example, if the instruction says: 'Ask your friend what time he gets up', you only need to say *Tu te lèves à quelle heure?*.

- The teacher will start the role-play unless otherwise stated.

- If you are allowed to make notes, do so, but don't be tempted to read a script.

- Don't spend too long on the preparation. You will need more time for the Foundation/Higher role-play.

In the test

- Be calm. You will have the instructions with you, so you don't have to remember what to do.

Foundation/Higher

At this level, there will always be an unpredictable task, i.e. one that is not specified on the candidate's card for you to prepare in advance. The scene will be set in English, and there will be either visual or verbal prompts for each task. The verbal prompts may vary from single words to full-sentence instructions in French, depending on the board.

Preparation

- Check any vocabulary you need and go over in your head what you will say for each of the tasks.
- Work out where the unpredictable element comes, and try to work out what it might be. For example, if you are telephoning to book a hotel room, you will probably be asked your name. If this is not one of the specified tasks, there's a good chance it might be the unpredictable one.

In the test

- Remember that you can only handle the unpredictable task if you understand what the teacher is asking you. You need to listen carefully.

Check yourself 2

Find Chapter 15 – Check yourself 2, Speaking on the CD (Track 35). Answer the questions, then compare your answers with the recording.

QUESTIONS

Q1 *Listen to the unpredictable questions. What do the people want to know? How would you reply? (You will sometimes need to invent the information asked for.) The situations are:*

a) You are arranging to meet someone.
b) You are booking a train ticket in advance.
c) You are on the telephone.
d) You are phoning to book a hotel room.
e) You are reporting a lost watch.

(Transcript: page 228)

REMEMBER! Cover the answers if you want to.

ANSWERS

A1
a) What time to meet.
b) What day is it for?
c) Your phone number.
d) Your name.
e) Where you lost your watch.

In preparing these role-plays, you would have been able to predict these as possible questions, given the situation.

TUTORIAL

T1
a) (On se retrouve) à huit heures?
b) (C'est pour) mardi.
c) (C'est) le deux cent cinquante-huit, quarante-huit, trente-deux. (*You would use your own number.*)
d) S M I T H (*You would use your own name.*)
e) (Je l'ai perdue) dans le métro.

In a), b) and e) you would need to make up the detail (time/day/place) unless it was included in the scene-setting.

Higher

These role-plays will always contain a problem to solve or something to negotiate – they will not be straightforward. The exception is the MEG Higher role-play, where the candidate must give an account of a series of events.

Preparation

- You really need to think yourself into the situation at this level, so that you can respond naturally however the situation develops.
- You can't write yourself a script in advance, since so much depends on what the teacher says.
- All you can do is to try to predict what sort of problem might arise, and make sure that you plan ways to cope.

In the test

- The main thing is to respond appropriately to what the teacher says, so again, listen carefully.
- Be sure to make all the points mentioned on the candidate's card, even if you have to go back over something.

Higher (MEG)

Remember that you are giving an account, so you must use the past tense.

Preparation

- Make sure you say something about every picture. You don't have to mention every detail, but they give you an idea of how much you should say overall, and if you can't think of any other details, you should probably make use of those suggested.
- Make sure you give full accounts, with descriptions and link words. Don't stick to the bare minimum.

In the test

- It's really a question of remembering what you've prepared. You will have the candidate's card to remind you, so it's not just a memory test.

Check yourself 3

 Find Chapter 15 – Check yourself 3, Speaking on the CD (Track 36). Answer the questions, then compare your answers with the recording.

QUESTIONS

Q1 *How would you do the following in French?*

a) Ask to see the manager.
b) Ask for your money back.
c) Say you bought it here yesterday.
d) Complain about the cleanliness of your room.
e) Explain that the dates are not suitable, and why.

Q2 *Listen to the unpredictable questions, and try to answer them.*

a) You are applying for a job in a café.
b) You are working at a Tourist Office.
c) You are reporting an accident.
d) You are talking to a friend about money.
e) You are buying a present for your young brother.

(Transcript: page 228)

ANSWERS

A1
a) Je voudrais voir le directeur,
s'il vous plaît.
b) Vous pouvez me rembourser?
c) Je l'ai acheté(e) ici hier.
d) On n'a pas nettoyé ma chambre.
e) Ces dates ne sont pas possibles. Je
rentre à l'école le deux septembre.

A2
a) Oui, j'ai travaillé dans le café de
mon oncle.
b) Il y a des musées, un château et
beaucoup de magasins.
c) J'étais dans le restaurant là-bas.
d) Oui, le week-end je travaille dans
un supermarché.
e) Il adore les petits trains et
les bandes dessinées.

Of course, you may have chosen different
details in your answers.

TUTORIAL

T1
a/b) *These are both quite standard ideas if you are
complaining. Remember to be polite.*
c) *Make sure you give **all** the relevant information.
It may be given in the scene-setting, or you may
have to make it up.*
d) *There are lots of different ways of expressing this:
Ma chambre est sale or Ma chambre n'est pas
propre, for example.*
e) *If you have to say that you can't do something,
make sure you prepare a reason – you can then
either volunteer it, or give it if asked.*

T2
a) *In a job interview, you are very likely to be asked
about experience, so if the scene-setting doesn't
tell you, make sure you prepare something
appropriate.*
b) *This situation is the reverse of the more common
one, since you are the one **giving** the
information. Again, it is fairly predictable.*
c/d/e) *These situations are not quite so predictable,
but the questions are easy to understand.
You have to think quickly to invent some
appropriate information.*

PRESENTATION AND DISCUSSION

This forms part of the Speaking Test for MEG and NEAB only, though similar
tasks may be done as part of the Coursework option with Edexcel (London).
If you are using one of the other exam boards, go on to the next section.

Both boards require you to speak for 1 minute (MEG) or $1\frac{1}{2}$ minutes (NEAB)
on a topic of your choice taken from one of the areas of experience. The
teacher will then ask you some questions about your Presentation.

Choosing your topic

You could choose a very familiar topic, such as M*a famille*, or M*on école*. You could
be more independent, and talk about M*on passe-temps préféré*. Or you could decide
to talk about M*es vacances en Italie* or L'*échange scolaire*. The choice is yours, but do
discuss it with your teacher, because your choice can affect the mark you get.

- If you choose a 'basic' topic, you may end up only demonstrating a
limited amount of the French that you know. It would be very easy,
for example, to talk about your school using short, familiar
sentences, giving few opinions, and entirely in the present. If you
are in fact able to express opinions clearly, and to refer to the past
and the future, this would certainly restrict your grade.

- If you choose an obscure topic (for example, if your hobby is bell-
ringing!), you need to do a lot of work on the vocabulary.

- Make sure that your teacher knows in advance what your
Presentation is going to be about. This will give him/her the chance
to plan some intelligent and helpful questions.

- Make sure that your first sentence says what the Presentation is
about. Your teacher might know, but the examiner listening to you
on cassette won't, unless you say so.

How much detail

You should include enough detail to make it interesting, but not so much that it becomes tedious. The main idea is to show off your knowledge of French.

- Try to avoid lists of vocabulary. For example, if you are talking about your hobby, give two or three of the key bits of equipment you need. If you are talking about your school, you don't need to list all the science labs one by one, nor to give the names of all the teachers.

- Try to avoid using English words. If your presentation is about La télévision, talk about the programmes in general terms – say J'aime les feuilletons (I like soaps), then give an example, rather than J'aime EastEnders. If you are talking about La musique say J'adore les groupes anglais rather than J'adore Oasis.

- It is possible with almost any topic to say something about the past and the future, as well as the present. Even an unpromising topic like Mon uniforme scolaire can produce sentences like A l'école primaire, je ne portais pas d'uniforme and Dans les écoles de l'avenir, il n'y aura pas d'uniforme.

Cue-cards

These are vital to keep what you are saying in order, and to stop you 'drying up'.

- Keep them to short phrases, or even key words.

- Don't have too many, otherwise you risk getting them mixed up.

- Number them, just in case you drop them on the floor just before the exam.

- Don't read from them (see Problem and Solution 5 on page 118).

- Although you may have written a script to give you confidence while practising, you will not be allowed to read from it, as it's against the rules. In any case, it would ruin your pronunciation.

Delivery

You should practise thoroughly, preferably recording yourself on cassette.

- You don't need to learn your Presentation off by heart (it's probably better if you don't, as you will sound more natural, and run less risk of 'forgetting your lines'), but when you go in to the exam you should know pretty well what you are going to say.

- Don't rush; speak clearly and steadily, without too much hesitation.

- Your practice should include timing. This will give you a good idea of whether you've got too much detail.

- Many of the topics lend themselves to the use of photographs and other visual aids, for example if you are talking about a holiday, or your family. However, don't have too many, and don't just restrict your Presentation to a description of a series of photos:
  Voici mon père. Voici ma mère. Voici la plage. Voici notre hôtel.
  It could get very dull, and doesn't allow much opportunity for demonstrating a range of language.

Predicting the questions

It's a good idea not to include every bit of information, so that you leave the teacher something to ask you. For example, if you are describing a holiday, and don't mention the accommodation, it's fairly certain that the teacher will ask about it.

- The teacher will not be trying to catch you out, but to encourage you to develop further what you have said.

- He/She will probably stick to the well-tried questions: 'What?'; 'Where?'; 'When?'; 'Who with?'; 'Why?'; 'How much?' 'How long?'.

GENERAL CONVERSATION

This is common to the Speaking Tests of all the exam boards. You will be expected to carry out a conversation with the teacher on a variety of topics from the syllabus (they may be chosen by the teacher, or at random, or you might have some choice). In some syllabuses, some topics are only available at Higher Level. You need to check the precise requirements of your board.

The main thing to remember about the General Conversation is that it is your chance to show off what you know. There is no point in knowing four tenses and having an enormous vocabulary if you don't use them.

Tenses

You must make sure that you refer to past, present and future events during the Conversation. Your teacher will ask you questions aimed at encouraging you to use different tenses – it's up to you to respond.

- Listen out for *tu as* or *tu es* (+ past participle), and when you hear it, make sure you answer in the past – *j'ai* or *je suis* (+ past participle).

- If the teacher asks you a question containing *tu vas* (+ infinitive), reply in the future with *je vais* (+ infinitive).

- It is important to note that if you don't refer to past, present and future, you will not get a Grade C!

Opinions

Have some ready-made expressions for expressing different opinions – not just the basic *j'aime/je n'aime pas/j'adore/je déteste*, but more complex ideas such as:
Je crois que – I think that
Il me semble que – It seems to me that
A mon avis – In my opinion
Je (ne) suis (pas) d'accord avec – I (don't) agree with
J'ai horreur de ça – I really hate that
J'en ai marre de – I'm sick of

Again, without expressing opinions, you won't get a Grade C.

Full accounts and descriptions

In the General Conversation, you are rewarded for the range of your language. To score well you need to include:

- some longer sentences, linked with words like *mais, alors, puis*

- some sentences containing *qui* and *que*

- a variety of adjectives and adverbs

- extra details, without being asked. In other words, if you are asked a question like *Tu as des frères ou des sœurs?*, you can launch into a description of them without waiting for any further questions:
  Oui, j'ai une sœur. Elle s'appelle Marie. Elle est plus âgée que moi – elle est à l'université où elle étudie les langues.

What not to do

Since the examiner can only assess what **you** say:

- Don't allow long pauses to develop.

- Don't let the teacher say more than you do.

- Don't hesitate before every word.

- Don't force the teacher to drag every word out of you. Volunteer some information.

- Don't be embarrassed to have a go. It doesn't have to be perfect to communicate.

Check yourself 4

 Find Chapter 15 – Check yourself 4, Speaking on the CD (Track 37). Answer the questions, then compare your answers with the recording.

QUESTIONS

Q1 *Answer these questions (which are also on the CD). Make sure you say more than the minimum needed.*

a) Que fais-tu pour t'amuser?
b) Où es-tu allé(e) en vacances l'année dernière?
c) Tu vas continuer tes études?
d) Parle-moi un peu de ta ville.

Q2 *Answer these questions (which are also on the CD). Make sure you use either a link word (puis, mais, parce que) or qui or que in your answer.*

a) Tu aimes l'école?
b) Tu t'entends bien avec ta mère?
c) Qu'est-ce que tu vas faire ce soir?
d) Que fais-tu le matin?

REMEMBER! Cover the answers if you want to.

ANSWERS

A1
a) J'aime bien lire et regarder la télé. Mais je suis aussi assez sportif, et je joue souvent au tennis et au badminton.
b) L'année dernière je suis allé(e) en Italie avec ma famille. Nous avons passé quinze jours à Florence. C'était super.
c) Oui, d'abord je retournerai à l'école pour passer mes examens. Après, je voudrais étudier les sciences à l'université.
d) C'est une grande ville industrielle dans le nord de l'Angleterre. J'aime bien habiter ici, car il y a beaucoup de distractions.

A2
a) Oui, d'habitude ça va, mais on a trop de devoirs, surtout en maths. C'est une matière que je trouve très difficile.
b) Oui, ma mère est sympa, et on parle de tout parce qu'elle comprend mes problèmes.
c) J'arriverai à la maison vers quatre heures, et je mangerai quelque chose. Puis, je ferai mes devoirs.
d) Avant de descendre dans la cuisine pour prendre le petit déjeuner, je m'habille.

TUTORIAL

T1
a) *It would have been quite easy to develop this by simply repeating j'aime with a long list, but the answer here adds a bit more variety of structure.*
b) *As well as the added detail, this answer gets in an opinion – and two different past tenses.*
c) *This answer is good because the sentences are long (which is good in itself) and it uses two different ways of talking about the future.*
d) *Adjectives are a good way of varying what you say, and adding extra information.*

T2
a) *This answer uses link words very successfully to combine three ideas into two sentences.*
b) *Parce que is an excellent way of explaining how you feel.*
c) *Words like puis help you to organise your ideas effectively.*
d) *Avant de is another good way of organising your ideas into a sequence.*

Don't worry if you don't come up with answers as good as these. They are simply to show you what is possible without learning lots of new words, tenses and so on. Try to introduce some of these ideas into what you say. Why not learn some whole phrases. such as elle comprend mes problèmes and je pense qu'il est important de, that you could use in a number of different circumstances?

EXAM PRACTICE

ROLE-PLAYS

Each of the following role-plays is marked with the name of the exam board on whose style it is based. You may, therefore, wish to concentrate on those role-plays which are closest in style to the ones you will be doing, though the others will give you valuable extra practice.

For each role-play, spend a few minutes working out (with the help of your dictionary) what you would say – and for the Foundation/Higher and Higher role-plays, trying to predict what the teacher might ask. You should probably spend about two minutes on a Foundation role-play, about three minutes on a Foundation/Higher, and five to six minutes on a Higher.

Then find Chapter 15 – Exam Practice, Speaking on the CD (Track 38). Listen to the sample student's answer and compare it with your own.

1

You are at a leisure centre in France.

- *You want to play tennis.*
- *There are four people.*
- *You need to find out the cost.*
- *You want to play for two hours.*

Your teacher will play the part of the assistant and will speak first.

FOUNDATION

[*In the style of* NEAB]

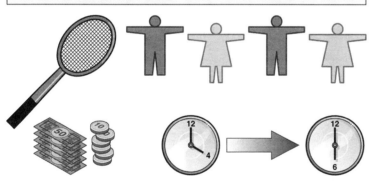

2 **AU CAFE**

You are at the café and need to buy two items from those given below. Remember to greet the waiter and end the conversation politely.

FOUNDATION

[*In the style of* EDEXCEL]

FOUNDATION

[In the style of MEG]

3 **Au camping**

SITUATION: You are shopping in France with your family.

Your teacher plays the part of the shopkeeper and will start the conversation.

FOUNDATION

[In the style of SEG]

4 Tu parles à ton correspondant de tes loisirs.
Ton correspondant parle d'abord.

1 **Saluez l'examinateur.**

2

3

4

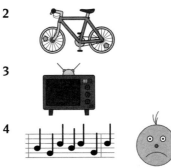

5 **Finissez poliment la conversation.**

FOUNDATION/HIGHER

[In the style of MEG]

5 **Au magasin de souvenirs**

SITUATION: You are on holiday in France with your family.
You go into a souvenir shop.
You want to buy a towel and another item.

Your teacher will play the part of the shop assistant and will start the conversation.

1 Saluez l'employé et dites ce que vous voulez acheter.

2 Répondez à la question du vendeur / de la vendeuse.

3 Choisissez la taille de la serviette.

4 Demandez un autre article et donnez-en 2 détails.

5 Expliquez le problème avec l'argent.

6 A LA GARE

FOUNDATION/HIGHER

[In the style of EDEXCEL]

You are in France on holiday, and you want to visit a friend in Nice. You go to the railway station. Remember to reply to the employee's questions.

The Examiner will begin the conversation.

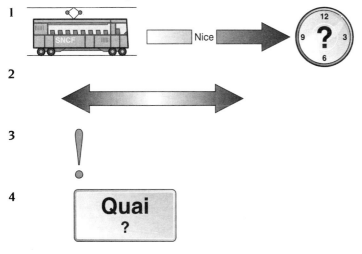

1

2

3

4

You are at a hotel in France.

FOUNDATION/HIGHER

[In the style of NEAB]

- Say you want a single room.
- **!**
- Find out what floor the room is on.
- Ask the price with breakfast.

When you see this – **!** – you will have to respond to something you have not prepared.

Your teacher will play the part of the receptionist and will speak first.

- Chambre.
- **!**
- Etage?
- Prix?

Vous parlez de votre petit emploi à votre ami français.
C'est à vous de commencer.

HIGHER

[In the style of SEG]

1 **Saluez l'examinateur.**

2

3

4

5 **Répondez à l'examinateur.**
6 **Finissez poliment la conversation.**

SITUATION: The notes and pictures below give an outline of a day spent in Normandy. Tell the examiner what happened. You need not mention every detail, but you must cover the whole day's events.

[In the style of MEG]

Be prepared to respond to any questions or comments from the examiner.

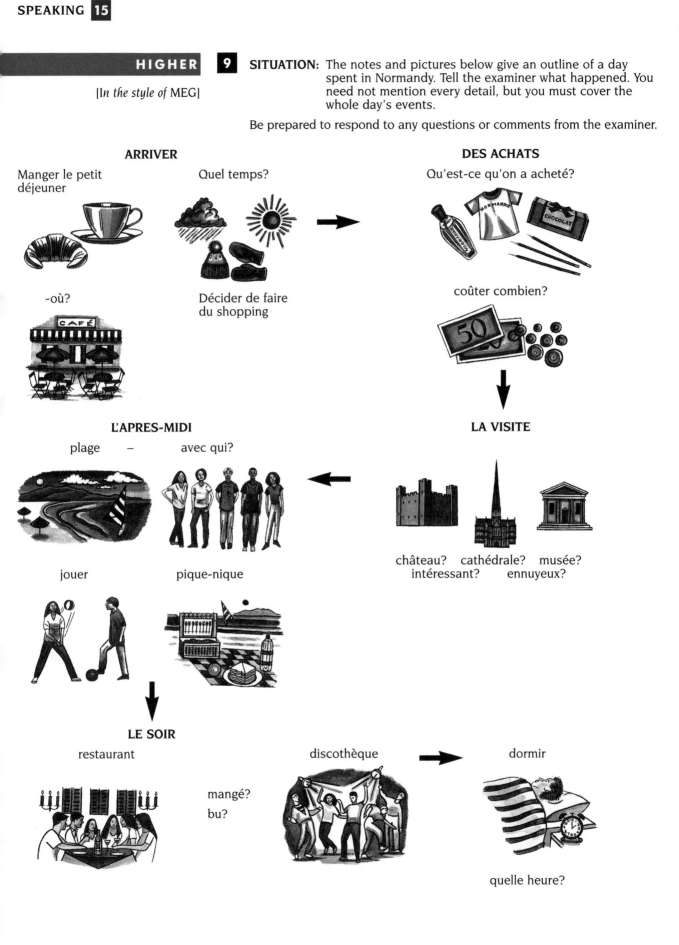

ARRIVER

Manger le petit déjeuner

Quel temps?

-où?

Décider de faire du shopping

DES ACHATS

Qu'est-ce qu'on a acheté?

coûter combien?

LA VISITE

château?   cathédrale?   musée?
intéressant?   ennuyeux?

L'APRES-MIDI

plage   –   avec qui?

jouer   pique-nique

LE SOIR

restaurant   discothèque   dormir

mangé?
bu?

quelle heure?

10 You have bought a radio. When you get back to the campsite, you try it, and it doesn't work. The following day, you take it back. The examiner will begin the conversation.

ELECTRO-MUSIQUE
Spécialiste hi-fi et CD
Prix imbattables
Garanti de deux ans

- OBJET ACHETÉ
- PROBLÈME
- SOLUTION

11 In France, you saw this advertisement for a job. You go to see the manager to ask about it.

LIBRAIRIE DU MOULIN
Grand choix de livres étrangers
Clientèle européenne

RECHERCHE
Vendeur/Vendeuse
- soir et week-end
- bon salaire

You notice that the advertisement does not mention the rate of pay, nor the exact hours worked. You would like to work there until you return to school on the 5th of September.

PRESENTATION AND DISCUSSION

You should only do this if your exam board has it as part of the Speaking Test. However, it would do no harm to listen to the CD – it might give you some useful ideas about things you could say about your family.

Prepare a $1\frac{1}{2}$ minute presentation about your family. Then, in Chapter 15 – Exam Practice, Speaking on the CD, find Track 39 and listen to the sample student's answer. Did you say the same sort of things? Did you manage to fit in a variety of tenses and structures? Did you anticipate the questions the teacher was likely to ask?

GENERAL CONVERSATION

First, listen to the questions which begin this section on the CD (Track 40), and answer each one as fully as you can. The topics covered are House and Home, Leisure and Education and Future Career. Give lots of detail, and don't forget that if the teacher asks a question in the past or the future, you should make sure that you use a verb in the past or the future in your reply. Then listen to the sample student's answer, and compare it with your own.

You will find the transcripts of the sample answers, with examiner's comments, on pages 228–234.

CHAPTER 16

READING AND RESPONDING

INTRODUCTION

Reading is generally thought to be the easiest of the four skills. It is certainly true that, when reading in their own language, people can almost always understand more than when listening, and much more than they can actually produce in speech or writing. However, there are some particular problems with reading.

Problem 1

Some of the material you are asked to read in the exam might be handwritten. Handwriting is always more difficult to read than print, and it can be even more so in a foreign language. In addition, French handwriting is quite different from English handwriting, and this can cause problems with recognising letters, which can lead to comprehension difficulties.

Solution 1

Make sure that you have seen some examples of French handwriting before the exam. You or a friend might have a French pen-friend, or there may be a French teacher at your school. You will be able to pick out the letters which you find hard to read, and so be prepared to meet them in the exam.

Problem 2

Because it is 'easier' than listening, passages in the Reading Test, especially at Higher Level, tend to be longer and more dense. This has implications for timing, as well as for understanding.

Solution 2

There are several strategies for dealing with a long text, some of which will be looked at later in this chapter, but one of the most important is to approach the text in the right way. You should always begin by reading through the whole passage to get the gist. You should then approach a detailed understanding via the questions. Usually, questions will be asked in the order that the information appears in the text. In other words, once you have found the answer to Question 1, the answer to Question 2 will appear later in the text. There may be exceptions to this, particularly when a question is asked about the gist of part of, or the whole, passage, but it is still a reasonable starting point.

Problem 3

You are much more likely to meet words that you do not know in reading than in the other skills.

Solution 3

Again, some of the strategies for coping with unknown words will be looked at later in this chapter, but the main thing is not to panic. You may not need to understand the word at all in order to answer the question.

Problem 4

Written language tends to be more formal than the spoken language, and to use more complex structures. In particular, you may meet two parts of the verb which you will probably not use, or meet in speech, and which you might have met rarely, if at all, in class. These are the past historic tense, which has the same meaning as the perfect tense but is found almost exclusively in literature and journalism, and the subjunctive, which is used in certain phrases, usually after *que*.

Solution 4

You will find a reference to these in the Grammar Summary but generally, for the purposes of reading, you simply need to recognise which verb they belong to. This is usually fairly easy – it's just a question of removing the ending and seeing what's left – though there are one or two irregular verbs where it's a bit more difficult.

Problem 5

Unlike in the Listening and the Speaking Tests, you have access to your dictionary throughout the Reading Test. This may seem to be an advantage rather than a problem, but that is only true if you use the dictionary effectively.

Solution 5

There is one great disadvantage in having a dictionary available in the Reading Test – you tend to use it! You can waste an awful lot of time in a short exam unless you follow this simple rule: don't use the dictionary until and unless you need to.

Problem 6

Because you have more control over reading than over listening, the questions often require closer attention to detail, since you can move about a text, and go back to the beginning, very easily in a printed passage.

Solution 6

Try to work systematically, studying a section at a time, and possibly ticking it when you think you have all the information. It's very tempting to jump about from paragraph to paragraph looking for a particular word or phrase, but you risk repeating what you have already done, and missing out just the part where the answer is.

USING THE DICTIONARY

As already mentioned, the dictionary is a great help in reading if it is used sparingly and sensibly, but it can lead to problems if you use it too much.

Before you use the dictionary

- Read the instructions and questions first.
- Read through the passage – without using the dictionary – to try to get the gist.
- Try to match up the questions with the appropriate paragraph or section of the text.
- Look out for the key words or phrases which might give away the answer – numbers (as in dates, times and prices) can often indicate where to find an answer.
- Then look at the questions, and see how many you can answer, still without using the dictionary.

When you are using the dictionary

- Use it first to make sure that you understand the questions or instructions which are causing you problems.
- If there are still parts of the passage which are giving problems, check the important words. These are more likely to be longer words.
- Make sure you look up the right word. For a verb, this will be the infinitive, for a noun the singular, and for an adjective the masculine singular. Trying to look up a word exactly as it is used in a passage can waste a lot of time.
- Make sure that the meaning you come up with makes sense in the context. Many words have more than one meaning, and you need to choose the one that fits. For example, you see an advert: *Réduction – toutes nos pellicules* -15%. You do not know *pellicules*, so you look it up, and you find *la pellicule* = film, and also *les pellicules* = dandruff. In this context, it clearly has the first meaning.

What you should not do

- Don't use the dictionary to look up words you know. This sounds obvious, but many candidates waste precious time 'just checking' on words they would have understood perfectly if they had not had a dictionary available.

- Don't try to look up every word you don't know – you won't get beyond the first or second long passage on the Higher paper.

- Don't let the fact that you will have a dictionary available stop you learning grammar and vocabulary. The more words you know without a dictionary, the more time you'll have to concentrate on working out the meaning of some of the more complex sentences.

STRATEGIES FOR UNDERSTANDING

There are many ways of understanding words that you have never met, without using a dictionary, but instead using grammatical markers and word patterns and similarities. The more of these strategies you can use, the more you will understand.

Verbs

If you are familiar with the various forms of verb ending, it will be easy enough to remove the ending, and get back to the stem of the verb, which can often be enough to enable you to identify it. For example, if you read *nous dînions*, you will know it's a verb. Remove the ending and you are left with *dîn...* . The infinitive is probably going to end in *-er*, giving *dîner*. Even if you have never met it as a verb, you can easily work out its meaning by comparing it with the familiar noun *le dîner*.

Adjectives

If you are familiar with irregular feminine and plural forms, you can again often get back to the stem of the word. For example, *nationaux* is much easier to understand if you know that *-aux* is the way in which words ending *-al* make their plural.

Nouns

Again, familiarity with irregular plural forms can save a lot of time struggling to work out what an 'unknown' word means.

French word patterns

- If *re-* is added to the front of a verb, it means the action is being done again: *revoir* – to see again.

- The ending *-erie* on many shops is well known, but less known is the ending *-er* or *-ier* to refer to someone who works in such a shop: *boucher; épicier*.

- The addition of *in-* (or *im-* before *b*, *m* or *p*) to the front of an adjective reverses its meaning, so *mangeable* means 'edible', *immangeable* means 'inedible'.

- The ending *-aine* added to numbers turns it into an approximate or round number: *une dizaine* – about 10.

French/English word patterns

- French nouns ending in *-té* often match English nouns ending in '-ty': *beauté*.

- French adverbs ending in *-ment* often match English adverbs ending in '-ly': *complètement*.

- French present participles ending in *-ant* often match English present participles ending in '-ing': *entrant*.

- French words which have a circumflex accent often match English words which have an 's': *forêt*.

- French words which begin with *dé-* often match English words which begin with 'dis-': *décourager*.

- French words which begin with *é-* or *es-* often match English words which begin with 's-': *espace*.

Similar words in English and French

These are far too many to list, and there are of course some which are 'false friends'. For example, *journée* has absolutely no connection with 'journey' – it means 'day'; and *un car* doesn't mean 'a car', but 'a coach'. However, it is certainly worth trying to make use of these similarities. If you are reading a passage in French and you come across a word which (within a letter or two) is the same as an English word, then try to fit it in the context. If it makes sense, then assume it's right. If you have time at the end of the Test to double-check using your dictionary, that's fine.

Check yourself 1

QUESTIONS

Q1 *Use your dictionary to find the meanings of the underlined words. Check how long it takes you.*

a) Le camion est monté sur le <u>trottoir</u>.
b) Il a <u>traduit</u> le roman en anglais.
c) A Noël, maman a acheté une <u>oie</u>.
d) Le chat a grimpé dans le <u>chêne</u>.
e) M. Dubois a mis ses affaires dans sa <u>serviette</u>.
f) Il y a maintenant des cartes à <u>puce</u>.
g) Elle <u>cueille</u> les fleurs dans le jardin.
h) Il a <u>couru</u> pour arriver à temps.

Q2 *Without using the dictionary, write down the meanings of the underlined words. Then check in the dictionary.*

a) J'ai passé des vacances <u>inoubliables</u>.
b) Je l'ai <u>revue</u> hier.
c) Je n'ai pas pu lire tes devoirs – ton <u>écriture</u> est affreuse.
d) Le <u>juge</u> l'a <u>condamné</u> à deux ans de <u>prison</u>.
e) Mme Dumas a été nommée <u>ministre</u> dans le <u>gouvernement</u>.
f) On a <u>assassiné</u> le président.
g) A la météo, on a annoncé une <u>tempête</u>.
h) Il n'y a pas d'<u>éponge</u> dans la salle de bains.

REMEMBER! Cover the answers if you want to.

ANSWERS

A1
a) pavement
b) translated
c) goose
d) oak tree
e) briefcase
f) micro-chip
g) picks
h) ran

TUTORIAL

T1
a/c/d) *There is only one meaning each time, so these are quite straightforward.*
b) *This is clearly the past participle of a verb, so you need to look up the infinitive* traduire. *If you're not sure what the infinitive is, try looking at the first four or five letters, and see if you find anything.*
e) *Briefcase or towel? Look at the context.*
f) *Micro-chip or flea? Which makes sense in the context?*
g) *See b). The infinitive here is* cueillir.
h) *See b). The infinitive here is* courir.

ANSWERS

A2
a) unforgettable
b) saw again
c) (hand)writing
d) judge ... condemned ... prison
e) minister ... government
f) assassinated
g) tempest/storm
h) sponge

TUTORIAL

T2
a) Oublier = *to forget*; in- *before a word* = '*un-*'; -able = '*-able*'.
b) Vu = *saw (past participle of* voir*)*; re = *again*.
c) *This is a bit harder. The word* écriture *is a noun (*ton*) from* écrire (*to write*).
d/e/f) *These are all close enough to the English.*
g) *The circumflex (*ê*) often indicates an added 's' in English.*
h) *Many words which begin* é- *or* es- *in French have an English equivalent beginning* 's-'.

HIGHER LEVEL PERFORMANCE

At Higher Level, you will be expected to be able to do a number of things which are not expected at Foundation Level.

Understand a variety of types of writing

- Authentic extracts from magazines and newspapers. These will include long and complex sentences, and a significant proportion of words which are not in the Minimum Core Vocabulary. These will not be tested, but you will need to be able to use the context, or one of the strategies referred to above, to help you understand the gist of the passage.

- Letters – either printed or in authentic handwriting – which include long sentences, unknown words, and possibly colloquial expressions.

- Extracts from fiction. These will be reasonably short, but may include structures such as the past historic and the subjunctive.

- Advertisements, where the message is not always explicit, and you need to deduce the answer.

Pick out the main points and themes

If a question is aimed at the theme or the main point of a passage, an answer which gives specific details will not score very highly, and may not score at all.

- This type of understanding is often tested through English. So if you read an article about a play, which says that the acting was bad, the dialogue was unconvincing and the sets were ridiculous, and you are asked what the author thought of the play, 'He didn't like it' – although it seems vague – is actually a better answer than 'The acting was bad'.

- Picking out the main point involves a similar technique, but is often tested through multiple-choice in French. So in an article about the environment, the author might include sentences such as: *Il faut utiliser moins les voitures*; *Nous devons tous éteindre la lumière quand nous quittons une pièce*; *On doit tenir fermées les portes et les fenêtres*. You might then be asked to choose the most suitable of the following sentences.
    L'auteur pense que le problème le plus important, c'est:
    A *le prix de l'électricité*
    B *la conservation de l'énergie*
    C *le manque de pétrole*
    D *le chauffage domestique*
All of these appear in the article, but only **B** could be counted as the most important problem.

Identify attitudes and opinions

As in listening, this is not a question of seeing and understanding words like *ennuyé* or *agacé*, but of interpreting that someone who says that she shouted at her brother when he borrowed her make-up was annoyed.

Make deductions from what you read

This is a question of reading a sentence like *Quand elle est rentrée au bureau, elle était toute bronzée* and deducing that she had been on holiday.

Answer questions using French which is not in the passage

If you read *Après le collège, je n'ai pas l'intention de continuer mes études, je préfère travailler*, you might be asked to complete the following sentence:

Elle va chercher ....

None of the words in the printed sentence will fit; you need to put *un emploi or du travail*.

Check yourself 2

QUESTION

Q1 *Read the following passage, then answer the questions. Answer in English.*

LA CARTE JEUNES

Les jeunes de l'an 2000 seront des consommateurs tout comme leurs parents. Ils achètent des tickets de cantine, des places de cinéma ou de concert, des CD .... Ils voudraient donc contrôler leur argent de poche comme les grandes personnes. Le Crédit Agricole met donc à leur disposition la carte bancaire de retrait. Ce n'est point une carte de crédit, mais elle permet aux plus de 12 ans de retirer de l'argent dans les distributeurs automatiques, dans les limites fixées par les parents.

   La carte encourage les jeunes à surveiller de près leurs dépenses. En plus, il y a l'aspect sécurité. On ne veut pas avoir trop d'argent dans sa poche quand on va en ville, et pourtant, si on voit une paire de baskets de rêve, qu'est-ce qu'on fait? Avec la carte jeunes, pas de problème – on se rend vite au distributeur le plus proche, et voilà!

a)   How are young people nowadays like their parents?
b)   What do young people these days need to do?
c)   What does the new card allow you to do?
d)   What limitation is put on its use?
e)   What two advantages does the card have?

REMEMBER! Cover the answers if you want to.

ANSWERS

A1
a)   They are consumers, too.
b)   They need to look after/be in charge of their money (like adults).
c)   To get money from an automatic cash dispenser/hole in the wall.
d)   Parents set a limit on withdrawals.
e)   (i) They can keep an eye on expenditure.
     (ii) They don't need to carry a large amount of cash.

TUTORIAL

T1
a)   You will probably need to look up consommateurs in your dictionary.
b)   This was clearly going to come after parents – see question a) – but it's a bit separated by the examples of what they buy.
c)   It doesn't really matter what word you use for distributeur automatique, as long as it's clear.
d)   You really have to think to get this meaning out of dans les limites fixées par les parents.
e)   (i) is not too difficult, but you have to understand the gist of the last two sentences to get the idea in (ii).

DIFFERENT TYPES OF READING

Skimming

This is particularly useful when you have a lot of text with a small number of quite specific questions – or even a single question. For example, you may have a series of short letters to a magazine, and you need to say which writer fulfils a certain requirement.

- You may simply need to look through each letter to find a single word. For example, if the question is *Qui parle anglais?*, you just need to skim through each letter to find the word *anglais*.

- You may need to find a certain category of word. For example, if the question is *Qui parle trois langues?*, you need to skim through each letter looking for words for languages, and note (don't trust to memory – write it down) the number you find for each person.

- You may need to find one detail for each person, and compare them. For example, if the question is *Qui est le plus jeune?*, you need to skim through each letter and note (again, write it down) the age of each person, and then select the youngest.

The important thing to remember in this type of question is that you are looking for a specific piece of information, and you can ignore everything else. In this type of question it is usually not necessary to read the passage first – you can go straight to the question.

Reading for detail

This is rather similar to skimming, but the questions may be a little less specific, or there may be a number of questions of detail about a single medium-length or long text. In order to find where in the passage the answer comes, it is useful to identify a key word.

- This may be something as precise as a number (time, date, etc.). For example, if the question is *Le voyage a duré combien de temps?*, you are clearly looking for a length of time, which will probably involve a number (though think of other possibilities too, such as *une demi-heure, une journée*).

- The key word might be a little less precise. If the question is *Le voyage était a) très bon? b) pas mal? c) mauvais?*, you need to find the place in the passage where the word for 'journey' appears – though of course the word might be *trajet* or *traversée* for example, as well as *voyage*.

Remember that almost always in this kind of question, the answers will appear in the passage in the same order as the questions appear on the paper. It is useful here to read the passage through quickly before studying the questions, so that you have an idea of the overall meaning – it can save time if you know which bits of the passage contain which ideas.

Reading for gist

This is often the most difficult sort of reading, since you really do need to have a good overall understanding of what you read, though it is not necessary to understand every detail. This sort of item will often have questions in English.

- You may be asked to identify someone's attitude:

    Michèle est contente de sa vie de famille.   VRAI?   FAUX?

    What Michèle says may include good and bad things about her family life, and you have to put everything together and come up with a decision based on the balance of what she says.

- You may be asked to identify the main point or theme of what you read. This may not be stated explicitly; you may have to deduce it from what is written.

It is important here to read the passage right through carefully, but at this stage don't worry about words that you don't understand. Ideas are often repeated in different ways, and understanding a particular word may not matter at all. Only use your dictionary if you are convinced that it is a key word.

Check yourself 3

QUESTIONS

Q1 *Pick out the detail.*

Louise   13 ans   Paris
J'adore la musique pop. J'aime aussi tous les sports, surtout la gymnastique. Je lis beaucoup – les magazines de mode, par exemple.

Maryse   14½ ans   Lyon
Mon passe-temps préféré, c'est l'équitation – j'adore les chevaux. J'aime aussi aller à l'étranger. Je suis déjà allée en Angleterre et aux Etats-Unis.

Luc   14 ans   Calais
Salut! Ce que je préfère, c'est échanger des lettres avec des jeunes d'autres pays. Je parle anglais et italien, et je voudrais un correspondant à New York.

a)   Qui s'intéresse aux vêtements?
b)   Qui parle d'autres langues?
c)   Qui aime écrire à d'autres jeunes?
d)   Qui aime les animaux?
e)   Qui est très sportive?

Q2 *Identify the attitude.*

1   Les jeunes, en ce moment, croient que tout leur est permis. Ils agressent les gens âgés dans la rue ou les petits à l'école. Ce qui est important, pour eux, c'est l'argent.

2   Mais ce n'est pas tous les jeunes, quand même. Il y en a qui essaient d'aider les autres. Ils font les courses des grands-parents, ou ils organisent des points de recyclage à l'école.

3   Pourquoi est-ce qu'on parle toujours des jeunes? Les personnes âgées sont souvent les moins polies, et si on parle d'être honnête, on ne pense pas aux hommes politiques.

4   Oui, il n'y a pas besoin d'être jeune pour être égoïste. Il y a pas mal de gens qui pensent trop à gagner de l'argent pour s'occuper de leurs enfants.

a)   pense qu'on doit plutôt critiquer les adultes.
b)   pense que les jeunes sont égoïstes.
c)   trouve que chez les jeunes, il y a du bon et du mauvais.
d)   pense que les parents ne sont pas toujours parfaits.
e)   pense que les adultes ne montrent pas toujours le bon exemple.

ANSWERS

A1
a) Louise
b) Luc
c) Luc
d) Maryse
e) Louise

A2
a) 3
b) 1
c) 2
d) 4
e) 3 OR 4

TUTORIAL

T1
a) *You might have been looking for an item of clothing here, but it's not always as easy as that!*
b) *Langues matches easily with anglais and italien.*
c) *You need to match écrire with either lettres or correspondant.*
d) *Maryse is the only one who mentions an animal.*
e) *Sportive is a general word, and although Maryse does mention one sport, Louise is the only one who refers to sport in general.*

T2
a) *There are two examples of bad adult behaviour, and the first sentence gives another clue to the general attitude.*
b) *The first comment is the only one which is completely critical of young people.*
c) *The first sentence accepts some criticism of the young, but the rest contains praise.*
d) *This is the only comment which refers to parents – indirectly, with the phrase leurs enfants.*
e) *Politicians not being honest is probably the clearest case of not setting a good example, but parents who are too busy earning money to give their children any attention is also a reasonable interpretation.*

DIFFERENT KINDS OF QUESTION

There are four basic question-types, but there are a number of variations within some of them.

Multiple-choice (pictures)

The aim is to choose the picture which best fits a word, a sentence, or a paragraph.

- Single vocabulary items. In these, you might have, for example, a list of jobs and a series of pictures illustrating certain jobs, and you have to link each picture to the right word.

- A similar technique can be used to test a number of vocabulary items together. For example, you might read: *Dans mon sac, il y avait mes clés, ma carte de crédit, et un flacon de parfum.* You then have four pictures of bags, showing different contents:

  A a ring, keys and a credit card
  B perfume, credit card and keys
  C credit card, perfume and 200F
  D keys, perfume and a diary

  The only choice which matches is **B**.

- The picture might be more general. For example, you read about someone's holiday, and have to decide which fits best:
  A a beach scene   **B** a mountain scene
  C a country scene   **D** a hiking scene

- A variation on this is a series of pictures to be put into the correct order according to what you read. At Foundation Level, this might take the form of a separate account (for example of a day in the country), followed by a series of pictures which you have to put in order. At Higher Level there might be a story from a picture magazine, including speech bubbles which are printed out of order, and you have to note the correct order. If you find this kind of exercise difficult – and you may do, no matter how good your French – it might be a good idea to leave this question until last. It can take a long time to sort out. However, if you do decide to leave this, or any other question, to be done later, make sure you go back to it, even if you only have time to more or less guess at the answers. You should never leave an answer blank, especially if it's just a question of choosing the correct letter or box to tick.

Multiple-choice (words)

Again, there are a number of types.

- One-word answers. These may take the form of an English sentence, followed by a number of one-word items (such as shop names) to choose from. For example:

  Where do you go to buy bread?
  A BOUCHERIE   **B** BOULANGERIE
  C CHARCUTERIE   **D** GARAGE

  At a higher level, you may be given a passage with blanks, and you have to choose from a list which word fits which blank. In this sort of exercise, there will often be more words in the list than there are blanks. A variation on this is a complete passage, followed by a series of sentences, each with a blank which you have to fill with a word from the original passage. When you are choosing words to fill a blank, it is often useful to know whether you are looking for a verb, an adjective or a noun.
  – If the blank comes after a subject pronoun (*je, tu, elle*, etc.) it must require a verb.
  – If the blank comes after a definite or indefinite article (*le/la/les* or *un/une*) it must require a noun.
  – If the blank comes between an article (see above) and a noun, it must require an adjective.

- Phrase or sentence answers. Often, these take the form of a number of sentences following a passage, of which you have to choose (by ticking or writing a letter) the two or three which are correct according to the passage.

Answers in French

Like the above, this can consist of one word, a phrase or a sentence in French. There will often be an example to show how long an answer is expected.

- At Foundation/Higher Level, the answer will often be largely taken from the text. For example, in a letter, you might read: *J'ai un frère.* One of the questions might be: *Elle a combien de frères?* The expected answer would be: *Elle a un frère.*

- You might be asked to fill in a form – for example with personal details, or details of lost property.

- At Higher Level, you may be asked to construct a sentence of your own to answer a question, but this will not usually require more than a fairly simple sentence, drawing on vocabulary from the original passage.

Answers in English

These are often used to test the most difficult ideas, and at Higher Level will almost certainly want more than simple details based on vocabulary.

- Open questions in English at Higher Level will often ask 'Why?', 'How?', 'In what circumstances?' or 'What difference?', and will test either gist understanding, or understanding of a complex idea or sentence.

- Multiple-choice answers in English may be used to test gist, or detailed understanding of a large section of text.

143

Check yourself 4

QUESTIONS

Q1 *Answer in French.*

Salut. Moi, ça ne va pas bien en ce moment. Je viens de finir mes examens, ça ne s'est pas bien passé, je t'assure. J'ai eu de très mauvaises notes, alors mon père m'a dit que je ne pouvais pas sortir pendant un mois. On s'est disputé, ce qui n'est pas habituel, car on s'entend pas mal d'habitude – c'est plutôt ma mère qui me critique – et le résultat – pas d'argent de poche!
J'espère que pour toi ça va mieux.
Sylvie

a) Pourquoi est-ce que le père de Sylvie n'est pas content d'elle?
b) Normalement, comment est-ce qu'ils s'entendent?
c) Avec qui est-ce qu'elle ne s'entend pas?
d) Quelle a été sa punition? [2 choses]

Q2 *Answer in English.*

Mathieu était mon meilleur copain. On faisait tout ensemble. On avait les mêmes goûts en musique, en cinéma, on aimait les mêmes livres. Et je crois que c'était ça le problème, car quand on a commencé à sortir avec les filles, on avait les mêmes goûts là aussi. D'abord, ça nous a fait rire, de tomber amoureux de la même jolie fille en même temps. Puis j'ai rencontré Nathalie, et tout a changé. Je voulais la garder pour moi – et Mathieu aussi. Maintenant, j'ai perdu et ma petite amie et mon copain, car on ne se parle plus.
Qu'est-ce que je peux faire?
Marc

a) Why were Marc and Mathieu best friends?
b) What happened when they saw a pretty girl?
c) How did they feel about this?
d) What was Marc's attitude to Nathalie?
e) In what way has Marc suffered more than Mathieu?

REMEMBER! Cover the answers if you want to.

ANSWERS

A1
a) mauvaises notes aux examens
b) bien
c) sa mère
d) pas d'argent de poche
    ne peut pas sortir (pendant un mois)

A2
a) They liked the same things/had the same tastes.
b) They both fell in love with her.
c) It made them laugh/they laughed.
d) He wanted her for himself.
e) He's lost his friend and his girlfriend/Nathalie.

TUTORIAL

T1
a) *There are other ways of expressing this, such as mauvais résultats, but the key vocabulary is there in the text.*
b) *One word is enough here – but it isn't in the text.*
c) *The mark would probably be given for mère on its own, but not for ma mère.*
d) *You could answer with a sentence, but these are the important ideas.*

T2
a) *Either of these ideas answers the question, but 'They did everything together' doesn't answer 'Why?'.*
b) *The word 'both' is needed for the mark.*
c) *Rire is the key word here.*
d) *Any expression of possessiveness (garder) would get the mark.*
e) *Both ideas are needed to score the mark.*

USING THE TEXT LAYOUT TO HELP UNDERSTANDING

Extracts from newspapers/magazines

- Headlines in large print will tell you what an article is about.

- Articles are often divided into paragraphs. If these have a sub-heading, again this will help with the gist. The paragraphs can also help to pinpoint a particular sort of information in a particular section.

- **Bold** print and *italics* are often used to draw attention to important points or key ideas.

- The photographs in an article, although they won't give away the answer to any of the questions, will give a clue to what the article is about.

- Figures, charts and tables are often used. Their purpose is to give information simply and clearly to the reader, but they can work for the candidate too.

Notices and advertisements

- Like newspaper articles, these make use of changes in print size to draw attention to particular information, and to separate one category of information from another. For example, opening times will often be in a different type-face from, for example, the address. This can help you, if you are looking for specific information.

- The use of centering, bullet points, etc. is also used to highlight certain pieces of information.

Letters

- Letters in French have more or less the same layout as letters in English, so the top right-hand corner will tell you where the letter was written, and the part at the end before the signature will simply be the closing greeting.

- If you are finding the handwriting difficult, it sometimes helps if you find a word that you do recognise, and compare the way the letters in that word are written with a word that you can't work out.

EXAM PRACTICE

1 You want to catch a train. Which sign should you follow?

Tick ONE box only.

| A | □ | PISCINE ⟩ | B | □ | GARE SNCF ⟩ |
| C | □ | BIBLIOTHEQUE ⟩ | D | □ | GARE ROUTIERE ⟩ | [1] |

2 Answer the questions in English.

> ## LA PETITE FERME
>
> entre Villeneuve et St-Maurice
>
> *ouverte à tous les enfants de 3 à 13 ans*
> de 10h à 18h
> fermée le lundi
>
> **lapins, chèvres, moutons, volaille**
>
> Oui, tu peux toucher!

a) Who is **La petite ferme** for? [2]
b) When is it closed? [1]
c) What are visitors allowed to do? [1]

3 Regarde ces extraits des lettres de quelques jeunes Français et Françaises.

> **Julie**
> Moi, j'ai trois frères et deux sœurs. D'habitude ça va, mais je n'aime pas partager une chambre avec ma petite sœur.
> Il n'y a pas beaucoup de place.

> **Alexandre**
> Chez moi, il y a seulement mes parents et moi. C'est bien, car ma mère me gâte, mais quelquefois je voudrais un frère ou une sœur pour jouer avec.

> **Aurélie**
> Je sors souvent avec ma sœur. Elle a deux ans de plus que moi, mais elle me parle comme à une amie, elle me prête ses vêtements et ses disques. C'est bien.

Qui dit quoi? Coche (✔) la bonne case.

	Julie	Alexandre	Aurélie
Je suis fils/fille unique.			
Je m'entends bien avec ma sœur.			
J'ai une assez grande famille.			

[3]

4 Regarde ces objets.

A B C

D E F

Où est-ce qu'on les trouve? Ecris la lettre dans la bonne case.

| CHAMBRE | | CUISINE | | SALON | |
| JARDIN | | SALLE DE BAINS | | SALLE A MANGER | | [6] |

5 Lis la lettre et réponds aux questions.

> Chère Dominique,
>
> Je suis enfin arrivée en France, après un voyage atroce. La mer n'était pas du tout calme, et j'ai été malade. En plus, il y avait beaucoup d'enfants qui ont crié toute la nuit.
>
> Le père de ma correspondante m'attendait au port, et m'a emmenée en voiture. Il a l'air assez sympa, sa femme aussi, et Nathalie est tout à fait comme dans ses lettres – très ouverte et bavarde. Je sens que je vais m'amuser avec elle.
>
> L'inconvénient, c'est la situation de leur maison. Elle se trouve assez loin des autres maisons mais elle donne sur la route nationale, alors il y a de la circulation jour et nuit. Tu sais, je n'ai pas l'habitude, car j'habite dans un coin assez tranquille. La nuit dernière, je n'ai pas dormi.
>
> Heureusement, la semaine prochaine, je vais partir à la mer avec la famille, et ils m'ont dit que la villa qu'ils ont louée n'est pas sur la route. Je l'espère!
>
> Grosses bises
> Amélie

Coche (✔) la bonne case.

a) Le voyage a été …
bon ☐ assez bon ☐ mauvais ☐

b) Amélie est …
contente ☐ assez contente ☐ pas contente ☐
de la famille.

c) La maison se trouve …
en ville ☐ près d'une ferme ☐ dans un village ☐

d) La semaine prochaine, Amélie espère …
aller à la plage ☐ rentrer à la maison ☐ bien dormir ☐ [4]

6 Voici un article du journal *Mon Quotidien*.

Choisis les mots qui conviennent. Complète le tableau.

2 ados passent 40h dans l'eau au milieu des requins

Prisonnières sur un cargo, deux adolescentes néo-zélandaises ont sauté dans une eau infestée de requins. Elles ont réussi à rejoindre la terre et ont survécu 18 jours en ....1........ du poisson.

Deux sœurs jumelles de 18 ans ont survécu 40h dans un ....2........ infesté de requins. Sarah et Joanne, deux Néo-Zélandaises s'étaient embarquées en cachette sur un cargo pour se rendre en Malaisie.

Le capitaine les a ....3.......... et enfermées dans les ....4........ .

Requins

Les ados ont réussi à ....5........ et se sont jetées à l'eau en ....6........ d'une hauteur équivalente à celle de 3 étages. Elles ont échappé par miracle aux ....7........ avant de rejoindre la côte, 36 km plus loin. Puis, elles se sont ....8........ et nourries durant 18 jours, avant d'être retrouvées par la police.

1	exemple: *mangeant*
2	
3	
4	
5	
6	
7	
8	

Choisis les mots dans la liste:
cuisines
requins
mer
s'échapper
océan
entrer
sautant
découvertes
mangeant
cachées

[7]

7 Lis cet article.

◆ **Beso – génie à 11 ans** ◆

Il a sa propre exposition dans une galerie à Londres. Il a déjà créé plus de 3 000 tableaux. Rien d'étonnant peut-être – mais à 11 ans?

Ce petit gamin géorgien peint depuis l'âge de 4 ans. Encore rien d'anormal, car tous les enfants aiment la peinture. Mais le directeur de la galerie d'art, Roy Miles, est convaincu qu'il a trouvé un vrai génie. Il a découvert l'artiste lors d'une visite en Géorgie.

Beso n'est pas d'une famille riche – tout au contraire – et comme tous les enfants de son pays il a connu la guerre et la violence. C'est ce qu'il peint!

Coche (✔) la case VRAI ou la case FAUX.

	VRAI	FAUX
a) Beso est de nationalité anglaise.	☐	☐
b) Il peint depuis sept ans.	☐	☐
c) Il est assez riche.	☐	☐
d) Ses peintures représentent les souffrances de son pays.	☐	☐

[4]

8

PROJETS D'AVENIR

Voici la réponse de Martine:

En ce moment, ça va pas mal à l'école, mais on verra après les examens l'année prochaine. Je voudrais faire des études supérieures – de préférence des études de commerce. J'ai envie de travailler à l'étranger pendant quelques années, avant de m'installer en France et mener une vie de famille.

Mon rêve serait de trouver un emploi dans une grande entreprise, et de passer un an en Italie, un an en Belgique et deux ou trois ans aux Etats-Unis. Heureusement, je parle assez bien anglais, et j'ai habité pendant trois ans à Rome, alors je parle couramment italien.

Pour finir les phrases, choisis parmi les expressions A à F.
Puis écris la bonne lettre dans la case.

1 Après le lycée, Martine voudrait ... ☐

2 Elle n'a pas encore envie ... ☐

3 Elle a l'intention ... ☐

4 Elle n'aura pas ... ☐

A ... de se marier.
B ... de problèmes avec les langues étrangères.
C ... d'enfants.
D ... de travailler dans plusieurs pays différents.
E ... travailler en Europe.
F ... continuer ses études.

[4]

HIGHER **9** Mets les phrases dans le bon ordre.

A Je ne sais jamais. Les fleurs sont belles, mais elles se fanent si vite.

B Bon. Je vais lui en parler tout de suite.

C Oui. J'avais pensé à un sac à main. Je sais qu'elle en a besoin.

D Dis, c'est l'anniversaire de maman la semaine prochaine.

E Demande à papa. Il t'avancera certainement un mois d'argent de poche.

F Oui, tu as raison. Qu'est-ce qu'on va lui acheter?

G Ce sera très cher, non? Pour l'instant, je n'ai pas un sou.

Numero	Phrase	
1	D	*Exemple*
2		
3		
4	C	*Exemple*
5		
6		
7	B	*Exemple*

[4]

HIGHER **10** Ecris le nom de la personne.

Tiphaine, Olivier et Sandrine parlent de la fête du cinéma, qui a lieu les 29, 30 juin et 1er juillet.

Tiphaine, 21 ans: J'y vais une fois par semaine. Ça dépend de ma bourse et de mon temps. Pendant la fête, je compte voir au moins 5 films, car pendant ces trois jours, on paie le premier film à plein tarif, et après on ne paie que 10 francs par film.

Olivier, 21 ans: Je vais au cinéma, bien sûr, mais pas de façon régulière. Si j'ai des examens, j'y vais pas. En général, j'y vais deux fois par mois. Les places sont tellement chères que je ne peux pas me permettre d'y aller trop souvent.

Sandrine, 20 ans: Pour moi, le cinéma, c'est un plaisir qui me permet de tout oublier et de changer de vie pendant deux heures. J'y vais tous les samedis, et assez souvent en semaine aussi. Ça change de la monotonie quotidienne et c'est une façon de se cultiver.

1 Qui n'a pas assez d'argent pour aller souvent au cinéma?
2 Qui trouve que les films sont un moyen de s'évader de la réalité?
3 Qui va profiter de la fête pour voir beaucoup de films?
4 Normalement, qui va le plus souvent au cinéma? [4]

11 Read this article, then answer the questions in English.

Vos papiers, s'il vous plaît!

Depuis 1993, la situation des 'sans papiers' en France est très difficile. Il s'agit d'immigrés qui sont en France depuis des années, et qui avant cette date auraient eu le droit d'y vivre. Mais ils sont maintenant considérés comme clandestins, et leur statut est illégal.

Pour protester, et pour demander leur régularisation, ils ont trouvé asile dans l'église St-Bernard à Paris.

Le cinquante-deuxième jour, la police a forcé les portes de l'église. A l'aide de brutalité physique et de gaz lacrymogène, les policiers ont mis fin à la résistance.

La question des immigrés joue un rôle de plus en plus important dans la politique française. Le Front National profite de la peur que ressentent beaucoup de Français face au chômage et aux problèmes sociaux des grandes villes.

Arif, lui, vit à Paris. Ce n'est pas un immigré – il est né en France, et il se considère comme français. "Les gens ont peur de ceux qui ne sont pas comme eux" dit-il. "S'il y a du chômage, c'est à cause des immigrés. Si les gens sont agressés dans la rue, c'est à cause des immigrés. Ce qu'ils ne disent pas, c'est que ce sont les immigrés qui sont les plus touchés par le chômage, et que les victimes des agressions, ce sont très souvent des immigrés."

a) How has the position of immigrants without papers changed since 1993?
b) What happened to end the asylum of the group of immigrants in St Bernard's Church?
c) Why is the National Front attracting more voters?
d) What is Arif's response to accusations that immigrants are responsible for unemployment and street violence?
e) How would you describe the general tone of the article? [5]

[Total: 46 marks]

You will find the answers and examiner's comments on pages 234–236.

INTRODUCTION

This chapter deals with the skills and techniques you will need to help you gain maximum credit in the most difficult of the language skills.

Most people find the accuracy needed to score highly in writing quite hard to achieve. If you have studied the topic-based chapters of this book thoroughly, you will have acquired all the structures you need to achieve a very high mark in writing. However, it is not only accuracy that counts. You also need to express ideas and opinions, and to give full and detailed accounts.

As in speaking, however, you do have one great advantage. There is always some choice of content, and therefore of language, in the Writing Test. Some boards actually give you a choice of question in the Writing Test. If this is the case for you, make sure you choose wisely. Don't spend too long on the choice, but don't simply go for the first option. Look at the topics, and ask yourself which one you feel happiest with. Do you know a lot of vocabulary in that topic? Do you have some ready-made phrases which would fit? Are there many words which you will **have** to use (for example in a narrative based on pictures) that you'll need to look up? More about the use of the dictionary later, but as in the other skills, the key rule is to use it as little as possible. Even if the paper set by your board doesn't give you any choice of question, you can still to some extent choose what to say.

Here are some of the problems which are specific to writing, with some suggestions as to how you might overcome them or avoid them.

Problem 1

Understanding the question.

Solution 1

Make sure that you are familiar with the layout of the Writing paper set by your own board. The general pattern will remain the same from year to year, and in particular the early questions will ask for similar things every year. However, in the later questions, and at Higher Level, you must make sure that you understand what you have to do, using your dictionary if necessary.

Problem 2

Deciding what you want to write.

Solution 2

There are a number of golden rules here.

- Don't start by working out in detail in English what you want to say, and then putting it into French. You will always end up trying to say things you have never learnt, you'll get the structures wrong, and have to look up lots of words.

- Don't be in too much of a rush to get started. Many candidates aim to finish in time to make a 'fair copy' of what they have written. This is usually a bad idea. You often end up simply copying the mistakes you made in the first draft (because you don't really have time to write all your answers twice), and adding a few new ones too as you rush to get finished.

- It's much better to start by making a plan. This needn't take long, nor be too full, but it will help you to know where you're going. If the question gives you a series of tasks to do (in French or in visual form), make a note – at this stage in English if you like – of what each task is, and of some useful words and phrases (in French). If your task is to reply to a French prompt, such as a letter which asks a number of questions, jot down in English the questions which are asked, and then list some useful French words and phrases.

Problem 3

Deciding how much to write.

Solution 3

Most boards actually suggest on the question paper the number of words you should write, and you should obviously follow these suggestions. NEAB does not specify a number of words, but at Foundation Level, Question 2 will require about 35 words, and Question 3 about 90 words, while at Higher Level, Question 1 will require about 90 words, and Question 2 about 120 words. For all boards, what really matters is carrying out the specified tasks, so you shouldn't spend too long counting the words, and if you find you've written a few words over the 'limit' you should certainly not spend ages trying to cut them out. However, if you write much less than the suggested number of words, you will probably lose marks.

Problem 4

Producing accurate work.

Solution 4

Unfortunately, there is no easy answer to this. However, there is one thing you can do to minimise inaccuracies, and that is to check your work. Simply reading over what you have written is not likely to highlight many mistakes, but a structured approach can really help. Try to leave yourself enough time at the end to go through the following check-list:

1   Make sure that verbs agree with their subject. Common errors are to put a singular ending after *ils* or *elles*, (often putting *-e* instead of *-ent*, or *-ait* instead of *-aient*). If you're in a hurry, you can at least check that after *tu* your verb ends in *-s* (it always should), and after *il/elle*/someone's name, the verb does not end in *-s* (it never should – perhaps *-t*, *-d* or *-e*, but never *-s*).

2   Make sure that all your perfect tense verbs have the correct part of *avoir* or *être* **as well as** the past participle. The commonest verb error of all is to write, for example, *je parlé* instead of *j'ai parlé*.

3   Check that if you've used an adjective with a feminine or plural noun, you've made the adjective feminine or plural too.

Problem 5

Completing all the tasks. If you forget to do one of the tasks – even one of the simple ones like the greeting at the beginning of a letter, or the ending of a letter – you will lose marks for content, and this might even affect the other marks for that question too.

Solution 5

Either on the question paper, or on your plan, tick each task as you do it. This makes it less likely that you'll leave one out.

USING THE DICTIONARY

Using the dictionary for the Writing Test requires a different skill from using it in the Reading Test. To begin with, you are using the other half of the dictionary! You should keep in mind the following points:

● Only use the dictionary when you need to – as little as possible.

● Words with different meanings are more of a problem when you are using the English/French section of the dictionary. How do you know that you've come up with the right word? For example, if you want to say in French 'the case is very light', and you look up the word 'light', you may well find all of the following: *lumière*; *clair*; *léger*; *allumer*. You probably don't know immediately which you want

153

– presumably you looked it up because you didn't know it. You need to double-check, therefore. If you know that the word you want is an adjective, then it's quite simple – you want the word which is marked *adj* in your dictionary. (Make sure you know your own dictionary and the abbreviations it uses.) Otherwise, you may have to cross-check by looking up *lumière, clair, léger* and *allumer* in the French/English section to make sure. You should always check carefully if the word you find doesn't seem at all familiar.

Check yourself 1

QUESTIONS

Q1 **Use *your dictionary to find a suitable French word for the words underlined.***

a) I've lost my <u>watch</u>.
b) He went to buy a <u>paper</u>.
c) She's broken her <u>nail</u>.
d) I'll give you a <u>ring</u> tomorrow.
e) You have no <u>right</u> to do that.

REMEMBER! Cover the answers if you want to.

ANSWERS

A1 a) montre
b) journal
c) ongle
d) coup de téléphone
e) droit

TUTORIAL

T1 a) *Most of the other meanings for 'watch' are verbs, which clearly won't fit here.*
b) *This should be quite clear, since you'll probably find the word 'newspaper' in brackets in the dictionary.*
c) *You probably need to look at the examples to get this right.*
d) *Here, the French phrase gives it away.*
e) *Droite is 'right' in the sense of the direction.*

DIFFERENT KINDS OF QUESTION

Each exam board uses different kinds of questions, but there are a number of basic types:

Foundation Tier

● Many boards have as the first question a simple list – single words or short (2-3 word) phrases. This usually carries relatively few marks, and is aimed at Grades F and G. The important thing here is to make sure you only include in the list items which are appropriate to the question. If you're asked to list things to buy for a picnic, don't put down *stylo*.

● The second question is likely to be a message (a postcard/fax/phone message) to be completed in 30-40 words. The tasks (probably five) are clearly specified in French and/or visually, and each will usually require a short sentence. This question is aimed at Grades D, E, F and G. The tasks only require the use of the present tense, in such sentences as: *J'habite une petite maison; J'aime les petits pois; Je joue au volley*.

● The third question will probably be a letter to be completed in 70-90 words. The tasks may be set out specifically in French (with or without some sort of French stimulus to help you, such as a letter or an advertisement), or you may simply be asked to reply to a letter which is printed on the question paper. This question is aimed at Grades C and D. The tasks will require the use of past, present and future, (don't forget you can often talk about the future by using *aller* and the infinitive – *Je vais passer les vacances à Paris*) and in addition to give reasons and express opinions.

Check yourself 2

QUESTIONS

Q1 *Write a French sentence to fulfil each task.*

a) Quelle est ta matière préférée?

b) Quelle est ta nationalité?
c) Dis quand tu veux travailler.
d) Que fais-tu?

e) Réductions?

Q2 *Write a French sentence to fulfil each task.* **10–20 words.**

a) Dimanche dernier – sortie en famille.
b) Quel est votre passe-temps préféré? Pourquoi?
c) Parlez de vos heures de cours au lycée et de vos devoirs à la maison.
d) Vous avez déjà travaillé?
e) Parlez de vos ambitions pour l'avenir.

REMEMBER! Cover the answers if you want to.

ANSWERS

A1 For example:
a) Je préfère l'histoire/la géographie/les maths.
b) Je suis anglais(e)/britannique/écossais(e)/gallois(e).
c) Je veux travailler au mois d'août.
d) Je joue au volley.
e) Est-ce qu'il y a des réductions (pour étudiants)?

A2 For example:
a) Dimanche dernier, je suis allé(e) au cinéma avec ma famille pour voir un film comique.
b) Je préfère les échecs, parce que je suis plus fort(e) que mon frère.
c) Au lycée j'ai cours de huit heures et demie à cinq heures, puis j'ai deux heures de devoirs.
d) Pendant les vacances, j'ai travaillé comme serveur dans un restaurant.
e) Je voudrais être médecin comme ma mère, car je veux aider les gens.

TUTORIAL

T1
a) *You just need to adapt the verb and choose one of the three subjects.*
b) *You need to know the appropriate nationality, and the je form of être.*
c) *You have to adapt tu veux to je veux, but the choice of time is yours.*
d) *Here, you have to supply both the verb and the noun.*
e) *Remember that a question mark prompts you to **ask** a question.*

T2
a) *Note the extra detail of the type of film.*
b) *Again, the explanation moves this up from a C.*
c) *Lots of detail, and a good long sentence with a link word.*
d) *A very simple sentence, but again with that extra detail of the precise job.*
e) *There are two added details here – comme ma mère and a reason.*
All these answers have the fullness which pulls them above Grade C – some of them would probably come in a Grade A piece of work.

Higher Tier

- The first question will probably be a letter to be completed in 70-90 words. The tasks may be set out specifically in French (with or without some sort of French stimulus to help you – such as a letter or an advertisement), or you may simply be asked to reply to a letter which is printed on the question paper. (This is in fact the same as the last question on the Foundation paper.) This question is aimed at Grades C and D. The tasks will require the use of past, present and future, (Don't forget you can often talk about the future by using *aller* and the infinitive – *Je vais passer les vacances à Paris*) and in addition to give reasons, and to express opinions.

- The second question will be a letter or an article to be completed in 120-150 words. Again, the tasks may be specified in French, (with or without some sort of French stimulus to help you), or you may be asked to write an account of a series of events outlined in a set of pictures. This question is aimed at Grades A*, A and B. It will often require the use of different tenses, but will also give more scope for a wide range of language, for longer and more detailed descriptions and accounts.

DIFFERENT KINDS OF WRITING

As can be seen above, the Higher Level questions (including the final question on the Foundation paper) may require a number of different forms of writing.

Letters

Whether you are asked to write a formal letter (to a hotel booking a room, or to a company applying for a job, for instance) or an informal letter (to a French-speaking friend), the opening and ending are important.

- Formal letters usually begin simply *Monsieur*, *Madame* or *Mademoiselle*. The ending for formal letters is, however, more complex. It is probably enough simply to know one: *Je vous prie d'agréer, Monsieur (Madame, Mademoiselle) l'expression de mes sentiments distingués*. Formal letters require you to use *vous* to the person you are writing to: *Pourriez-vous m'envoyer une liste des hôtels?* It is important to be consistent in this, and to remember to use *votre* and *vos*. Finally, letters will often require you to ask questions. In a formal letter you should use a formal way of asking a question: *Est-ce qu'il y a un musée dans la ville?* or *Y a-t-il un musée dans la ville?*

- With informal letters, it is normal to begin with *Cher* (*Cher Paul*) or *Chère* (*Chère Marie*). There are several possible endings, varying from the fairly formal *A bientôt* or *Amitiés* to the very familiar *Grosses bises* – only to be used to someone you know well! In informal letters, you will be expected to use *tu* to the person you are writing to. Again, it is important to be consistent, and to use *ton/ta/tes*, and *toi*. Informal letters will usually require you to ask at least one question, but it is quite appropriate to use the colloquial question form, which simply involves the use of a question mark: *Tu as un animal chez toi?*

Articles

- These are often not very different from letters, apart from the opening and ending referred to above.

- They are, however, more likely to stick to one subject – where a letter might cover a variety of different topics. It is more important, therefore, (even if the tasks don't ensure this) to make sure that what you write is arranged in some sort of logical order.

- You are not likely to need to ask questions in an article, so for the sake of variety you might try to use *nous* instead of *je* from time to time: *Je suis allé(e) en France avec mon frère; Nous avons pris le train.*

Accounts

- These may well be presented as part of a letter, but will not need the opening and ending.

- Accounts are always in the past, but if possible, you should try to get in at least one future. At the end of almost any account, for example, you could put in a sentence like *J'y retournerai l'année prochaine, car je me suis bien amusé(e).*

- If the account is based on a series of pictures, you don't necessarily need to mention every detail of each picture, but you should make sure that you at least refer to each picture. In fact, when you are making your plan, it is often easier to assume that you will write about the same amount about each picture. So, if you have to write about 150 words based on six pictures, you would expect to write between 20 and 30 words about each picture. This ensures that your account is reasonably balanced.

Check yourself 3

QUESTIONS

Q1 *Write one or two sentences in French to complete the following tasks.*

a) Write one or two sentences, including the opening, of a letter booking a hotel room for your family, giving dates and details of room(s).

b) You have been asked to write an article about your holiday. Write the one or two sentences needed to complete this task:
– *Vos projets pour l'année prochaine.*

c) You are writing a letter to apply for a job in a restaurant. Write the one or two sentences needed to complete this task:
– *Des petits jobs que vous avez déjà eus.*

Q2 *Write a sentence in the past or in the future which would fit each of these topics.*

a) An article about your school. (past or future)

b) A letter inviting your penfriend to come to Britain. (past)

c) A description of a famous French person. (future)

d) An account of the school exchange visit to Normandy. (future)

e) A letter telling your penfriend about your plans for a holiday in Florida next year. (past)

ANSWERS

A1

a) Monsieur,
Je voudrais réserver deux chambres pour deux personnes avec salle de bains. Je voudrais les chambres du huit au douze juin.

b) L'année prochaine je voudrais bien revenir ici, car je me suis bien amusé(e). Mais je préférerais un hôtel plus près de la plage.

c) Depuis le mois de janvier, je travaille dans le café de ma tante le week-end. Avant ça, j'ai travaillé dans un supermarché.

A2

a) J'ai commencé à ce collège il y a trois ans, quand j'avais douze ans.
OR
L'année prochaine, j'irai au lycée pour étudier les langues et l'histoire.

b) On s'est bien amusées il y a deux ans, quand tu es venue en Angleterre pour la première fois.

c) Au mois de juin il donnera un concert à Sheffield – la semaine prochaine je vais faire la queue pour acheter mon billet.

d) Je voudrais bien revenir en Normandie avec ma famille – je suis sûr(e) qu'ils trouveraient le paysage très beau.

e) Je ne suis jamais allé(e) aux Etats-Unis, tu sais, alors j'attends le mois de juillet avec impatience.

TUTORIAL

T1

a) *This is a fairly straightforward task. The thing is to make sure you include all the necessary information – details of room(s) and dates.*

b) *The first sentence actually completes the task, but going on allows the use of the conditional, and includes an expression of opinion.*

c) *Depuis is a good construction to use (check the tense in the Grammar Summary), and this gives lots of detail, as well as including a past tense.*

T2

a) *With a little imagination, there is always something you can say in the past or the future. It's always a good idea to go beyond a minimum statement of facts, and add some extra detail, such as when or why. Of course, it would do no harm to include both these sentences – then you've got the past and the future out of the way.*

b) *Another example of going beyond the minimum. Note the agreements (amusées, venue) used by this female writer.*

c) *Two futures for the price of one (donnera and vais aller).*

d) *The conditional refers to a future event and adds more variety, as well as expressing an opinion.*

e) *Don't forget the value of negative statements. They can add variety as well as giving more detail.*

HIGHER LEVEL PERFORMANCE

The following tips will all contribute to moving your written work up to and beyond a Grade C. Remember that it is a **requirement** for Grade C that candidates refer to past, present and future events, and express opinions.

- Each answer should contain references to past, present and future events, and most questions will be designed to encourage use of a variety of tenses. This is not as demanding as it might sound: the perfect tense is easier than the present since there are fewer irregular forms, and the future can usually be expressed by *aller* and the infinitive. It only takes a little imagination to include at least one past and one future in almost any answer. For example, if you have to write about your favourite pop personality, you could simply say where you saw him (*Je l'ai vu à Manchester*) and where he will be playing next (*L'année prochaine, il va chanter à Birmingham*).

- One of the things which most clearly distinguishes a Grade A/A* piece of work from a Grade C is the length of the sentences produced. It is not difficult to increase the length of your sentences without greatly increasing the complexity of what you write. Simply by using link words such as *mais*, *puis*, *alors* and *donc*, you can

combine two sentences into one, and avoid the almost childish impression that a series of short sentences can give. For example:
> *J'ai pris le petit déjeuner, puis je suis parti(e) pour l'école.*
> *Je voudrais une glace, mais je n'ai pas assez d'argent.*

- Use of *qui* and *que* clauses is another indication of that higher level of language you are looking for, for example:
> *L'homme que j'ai vu était grand et mince.*
> *Chez nous, c'est mon père qui s'occupe du jardin.*

- Make sure you have some phrases ready for expressing your opinion, for example:
> *A mon avis* – In my opinion
> *Je pense que/Je crois que* – I think that
> *Il me semble que* – It seems to me that

- Writing at a higher level doesn't just mean writing longer sentences, but writing more fully. Don't just stick to the bare outline.
  - Fill in the detail with adjectives:
  > *On devait porter un uniforme **rouge** et **jaune**.*
  - Or adverbs:
  > ***Soudain** j'ai entendu un bruit.*
  - Give explanations:
  > *Je me suis couché(e) de bonne heure **car j'étais fatigué(e)**.*
  - Give some background information:
  > *Quand je suis arrivé(e), **il pleuvait**.*

- Finally, use as wide a variety of language as you can. Just because you've included a perfect tense and a future tense, you don't have to stop at that.
  - Try adding an imperfect:
  > *Mon père **était** très fâché quand il a vu notre chambre.*
  - Or a conditional:
  > *Si je gagnais à la loterie, **j'achèterais** une belle moto.*
  - And try to avoid repeating words if you can. It isn't always possible, but you can usually manage it with a bit of thought, often by using pronouns. If you've already referred to your case, you can say *Je l'ai laissée dans le train*, and avoid repeating *valise*.

MAKING USE OF THE FRENCH WHICH IS ON THE PAPER

Clearly, you are not going to get any credit for simply copying phrases or sentences from a letter or an advertisement which is printed on the question paper. However, the material is there to help you, and as long as you change or adapt it in some way, it becomes your language, and will be marked accordingly.

- Sometimes, the stimulus material has to be understood in order to carry out the task. If you have the instruction *Lisez cette lettre et répondez aux questions de votre correspondant*, then you must make sure you find the questions and understand them before you start answering them.

- However, often the stimulus is there to give you a sort of model. This is especially true at Foundation Level, but even at Higher Level you may find useful vocabulary or phrases. For example, a job advertisement will almost certainly contain useful words like *salaire* or *expérience*, and there is no reason not to make use of them in your answer.

- If the tasks are specified by means of questions in French, then you can often at least begin your answer by adapting the question:
> *Allez-vous continuer vos études?*
> *Oui, je vais continuer mes études au lycée, car j'espère aller à l'université.*

159

Check yourself 4

REMEMBER! Cover the answers if you want to.

QUESTIONS

Q1 *The following groups of sentences are too short to score highly. How would you improve them?*

a) Je me suis levé. J'ai pris le petit déjeuner. Je suis parti pour l'école.
b) Nous sommes allés au parc. Nous avons pris un pique-nique. Il a plu. Nous sommes rentrés à la maison.
c) Mon école est grande. Il y a mille élèves. Il y a soixante professeurs.
d) Le sac est en cuir marron. Le sac est petit. Dans le sac, il y a des clés.

Q2 *Answer the following questions which your penfriend asks in a letter. (20–30 words)*

a) Qu'est-ce que tu voudrais comme emploi? Pourquoi?
b) Qu'as-tu fait le week-end dernier?
c) Parle-moi un peu de la ville où tu habites.
d) Quels sont tes passe-temps préférés?
e) Tu as passé de bonnes vacances?

ANSWERS

A1
a) Je me suis levé, et puis j'ai pris le petit déjeuner avant de partir pour l'école.
b) Nous sommes allés au parc pour prendre un pique-nique, mais après il a plu, alors nous sommes rentrés à la maison.
c) L'école où je vais est grande, avec mille élèves et soixante professeurs.
d) C'est un petit sac en cuir marron, avec mes clés dedans.

A2
a) Si je réussis à mes examens, je voudrais être informaticien(ne), parce que c'est l'emploi de l'avenir, et on peut gagner beaucoup d'argent.
b) Samedi, je suis allée en ville, où j'ai acheté une nouvelle robe. Puis, le soir, je suis allée au cinéma avec Marc. Dimanche, j'ai fait mes devoirs.
c) La ville où j'habite est assez petite. Il y a des magasins, mais il n'y a pas de distractions. Pour faire des courses ou aller au cinéma, il faut aller à Middlesbrough.
d) J'adore la musique, et je joue dans un groupe de rock – moi, je joue de la batterie. Nous sommes assez populaires, et nous jouons aux boums de nos copains.
e) Je suis allé(e) en Espagne avec mes parents. Il a fait très beau, et l'hôtel était bien, mais j'aurais préféré être avec mes copains.

TUTORIAL

T1 *There are many possibilities for improving these answers. If you got something different, that's fine, as long as it gets rid of the short sentences, and avoids repetition.*
a) *Avant de (+ infinitive) is a good expression which links two sentences effectively.*
b) *Using pour (+ infinitive) gives a reason, and links two sentences, as do mais and alors.*
c) *The first half of the sentence is more impressive than the simple Mon école est grande, while the other two sentences are neatly linked by avec.*
d) *Again, a little re-organisaton joins all three sentences together into one neat sentence.*

T2 *Don't forget, we're trying to move up to the higher grades here, so don't just give the bare facts – add descriptions, explanations, opinions, and other interesting details.*
a) *The si clause at the beginning, and the two reasons, combine to make this a really good sentence.*
b) *This is a full answer, which expands on the basic facts to add interest.*
c) *Although there is no phrase like Je pense que, this sentence includes fact and opinion, as well as the contrast in the second sentence.*
d) *The second sentence adds some unexpected personalised detail, rather than the usual description of a hobby.*
e) *Three tenses in one sentence here, and the conditional is another way of expressing an opinion.*

EXAM PRACTICE

Though the instructions and layout might vary from board to board, the tasks required by these questions could be required by any of the boards. There are more questions than would be found on any single examination paper, in order to cover as wide a variety of question-types as possible. You should make sure you look at the syllabus for your board, and past question papers, to check how many questions there will be on your paper. Some boards offer candidates a choice of questions as follows:

Edexcel (London)

Foundation: Candidates choose either Section 1 (Questions 1 and 2) or Section 2 (Questions 3 and 4) and answer a compulsory Question 5.
Higher: Candidates answer a compulsory Question 1 (which is the same as Question 5 for Foundation) and choose either Section 2 (Questions 3 and 4) or Section 3 (Questions 4 and 5).

MEG

Foundation: Candidates answer Section 1 (Questions 1 and 2) and in Section 2 choose either Question 1 or Question 2).
Higher: In Section 2 (which is the same as Section 2 Foundation), candidates choose either Question 1 or Question 2 and similarly in Section 3 candidates choose either Question 1 or Question 2.

WJEC

Foundation: Candidates answer Question 1, Question 2 and either Question 3(a) or 3(b).
Higher: Candidates answer either Question 1(a) or 1(b) (which are the same as Questions 3(a) and 3(b) Foundation) and Question 2(a) or 2(b) or 2(c).

SEG

Foundation & Higher: Writing is assessed in two of the four modules, each requiring the completion of two tasks.

The Writing papers of the other boards do not offer candidates any choices.

1   Tu vas partir en France en vacances.   **FOUNDATION**

Qu'est-ce que tu achètes?

Exemple	lunettes de soleil
1	
2	
3	
4	
5	
6	
7	
8	
9	
10	

FOUNDATION **2** Votre correspondant(e) va bientôt venir en Angleterre.

Ecrivez, **en français**, CINQ (5) ACTIVITES DIFFERENTES, pour décrire une journée typique chez vous.

Exemple

7h30	*se lever* ....
8h30	....
12h	....
16h	....
19h	....
22h30	....

FOUNDATION **3** You have received this postcard from your friend Amélie.

Je passe deux semaines de vacances. Je suis à Antibes, dans le sud-est de la France. Il fait très chaud. Nous jouons au volley sur la plage. Le soir, on va danser.

Amélie

Vous êtes en vacances en France.

Regardez les illustrations et écrivez une carte postale à Amélie.

– Où êtes-vous? (Donnez deux détails)

– Où logez-vous?

– Quel temps fait-il?

– Que faites-vous?

– Quand est-ce que vous rentrez?

4 **Mon école**

Ecrivez une carte postale **en français; maximum 40 mots**.

Exemples

– Vous allez à quelle sorte d'école?

– Comment est votre école?

– Où est votre école?

– Comment allez-vous à l'école?

– Vous préférez quelle matière?

5 Tu cherches un(e) correspondant(e) en France.

Ecris un paragraphe (environ 30 mots) pour donner des renseignements sur toi.

● ta famille
● tes loisirs
● la ville où tu habites
● l'école
● tes vacances en France

6 Votre correspondant(e) va venir vous voir en Angleterre. Vous faites des projets pour sa visite.

Complétez ce programme. **Ecrivez 30 mots environ.**

Lundi Matin: Excursion	....
	....
	....
Mardi Matin:	....
	....
Après-midi:	....
	....
Soir: grands-parents	....
Mercredi Matin: Départ en vacances	....
	....

7 Regardez cette lettre.

> Salut!
> Enfin, j'ai trouvé un petit job.
> Je travaille dans un petit magasin de vêtements,
> trois soirs par semaine et le samedi.
>
> C'est un travail assez intéressant. Tu sais que
> j'ai toujours aimé la mode.
> En plus, je gagne 45F de l'heure.
> Et toi? Tu travailles? Combien est-ce que
> tu gagnes? Tu aimes le travail? Avec
> l'argent que j'ai gagné, j'ai acheté une
> guitare, et maman me paie des leçons.
> Tu aimes la musique, toi?
>   Rachid

Ecrivez une lettre à votre ami Rachid.
– Commencez et terminez votre lettre avec les formules nécessaires.

Répondez à ces questions:
– Vous avez un emploi? (Où? Heures?)
– Vous aimez le travail? Pourquoi?

Si vous n'avez pas d'emploi, dites pourquoi. (Donnez deux raisons.)
– Comment dépensez-vous votre argent?
– Quel est votre passe-temps préféré?
– Quelle est votre matière préférée à l'école?

Posez-lui:
– une question sur la musique.

8 Répondez à cette lettre, parue dans un magazine pour les jeunes.

Ecrivez 100–120 mots.

Parlez de:

1 comment vous aidez à la maison

2 votre avis sur ce que dit Nathalie dans sa lettre

3 ce que vous pensez sur ces questions.

> Je viens de remarquer une différence entre les garçons et les filles. Et à mon avis, ce n'est pas juste!
>
> I   Les garçons ne font jamais la vaisselle.
> 2   Ils laissent leurs affaires partout – souvent par terre.
> 3   C'est toujours eux qui choisissent la chaîne de télé qu'on va regarder.
> 4   Ils peuvent rentrer à la maison quand ils veulent.
>
> Je ne comprends pas. Pourquoi ces différences?
>
>   Nathalie

9 Ecrivez 70 à 80 mots **en français**.

Vous lisez cette annonce dans un magazine français.

> ## Hôtel du Lion d'or
> *recherche serveurs/serveuses*
> pour les mois de juillet/août/septembre
> pour travailler dans son restaurant ****

Vous voudriez travailler en France pendant les vacances. Ecrivez une lettre à l'hôtel avec les détails suivants:
– nom, âge et nationalité
– les dates où vous pouvez travailler
– les détails du travail que vous avez déjà fait
– vos passe-temps
– Posez une question sur le travail que vous ferez.

10 Tu écris à un(e) ami(e) français(e).

Regarde ces notes.

vendredi soir	– 16h00	café
	– 19h45	cinéma
	– 22h00	boum chez Laura
	– 01h30	retour à la maison

Ecris une lettre (environ 70 mots) pour raconter ta soirée.

N'oublie pas de donner tes impressions.

11 Imagine ta vie quotidienne si tu étais riche. Invente les détails.

Ecris 100–120 mots sur …
– ta matinée
– tes activités de la journée
– tes repas
– tes sorties
– tes passe-temps
– ce que tu penses de ta nouvelle vie.

12 Le week-end dernier, vous êtes allé(e) faire du camping avec un(e) ami(e).

Ecrivez une lettre à votre correspondant(e) français(e) pour lui raconter ce qui s'est passé.

Parlez de ce que vous avez fait, et du temps qu'il a fait. Dites ce que vous avez pensé du week-end, et si cette excursion vous a plu.

Ecrivez 110–120 mots.

COMMENCEZ VOTRE LETTRE APRÈS CETTE INTRODUCTION.

le 13 juillet 1997

Merci de ta lettre. Ici, tout le monde va bien. J'espère que vous allez bien, aussi, toi et ta famille.

13 Regardez cette annonce dans un journal français
et répondez aux questions.

ETUDIANTS EN ANGLAIS

Dans un prochain numéro, nous avons l'intention de présenter un
article sur les expériences des étudiants qui ont passé quelque temps
en Angleterre pour perfectionner leur anglais.

Répondez aux questions suivantes, s'il vous plaît.

1 Où avez-vous logé?
2 Comment avez-vous trouvé le logement?
3 Pourquoi?
4 Quelle langue avez-vous parlée pendant votre séjour?
5 Est-ce que ce séjour linguistique a réussi?
6 Quel a été le meilleur moment du séjour?

Voudriez-vous faire un séjour similaire en Allemagne
ou en Espagne? Pourquoi (pas)?

14 Tu viens de passer un week-end à Paris.

Ecris un article (environ 150 mots) pour raconter ton séjour. N'oublie
pas de donner tes opinions.

15 Ecrivez un article en français. Parlez du travail que vous avez fait l'année
dernière.

*You will find the sample answers
and examiner's comments on pages
237–244.*

Ecrivez 120 mots environ.

Précisez:
Où? Quelles dates? Genre de travail? Problèmes?
Votre opinion.
Vos projets de travail après l'école.

166

NOUNS

See Chapter 3

The first thing to be aware of about any noun in French is whether it is masculine or feminine. It is almost impossible to use a noun correctly unless you know this – you can't correctly use an article (*le/la* or *un/une*) or an adjective, for instance. Unfortunately, there is no useful short-cut to this knowledge. It is always best, when learning a new noun, to learn it together with the definite article, or (if it begins with a vowel) the indefinite article:

> *le stylo   un animal   la chaise   une école*

Most nouns in French make their plural by adding an *-s*, but remember that this is always silent. When you are listening, the only way to identify the fact that a noun is plural is by the article (*les*), or if there is a number in front of it:

> *les cahiers   trois enfants*

As always, there are a number of exceptions.

- Nouns which end in *-s*, *-x* or *-z* in the singular do not change in the plural.

- Nouns which end in *-au*, *-eau* or *-eu* add *-x* to make their plural:

le bureau	*les bureaux*	offices
le cadeau	*les cadeaux*	presents
le chapeau	*les chapeaux*	hats
le château	*les châteaux*	castles
	les cheveux	hair (always plural in French)
le couteau	*les couteaux*	knives
l'eau	*les eaux*	waters
le feu	*les feux*	traffic lights

  (**Note:** *le feu* also means 'fire'; *les feux* also means 'headlights')

le gâteau	*les gâteaux*	cakes
le jeu	*les jeux*	games
le jumeau	*les jumeaux*	twins

  (**Note:** feminine *jumelle[s]*)

le manteau	*les manteaux*	coats
le tableau	*les tableaux*	pictures

- Six nouns ending in *-ou*, which are in fairly common use, add *-x* in the plural:

le bijou	*les bijoux*	jewels
le caillou	*les cailloux*	pebbles
le chou	*les choux*	cabbages
le genou	*les genoux*	knees
le hibou	*les hiboux*	owls
le joujou	*les joujoux*	toys

- Nouns which end in *-al* make their plural in *-aux*:

un animal	*les animaux*	animals
le cheval	*les chevaux*	horses
le journal	*les journaux*	newspapers

- Some nouns have quite irregular plurals:

un œil	*les yeux*	eyes

Some nouns which refer to people or animals have a different form for the feminine:

un acteur	*une actrice*	an actress
un boulanger	*une boulangère*	a baker

(**Note:** also *boucher/bouchère* and other jobs ending *-er*)

un directeur	*une directrice*	a manager/headteacher
un informaticien	*une informaticienne*	a computer specialist

(**Note:** also *électricien/électricienne* and other jobs ending *-ien*)

un serveur	*une serveuse*	a waitress
un vendeur	*une vendeuse*	a shop assistant
un chat	*une chatte*	a cat
un chien	*une chienne*	a dog

See Chapter 3

ARTICLES

un/une

The indefinite article is used in much the same way as 'a/an' in English.
However, it is left out when talking about people's jobs:
> *Ma mère est professeur.* – My mother is a teacher.

du/de la/de l'/des

These words (which mean 'some') become simply *de* (or *d'* before a vowel)
after a negative:
> *J'ai de l'argent.* – I have some money.
> *Je n'ai pas **d'**argent.* – I don't have any money.
> *Tu as de la limonade?* – Do you have any lemonade?
> *Tu n'as pas **de** limonade?* – Don't you have any lemonade?

le/la/l'/les

The definite article is used more often in French than in English. In particular,
it is used when referring to a general idea:
> *Il aime le sport.* – He likes sport.
> *Je ne regarde jamais les films d'épouvante.* – I never watch horror films.

à + le/la/l'/les

These combine together in the following ways:
le cinéma: *Je vais **au** cinéma.* – I go to the cinema.
la pharmacie: *Elle m'a vu **à la** pharmacie.* – She saw me at the chemist's.
l'école: *Nous allons **à l'**école ensemble.* – We go to school together.
les Etats-Unis: *Ils sont allés **aux** Etats-Unis.* – They went to the United States.

de + le/la/l'/les

These combine together in the following ways:
le professeur: *C'est le stylo **du** professeur.* – It's the teacher's pen.
la mairie: *Voilà la porte **de la** mairie.* – There's the door of the town hall.
l'exercice: *On arrive à la fin **de l'**exercice.* – We're getting to the end of
                                 the exercise.
les étudiants: *J'ai mangé dans la cantine **des** étudiants.* – I ate in the students'
                                 canteen.

See Chapter 4

ADJECTIVES

Most adjectives come after the noun they describe:
> *un film amusant* – an amusing film

However, there are some very common exceptions, which come before:
beau   beautiful/handsome/nice/fine
bon   good
grand   big/tall/large
gros   fat/big
jeune   young
joli   pretty
long   long
mauvais   bad
nouveau   new
petit   small/little
vieux   old
(**Note:** *propre* changes in meaning according to its position:
ma propre chambre   my own room
une chambre propre   a clean room)

If the noun which it describes is plural, the adjective adds an -s:

le petit enfant *les petit enfants* small children

However, there are some very common exceptions:

- Adjectives which end in -s or -x do not change in the plural:
  le crayon gris *les crayons gris* grey pencils
  le vieux bâtiment *les vieux bâtiments* old buildings

- Adjectives which end in -u make their plural in -x:
  le beau cadeau *les beaux cadeaux* nice presents
  le nouveau disque *les nouveaux disques* new records

If the noun which it describes is feminine, the adjective adds an -e:

petit *petite* small

However, there are some very common exceptions:

- Adjectives which already end in -e do not change in the feminine:
  un jeune homme – a young man
  une jeune fille – a young girl

- Adjectives which end in -ien make their feminine in -ienne:
  italien *italienne* Italian

- The following adjectives have irregular feminine forms:

agressif	*agressive*	aggressive
*beau/*bel*	*belle*	beautiful
blanc	*blanche*	white
bon	*bonne*	good
cher	*chère*	dear/expensive
favori	*favorite*	favourite
gentil	*gentille*	nice/kind
gros	*grosse*	fat
long	*longue*	long
neuf	*neuve*	(brand) new
*nouveau/*nouvel*	*nouvelle*	new
premier	*première*	first
*vieux/*vieil*	*vieille*	old

  * before a vowel

Some adjectives do not change in the feminine or the plural:

marron brown
sympa nice (of people)

DEMONSTRATIVES

See Chapter 11

DEMONSTRATIVE ADJECTIVES

*ce/*cet* **(masculine)** *cette* **(feminine)** *ces* **(plural)**

ce magasin – this/that shop
cet animal – this/that animal
cette école – this/that school
ces enfants – these/those children

* before a vowel

If it is really necessary, you can distinguish between 'this' and 'that' by adding -ci or -là to the noun:

ce bâtiment-ci – this building
cet hôtel-là – that hotel
ces jupes-là – those skirts
ces verres-ci – these glasses

DEMONSTRATIVE PRONOUNS

celui (masculine)   **celle** (feminine)
ceux (masculine plural)   **celles** (feminine plural)

These are used to distinguish between two similar people or objects:

Je voudrais des pommes, celles   – I'd like some apples, the ones
à 12 francs.   at 12 francs.
On va au même restaurant, celui   – Shall we go to the same
où on est allé la semaine   restaurant, the one we
dernière?   went to last week?

Again, if it is really necessary, you can distinguish by adding *-ci* or *-là*.

Où est ton sac? Celui-ci est à moi. – Where is your bag? This one is mine.

When no noun is specified, use *ceci* for 'this' and *cela* (often shortened to *ça*) for 'that':

Je n'aime pas ceci. – I don't like this.
J'ai horreur de ça (cela). – I hate that.

See Chapter 4

POSSESSIVES

POSSESSIVE ADJECTIVES

These come before the noun and, like other adjectives, they have different forms according to the noun they go with:

Masculine	Feminine	Plural	
mon	ma/*mon	mes	my
ton	ta/*ton	tes	your (see Subject pronouns)
son	sa/*son	ses	his/her/its
notre	notre	nos	our
votre	votre	vos	your (see Subject pronouns)
leur	leur	leurs	their

* before a vowel

Claire m'a donné son numéro de téléphone. – Claire gave me her phone number.
Alain m'a prêté sa veste. – Alan lent me his jacket.
Je ne connais pas son adresse. – I don't know his/her address.

Note: The French does not indicate whether the person referred to is male or female.

POSSESSIVE PRONOUNS

Note: You need to be able to understand these, but will not be expected to use them.

Singular		Plural		
Masculine	**Feminine**	**Masculine**	**Feminine**	
le mien	la mienne	les miens	les miennes	mine
le tien	la tienne	les tiens	les tiennes	yours
le sien	la sienne	les siens	les siennes	his/hers
le nôtre	la nôtre	les nôtres	les nôtres	ours
le vôtre	la vôtre	les vôtres	les vôtres	yours
le leur	la leur	les leurs	les leurs	theirs

Use the appropriate word depending on whether the item is masculine, feminine or plural:

Marie, j'ai oublié mon stylo. – Marie, I've forgotten my pen.
Tu me prêtes le tien?   Will you lend me yours?

Possession can also be indicated as follows:
Cette montre est à qui? Elle est à moi. – Whose is this watch? It's mine.

 See also Chapter 6

INDEFINITES

See Chapter 13

INDEFINITE ADJECTIVES

autre   **other**
> *Je n'aime pas les autres profs.* – I don't like the other teachers.

tout/toute/tous/toutes   **all**
> *tout le temps* – all the time
> *toutes les pommes* – all the apples

même   **same**
> *Elle n'a pas les mêmes goûts que moi.* – She doesn't have the same tastes as me.

chaque   **each**
> *Répondez à chaque question.* – Answer each question.

quelque/quelques   **some**
> *J'ai acheté quelques cadeaux.* – I've bought some presents.

plusieurs   **several**
> *Ils ont plusieurs enfants.* – They have several children.

n'importe quel/quelle   **any**
> *à n'importe quelle heure* – at any time

INDEFINITE ADVERBS

n'importe comment   **no matter how**
> *Tu peux le faire n'importe comment.* – It doesn't matter how you do it.

n'importe où   **no matter where**
> *On peut manger n'importe où.* – We can eat anywhere.

INDEFINITE PRONOUNS

n'importe qui   **no matter who**
> *N'importe qui peut le faire.* – Anybody can do it.

quelque chose   **something**
> *Vous avez quelque chose pour le rhume?* – Do you have something for a cold?

quelqu'un   **someone/somebody**
> *Il y a quelqu'un dans ma chambre.* – There's somebody in my bedroom.

autre/autres   **other**
> *Je vais le dire aux autres.* – I'll go and tell the others.

tout   **all**
> *On y va tous* (in this case the 's' is pronounced) – We'll all go.

quelques-uns/unes   **some**
> *Il y avait des cartes. J'en ai* – There were some post-cards.
> *acheté quelques-unes.*   I bought some.

plusieurs   **several**
> *J'en ai plusieurs.* – I have several of them.

chacun/chacune   **each**
> *Elle nous a donné cinq livres chacun.* – She gave us five pounds each.

pas grand-chose   **not much**
> *On n'a pas fait grand-chose.* – We didn't do much.

See Chapter 8

ADVERBS

Adverbs describe how an action is done.

Just as we can often turn an adjective into an adverb in English by adding '-ly', many French adjectives can be made into adverbs by adding *-ment* to the feminine form:
> *lent* – slow → *lentement* – slowly

However, a number of the more common adverbs do not follow this pattern:

bien	well
énormément	enormously
évidemment	obviously
mal	badly
récemment	recently
soudain	suddenly
souvent	often
vite	quickly
vraiment	really

Adverbs usually come after the verb:
> *Il va souvent en ville.* – He often goes to town.

In the perfect tense, the adverb often comes before the past participle:
> *Tu as bien dormi?* – Did you sleep well?

Sometimes, the position of the adverb changes the meaning of the sentence:
> *Je ne peux vraiment pas lui parler.* – I really can't talk to him.
> *Je ne peux pas vraiment lui parler.* – I can't really talk to him.

INTENSIFIERS

The following indicate how much the quality expressed by an adjective or an adverb is true:

très   **very**
> *Elle était très fâchée.* – She was very angry.
> *Ils parlent très vite.* – They speak very quickly.

trop   **too**
> *Je suis trop fatigué(e).* – I'm too tired.
> *Le groupe joue trop fort.* – The group plays too loudly.

assez   **quite**
> *Il est assez petit.* – He's quite small.
> *Tu parles assez bien le français.* – You speak French quite well.

peu   **little**
This is often used instead of *pas très* (not very):
> *C'est peu probable.* – It's not very likely.

tout   **completely/quite/all/utterly**
Tout becomes *toute* when the adjective is feminine, unless the adjective begins with a vowel or a silent 'h':
> *Elle était tout heureuse.* – She was utterly happy.
> *Elle était toute seule.* – She was all alone.

tellement   **so**

J'étais tellement content(e). – I was so pleased.

Il est parti tellement vite. – He left so quickly.

si   **so**

Elle est si inquiète. – She is so worried.

Ils parlent si lentement. – They speak so slowly.

The following can be used to indicate how completely the action of a verb is achieved:

tout à fait   **completely**

Je n'ai pas tout à fait compris. – I didn't completely understand.

presque   **almost/nearly**

Elle a presque fini ses devoirs. – She's nearly finished her homework.

beaucoup   **a lot/very much**

Il me manque beaucoup. – I miss him a lot.

These three (as well as *pas beaucoup, pas tout à fait* and *un peu*) often stand alone as a one-word answer to a question:

Tu as fini? – Pas tout à fait.

Have you finished? – Not quite.

Vous avez aimé le film? – Beaucoup.

Did you like the film? – Very much.

Tu as manqué le car? – Presque.

Did you miss the coach? – Nearly.

Vous parlez français? – Un peu.

Do you speak French? – A little.

COMPARATIVE

See Chapter 7

ADJECTIVES

When comparing people or objects using adjectives, (which we often do in English by adding '-er' to the adjective, e.g. 'longer') it is necessary to put *plus, aussi,* or *moins* before the adjective, and *que* after it:

Luc est plus grand que Philippe.   – Luc is taller (literally: more tall) than Philippe.

Je suis aussi intelligent(e) que toi.   – I'm as intelligent as you.

Ma maison est moins grande que la tienne.   – My house is not as big (literally: less big) as yours.

There are some common exceptions:

bon → meilleur   good → better

Amar est meilleur que moi. – Amar is better than me.

mauvais → pire   bad → worse

Mes résultats sont pires que les tiens. – My results are worse than yours.

ADVERBS

Adverbs can be used in comparisons in the same way as adjectives:

Elle parle aussi bien que moi. – She speaks as well as me.

Le chat court plus vite que la souris. – The cat runs faster than the mouse.

There are similar exceptions here:

bien → mieux   well → better

Elle parle l'anglais mieux que moi. – She speaks English better than me.

mal → pire   badly → worse

Tu joues pire que moi. – You play worse than me.

See Chapter 11

SUPERLATIVE

ADJECTIVES

The superlative (which we often do in English by adding '-est' to the adjective, e.g. 'longest') is formed in French by putting *le plus, la plus* or *les plus* before the adjective:

C'est le sport le plus intéressant. – It is the most interesting sport.
Tu as la plus grande maison. – You have the biggest house.
C'est le meilleur joueur de l'équipe. – He's the best player in the team.

ADVERBS

The superlative of adverbs is formed by putting *le plus* before the adverb:

Ce sont les Italiens qui parlent – It's the Italians who speak
le plus vite. the fastest.

See Chapter 6

PRONOUNS

SUBJECT PRONOUNS

je (*j'* before a vowel)	I
tu (used to a friend, relative or animal)	you
il (used for a masculine person or thing)	he/it
elle (used fo a feminine person or thing)	she/it
on (often used to mean 'we' in speech)	one (we)
nous	we
vous (to a stranger, an adult, or more than one person)	you
ils (used for masculine people/things, or for a mixed group)	they
elles (used for feminine people/things)	they

OBJECT PRONOUNS

me (*m'* before vowel)	me
te (*t'* before vowel)	you (see note on *tu* above)
le (*l'* before vowel)	him/it
la (*l'* before vowel)	her/it
nous	us
vous	you (see note on *vous* above)
les	them (people or things)

Note that object pronouns come before the verb:

Il m'a frappé. – He hit me.
Je l'ai entendu. – I heard him.
Je peux vous aider? – Can I help you?

The pronouns *lui* and *leur*

These pronouns mean 'to him/her' and 'to them':

Je lui ai donné un cadeau. – I gave a present to him/her.
Elle leur a parlé. – She spoke to them.

(**Note:** The word 'to' is often missed out in English: I gave him a present.)

The pronouns *y* and *en*

The pronoun *y* refers to a place:

Tu es déjà allé en Italie?	– Have you ever been to Italy?
J'y vais l'année prochaine.	– I'm going (there) next year.

The pronoun *en* refers to a quantity:

Vous avez des pommes?	– Do you have any apples?
J'en ai beaucoup.	– I have a lot (of them).

In English we often omit these words, but they are never left out in French.

POSITION OF PRONOUNS

It is sometimes useful to use more than one of these pronouns in a sentence. In this case, there is a fixed order in which they must be used:

1 *je/tu/il/elle/on/nous/vous/ils/elles*
2 *me/te/nous/vous*
3 *le/la/l'/les*
4 *lui/leur*
5 *y*
6 *en*

followed by the verb.

Je voudrais un sandwich. – Il n'y en a plus.
I'd like a sandwich. – There aren't any left.
Où est le cadeau de Marie? – Je le lui ai déjà donné.
Where is Mary's present? – I've already given it to her.

With commands this order changes, in that (2) and (3) change places. Also, *me* becomes *moi* (*m'* before a vowel) and *te* becomes *toi* (*t'* before a vowel). Notice the use of hyphens:

Ça, c'est mon stylo. Donnez-le-moi. – That's my pen. Give it to me.
Tu aimes les cerises? Prends-en. – Do you like cherries? Take some.

See also Chapter 1

EMPHATIC PRONOUNS

moi	*nous*
toi	*vous*
lui	*eux*
elle	*elles*

These are used in a number of ways:

- To add emphasis to the pronoun, where in English we might underline it:
  Je ne sais pas, moi. – I don't know.

- In short phrases where there is no verb:
  J'adore le sport. Et toi? – I love sport. How about you?

- After *que*:
  Je suis plus grand(e) que toi. – I'm taller than you.

- With prepositions:
  après vous – after you
  avant toi – before you
  avec lui – with him
  de vous – from you
  devant elle – in front of her
  pour nous – for us
  sans elles – without them

- With *c'est*:
  C'est moi. – It's me.

- With commands:
  Donne-le-moi. – Give it to me.

- To indicate who something belongs to:
  Il est à qui, ce livre? – *Il est à moi.*
  Whose is this book? – It's mine.

- In combination with *-même* as follows:

moi-même	myself
toi-même	yourself
lui-même	himself
elle-même	herself
nous-mêmes	ourselves
vous-même(s)	yourself/yourselves
eux-mêmes	themselves
elles-mêmes	themselves

RELATIVE PRONOUNS

qui which/who
The pronoun *qui* is always the subject of the verb which follows it:

Voilà le bus qui va en ville.	– There's the bus which goes to town.
Je voudrais remercier l'automobiliste qui s'est arrêté.	– I'd like to thank the motorist who stopped.

que which/that/whom
The pronoun *que* is always the object of the verb which follows it:

Voici la robe que j'ai achetée.	– Here is the dress (which) I bought.
Voilà les garçons que nous avons vus hier.	– There are the boys (whom) we saw yesterday.

Note: In English we often leave out the words 'which' or 'whom'.

dont   of which/of whom

Voilà le garçon dont je t'ai parlé.	– There's the boy I talked to you about (literally: of whom I talked to you).

ce qui/ce que
These are are used when the pronoun is linked to two different verbs:
Montre-moi ce que tu as fait. – Show me what you have made.
('what' is the object of both *montrer* and *faire*)
Dis-moi ce qui va se passer. – Tell me what's going to happen.
('what' is the object of dire and the subject of *se passer*)

lequel/laquelle/lesquels/lesquelles
These are used with prepositions. They must agree with the noun to which they refer:

Voici la boîte dans laquelle j'ai trouvé l'argent.	– Here is the box in which I found the money.

When used after *à* or *de* these words become:

auquel	*à laquelle*	*auxquels*	*auxquelles*
duquel	*de laquelle*	*desquels*	*desquelles*

Lequel, etc. can also be used as a one-word question:
Voilà la voiture de mon père. – *Laquelle?*
That's my father's car. – Which one?

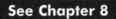
See Chapter 8

NUMBERS

Once you have learnt the basic numbers 1–19, and the words for 20, 30, 40, 50, 60, 70, 80, 90, 100 and 1000, you can build up all the numbers in very much the same way as in English:
6 = *six*; 20 = *vingt*; 26 = *vingt-six*

1	un	6	six	11	onze	16	seize
2	deux	7	sept	12	douze	17	dix-sept
3	trois	8	huit	13	treize	18	dix-huit
4	quatre	9	neuf	14	quatorze	19	dix-neuf
5	cinq	10	dix	15	quinze	20	vingt

21	vingt et un	30	trente
22	vingt-deux	34	trente-quatre
23	vingt-trois	35	trente-cinq
		36	trente-six

40	quarante	80	quatre-vingts
50	cinquante	81	quatre-vingt-un
60	soixante	82	quatre-vingt-deux
70	soixante-dix	90	quatre-vingt-dix
71	soixante et onze	91	quatre-vingt-onze
72	soixante-douze	92	quatre-vingt-douze

100 cent
200 deux cents
201 deux cent un
999 neuf cent quatre-vingt-dix-neuf
1 000 mille (no word for 'a')
5 000 cinq mille
1998 mille neuf cent quatre-vingt-dix-huit
1 000 000 un million
1 000 000 000 un milliard (a billion)

Apart from the numbers 1–10, you will not normally need to write out a number as a word, so you don't need to worry too much about spelling, use of hyphens, etc. For example, if you were writing about your family, you might write: *J'ai deux sœurs*, but you would probably write: *Ma sœur a 15 ans*. However, you need to take special care about learning to understand numbers, as they are always tested – particularly in the Listening Test – and cause many candidates to lose marks.

To make words such as 2nd, 3rd, 4th, etc., simply add *-ième* to the number:
  deux – 2 → deuxième – 2nd

The only exception is *premier* (1st), but two other numbers require a slight spelling change:
  neuf – 9 → neuvième – 9th
  cinq – 5 → cinquième – 5th

Remember that in telephone numbers, the digits are paired. For example, 04 93 45 57 24 is said as follows:
  le zéro-quatre, quatre-vingt-treize, quarante-cinq, cinquante-sept, vingt-quatre

All French telephone numbers now consist of ten digits, commencing 01, 02, 03, 04 or 05 depending on the area. If you need to say an English telephone number which has an odd number of digits, you should put together the first three digits, and pair the rest:
  01592 300158 → 015 92 30 01 58 (*zéro-quinze, quatre-vingt-douze, trente, zéro-un, cinquante-huit*).

QUANTITIES

See Chapter 8

These can be expressed in terms of the container (e.g. *un paquet*), or as weights or measures:

un kilo	a kilogram/1 000 grams (approx. 2.2lbs)
un demi-kilo	half a kilogram/500 grams (approx. 1lb)
x grammes	x grams
une livre	a pound/500 grams
	a pound (sterling)
un litre	a litre /1 000 millilitres (approx. $1\frac{1}{2}$ pints)
un demi-litre	half a litre/500 millilitres (just under a pint)

       un kilomètre   a kilometre (1 000 metres) just over $\frac{1}{2}$ a mile
       un mètre   a metre (just over a yard)
(The approximate equivalents are given to help you avoid 'silly' mistakes like asking for 10 kilos [about 22 lbs] of ham!)

It is useful to be able to express your own weight and height in metric measurements:
       Je mesure un mètre soixante-dix. – I'm 5ft 7 (approx.).
       Je fais quarante-cinq kilos. – I'm 7 stone (approx.).

In all cases, the quantity is followed by *de* before the item:
       Cent grammes de beurre. – 100 grams of butter.

Fractions are also sometimes used to express quantity:
       une demi-heure   half an hour
       un demi-frère   a half-brother/stepbrother
       un quart d'heure a quarter of an hour

But notice if the word 'half' is used alone:
       Tu en veux combien? – *La moitié.*
       How much do you want? – Half.

Other expressions of quantity include:
       beaucoup   a lot
       assez   enough
       un peu   a little
       (pas) trop   (not) too much
       tant   so much
       Tu ne devrais pas manger tant de sel. – You shouldn't eat so much salt.

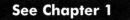

See Chapter 1

DATES

The months do not have a capital letter:
       janvier   *février*   *mars*   *avril*   *mai*   *juin*
       juillet   *août*   *septembre* *octobre*   *novembre* *décembre*

In dates, you always use *le* + a number + month:
       Aujourd'hui nous sommes le dix-sept juillet. – Today it's the 17th July.

The exception is on the first of the month:
       Mon anniversaire, c'est le premier mars. – My birthday is on the 1st March.

To express a range of dates ('from ... to'), use *du ... au*:
       Je voudrais réserver une chambre du   – I'd like to book a room from the
       trois au neuf juin.   3rd to the 9th of June.

You don't need a word for 'on' when referring to dates:
       Il arrive le cinq octobre. – He's arriving on the 5th October.

The days do not have a capital letter:
       lundi   *mardi*   *mercredi*   *jeudi*   *vendredi*   *samedi*   *dimanche*

You do not need a word for 'on' when referring to days:
       Je vais à la piscine jeudi. – I'm going to the swimming pool on Thursday.

But notice:
       Je vais à la piscine le jeudi. – I go to the swimming pool on Thursdays
                                   (every Thursday).

TIME

See Chapter 1

The most common, and easiest, way of expressing the time is by using a number followed by *heure(s)* – if necessary followed by another number to indicate 'minutes':

> *Il est six heures.* – It's six o'clock.
> *Il est une heure dix.* – It's one ten (ten past one).

If it is necessary to be clear whether the time is am or pm, use *du matin* or *du soir*:

> *Elle est rentrée à deux heures du matin.* – She came home at 2am (two in the morning).

On timetables, the twenty-four hour clock is used:

> *Le train part à quatorze heures trente.* – The train leaves at 14.30 (2.30pm).

In writing, for example on a poster, the time is usually written with the letter '*h*' between the hours and minutes, not a dot as in English:

> 20*h*30.

In conversation, you may hear the following expressions:

> *Je déjeune **à midi**.* – I have lunch at midday.
> *Il s'est couché **à minuit**.* – He went to bed at midnight.
> *Il est deux heures **et quart**.* – It's quarter past two.
> *Je vais arriver à trois heures **et demie**.* – I'll be arriving at half past three.
> *On a mangé à sept heures **moins le quart**.* – We ate at quarter to seven.
> *Le film commence à neuf heures* – The film starts at five/ten/twenty/
> ***moins** cinq/dix/vingt/vingt-cinq.*   twenty-five to nine.

To express a range of times ('from ... to') use *de ... à*:

> *Le dîner est de sept heures à neuf heures* – Dinner is from 7 o'clock
> *et demie.*   to half past nine.

The use of *depuis* to express the duration of an action in the past needs careful attention to the tense of the verb. Use the present tense instead of the English 'has/have been' and the imperfect tense instead of 'had been':

> *Tu apprends l'anglais depuis combien de temps?* – How long have you been learning English?
> *Je t'attends depuis dix minutes.* – I have been waiting for you for 10 minutes.
> *Je regardais le film depuis un quart d'heure.* – I had been watching the film for quarter of an hour.

The word *depuis* can also mean 'since':

> *Il est là depuis cinq heures et quart.* – He has been here since quarter past five.

Here are some other useful time expressions:

une journée	a day
une semaine	a week
quinze jours	a fortnight
un mois	a month
un an	a year
un siècle	a century

> *Le film dure vingt minutes.* – The film lasts 20 minutes.
> *J'ai passé une heure dans le jardin.* – I spent an hour in the garden.
> *Il y a un bus toutes les vingt-cinq minutes.* – There's a bus every 25 minutes.

(But note: ***tous** les quarts d'heure* because *quart* is masculine.)

PREPOSITIONS

Some of the more common prepositions cause problems because there is no exact overlap between French and English.

about   *au sujet de* (on the subject of)

> *Mon père a voulu me parler au sujet* – My father wanted to talk to me
> *de mes examens.*   about my exams.

vers (approximately)
Elle est arrivée vers neuf heures. – She arrived about nine o'clock.

as far as *jusqu'à*
Continuez jusqu'aux feux rouges. – Carry on as far as the traffic lights.

before *avant*
Elle a mangé avant de partir. – She ate before she left.
déjà (already)
J'ai déjà vu ce film. – I've already seen this film./I've seen this film before.

by *à* (means of transport)
à bicyclette/vélo/moto – by bicycle/bike/motorbike
en (means of transport)
en auto/autobus/avion/bateau/train/voiture – by car/bus/plane/boat/train/car
par
Le président a été tué par un assassin. – The president was killed by an
assassin.

for *pendant* (time during which)
J'ai dormi pendant trois heures. – I slept for three hours.
pour (time in the future)
J'irai en France pour deux semaines. – I will go to France for two weeks.
depuis
Je la connais depuis deux ans. – I've known her for two years.
(See also page 179: Time.)

in *à* (with names of towns/cities)
à Paris – in Paris
au (with names of masculine countries)
au Maroc/Portugal/Pays de Galles – in Morocco/Portugal/Wales
aux (with names of countries which are plural)
aux Antilles/Pays-Bas/Etats-Unis – in the West Indies/Netherlands/
United States
dans (inside)
Maman est dans le salon. – Mum is in the living room.
en (with names of most countries)
en Afrique/Allemagne/Angleterre/ – in Africa/Germany/England/
Ecosse/France/Italie Scotland/France/Italy

on *à*
à droite/à gauche – on the left/on the right
à pied – on foot
dans (with means of transport)
Je l'ai vu dans le train. – I saw him on the train.
en
en vacances – on holiday
sur
Le livre est sur la table. – The book is on the table.

since *depuis*
Je suis en Suisse depuis le onze février. – I've been in Switzerland since the
11th February.

until *jusqu'à*
Je serai là jusqu'à huit heures. – I will be there until 8 o'clock.

CONJUNCTIONS

These are linking words, which are useful if you want to create a more
complex sentence. Here are some of the most common ones:

alors	so
car	for (because)
donc	so, therefore
et	and
mais	but
ou	or

parce que   because
quand   when
(This is often used with a future tense in French:
Je viendrai te voir quand j'aurai le temps. – I'll come and see you when I
have time.)
si   if
(This is followed by either the present or the imperfect tense:
Si je gagne, je t'achèterai un cadeau. – If I win I'll buy you a present.
Si je gagnais à la loterie, j'achèterais une voiture. – If I won the lottery, I
would buy a car.)

INTERROGATIVES

See Chapter 9

A question may be formed simply by 'inversion', i.e. putting the verb in front
of the subject pronoun:
Tu aimes le chocolat. – You like chocolate.
Aimes-tu le chocolat? – Do you like chocolate?

Alternatively, the phrase *est-ce que* can be put in front of the statement:
Tu vas en ville. – You are going to town.
Est-ce que tu vas en ville? – Are you going to town?

In speech only, the question can be made by simply using a rising tone:
On va au cinéma. – We're going to the cinema.
On va au cinéma? – Shall we go to the cinema?

Many questions are introduced by special words:
Combien
Combien de frères as-tu? – How many brothers have you got?
Combien d'argent avez-vous? – How much money have you got?
Comment
Comment t'appelles-tu? – What is your name?
Comment est ta sœur? – What's your sister like?
Comment vas-tu? – How are you?
Où
Où allons-nous? – Where are we going?
Pourquoi
Pourquoi n'aimes-tu pas l'école? – Why don't you like school?
Quand
Quand allez-vous arriver? – When will you arrive?
Qui
Qui va m'aider? – Who is going to help me?
Que
Que fais-tu? – What are you doing?
Qu'est-ce que
Qu'est-ce qu'on fait cet après-midi? – What shall we do this afternoon?
Quel
Quel âge as-tu? – How old are you?
Quelle est la date? – What is the date?
Qu'est-ce qui
Qu'est-ce qui se passe? – What's happening?

VERBS

See Chapter 2

THE PRESENT TENSE

The French present tense is the equivalent of the English 'I speak', 'I am
speaking' and 'I do speak'.

There are three main types of French verb, each of which works through a series of endings. You must start from the infinitive, which is the form of the verb you will find in the dictionary.

	ER *parler*	IR *finir*	RE *vendre*
je	-e	-is	-s
tu	-es	-is	-s
*il/elle/on**	-e	-it	—
nous	-ons	-issons	-ons
vous	-ez	-issez	-ez
*ils/elles***	-ent	-issent	-ent

* Use these endings if the subject is a person's name, or any other noun in the singular:

    Le professeur choisit le cahier.

**Use these endings if the subject is the name of more than one person, or a plural noun:

    Les enfants regardent la télé.

See Chapter 2 page 13 for details of pronunciation, and for *er* verbs with minor irregularities.

You will find lists of the most common *er*, *ir* and *re* verbs on pages 191–193.

Reflexive verbs are usually *er* verbs, which have the addition of an extra pronoun. The present tense endings are the same as for all other *er* verbs:

      se coucher

je me couche	*nous nous couchons*
tu te couches	*vous vous couchez*
il/elle/on se couche	*ils/elles se couchent*

The infinitive of these verbs is easily identifiable by the *se* (*s'* before a vowel). There is a list of the most common reflexive verbs in Chapter 2, page 14.

Irregular verbs

The following verbs do not follow the pattern of regular *er*, *ir* or *re* verbs, and you need to learn them individually:

ALLER – to go	*S'ASSEOIR* – to sit down
je vais	In the present tense, rarely used
tu vas	except as a command:
il/elle/on va	*Assieds-toi!* – Sit down!
nous allons	*Asseyez-vous!* – Sit down!
vous allez	
ils/elles vont	

APPRENDRE – to learn (see *PRENDRE*)

AVOIR – to have	*BOIRE* – to drink
j'ai	*je bois*
tu as	*tu bois*
il/elle/on a	*il/elle/on boit*
nous avons	*nous buvons*
vous avez	*vous buvez*
ils/elles ont	*ils/elles boivent*

COMPRENDRE – to understand (see *PRENDRE*)

CONDUIRE – to drive	*CONNAITRE* – to know (a person)
je conduis	*je connais*
tu conduis	*tu connais*
il/elle/on conduit	*il/elle/on connaît*
nous conduisons	*nous connaissons*
vous conduisez	*vous connaissez*
ils/elles conduisent	*ils/elles connaissent*

CROIRE – to think/believe
je crois
tu crois
il/elle/on croit
nous croyons
vous croyez
ils/elles croient

COUVRIR – to cover (see *OUVRIR*)

DECRIRE – to describe (see *ECRIRE*)

DEVENIR – to become (see *VENIR*)

DEVOIR – to have to/should/must
je dois
tu dois
il/elle/on doit
nous devons
vous devez
ils/elles doivent

DORMIR – to sleep
je dors
tu dors
il/elle/on dort
nous dormons
vous dormez
ils/elles dorment

ETRE – to be
je suis
tu es
il/elle/on est
nous sommes
vous êtes
ils/elles sont

LIRE – to read
je lis
tu lis
il/elle/on lit
nous lisons
vous lisez
ils/elles lisent

OFFRIR – to offer (see *OUVRIR*)

OUVRIR – to open
j'ouvre
tu ouvres
il/elle/on ouvre
nous ouvrons
vous ouvrez
ils/elles ouvrent
(*COUVRIR* – to cover)
(*OFFRIR* – to offer)

PLAIRE – to please
Only used in certain phrases:
s'il te/vous plaît – please
Ça (ne) me plaît (pas) – I (don't) like it.
Ça te/vous plaît? – Do you like it?

COURIR – to run
je cours
tu cours
il/elle/on court
nous courons
vous courez
ils/elles courent

DIRE – to say
je dis
tu dis
il/elle/on dit
nous disons
vous dites
ils/elles disent

ECRIRE – to write
j'écris
tu écris
il/elle/on écrit
nous écrivons
vous écrivez
ils/elles écrivent
(*DECRIRE* – to describe)

FAIRE – to make/do
je fais
tu fais
il/elle/on fait
nous faisons
vous faites
ils/elles font

METTRE – to put (on)
je mets
tu mets
il/elle/on met
nous mettons
vous mettez
ils/elles mettent

PARTIR – to leave
je pars
tu pars
il/elle/on part
nous partons
vous partez
ils/elles partent
(*SORTIR* – to go out)

POUVOIR – to be able/can
je peux
tu peux
il/elle/on peut
nous pouvons
vous pouvez
ils/elles peuvent

183

PRENDRE – to take
je prends
tu prends
il/elle/on prend
nous prenons
vous prenez
ils/elles prennent
(APPRENDRE – to learn)
(COMPRENDRE – to understand)

RECEVOIR – to receive
je reçois
tu reçois
il/elle/on reçoit
nous recevons
vous recevez
ils/elles reçoivent

RIRE – to laugh
je ris
tu ris
il/elle/on rit
nous rions
vous riez
ils/elles rient

SAVOIR – to know (a fact)
je sais
tu sais
il/elle/on sait
nous savons
vous savez
ils/elles savent

SERVIR – to serve
je sers
tu sers
il/elle/on sert
nous servons
vous servez
ils/elles servent
SORTIR – to go out (see PARTIR)
TENIR – to hold (see VENIR)

SUIVRE – to follow
je suis
tu suis
il/elle/on suit
nous suivons
vous suivez
ils/elles suivent

VENIR – to come
je viens
tu viens
il/elle/on vient
nous venons
vous venez
ils/elles viennent
(DEVENIR – to become)
(TENIR – to hold)

VOIR – to see
je vois
tu vois
il/elle/on voit
nous voyons
vous voyez
ils/elles voient

VOULOIR – to want (to)
je veux
tu veux
il/elle/on veut
nous voulons
vous voulez
ils/elles veulent

IMPERSONAL VERBS

These are verbs which are only used in the third person singular. The most common examples are probably the weather expressions:

	Present	Imperfect	Perfect	Future
geler – to freeze	*Il gèle*	*Il gelait*	*Il a gelé*	*Il gèlera*
neiger – to snow	*Il neige*	*Il neigeait*	*Il a neigé*	*Il neigera*
pleuvoir – to rain	*Il pleut*	*Il pleuvait*	*Il a plu*	*Il pleuvra*

The phrase *il y a* (there is/are) is also common:

Dans ma chambre, il y a un lit et une armoire.	– In my bedroom there is a bed and a wardrobe.
Dans mon sac, il y avait mes clés.	– In my bag there were my keys.
Il y a eu un embouteillage.	– There was a traffic jam.
Demain, il y aura du soleil partout.	– Tomorrow there will be sunshine everywhere.

You also need to be able to recognise *il faut* (it is necessary), though you can usually use *je dois* if you prefer:

Dépêche-toi! Il faut partir. – Hurry up! We must leave.

THE IMPERFECT TENSE

See Chapter 12

This is the tense you should use for descriptions in the past. It is often the equivalent of the English 'was/were ...-ing' or 'used to ...'. To form the imperfect tense, you need to know the *nous* form of the present tense, and remove the *-ons* (e.g. *regardons → regard*) before adding the following endings:

je	*-ais*	*nous*	*-ions*
tu	*-ais*	*vous*	*-iez*
il/elle/on	*-ait*	*ils/elles*	*-aient*

e.g. *je regardais*
tu regardais
il/elle/on regardait
nous regardions
vous regardiez
ils/elles regardaient

There is only one exception to this rule, though it uses the same endings:

être – **to be**
j'étais
tu étais
il/elle/on était
nous étions
vous étiez
ils/elles étaient

THE PERFECT TENSE

See Chapter 5

This tense is used to refer to events in the past. It is made up of two parts:

The present tense of *avoir*	**The past participle**
j'ai	*...é* (for *er* verbs)
tu as	
il/elle/on a	*...i* (for *ir* verbs)
nous avons	
vous avez	*...u* (for *re* verbs)
ils/elles ont	

e.g. *j'ai quitté* – I left/I have left
tu as mangé – you ate/you have eaten
il/elle/on a fini – he/she/one finished/has finished
nous avons choisi – we chose/we have chosen
vous avez répondu – you answered/have answered
ils/elles ont rendu – they gave back/have given back

A small number of common verbs use *être* instead of *avoir*:

je suis
tu es
il/elle/on est
nous sommes
vous êtes
ils/elles sont

It is important to learn these verbs. Some people find a memory aid helpful, such as the sentence ATV AND MRS PERM, where each letter is the first letter of one of the verbs (*devenir* and *revenir* being based on *venir*, and *rentrer* based on *entrer*). The verbs are:

aller	to go	*partir*	to leave
arriver	to arrive	*rentrer*	to go back
descendre	to go down	*rester*	to stay/remain
devenir	to become	*retourner*	to return
entrer	to go in	*revenir*	to come back
monter	to go up	*sortir*	to go out
mourir	to die	*tomber*	to fall
naître	to be born	*venir*	to come

When the perfect tense is made with *être*, the past participle must agree with the subject:

> *je suis arrivé(e)* – I arrived/have arrived
> *tu es sorti(e)* – you went out/have gone out
> *il est parti* – he left/has left
> *elle est tombée* – she fell/has fallen
> *nous sommes venu(e)s* – we came/have come
> *vous êtes allé(e)(s)* – you went/have gone
> *ils sont descendus* – they went down/have gone down
> *elles sont entrées* – they went in/have gone in

Reflexive verbs also make the perfect tense using *être*:

> *je me suis couché(e)* – I went to bed
> *tu t'es habillé(e)* – you got dressed
> *il s'est réveillé* – he woke up
> *elle s'est levée* – she got up
> *nous nous sommes arrêté(e)s* – we stopped
> *vous vous êtes baigné(e)(s)* – you bathed
> *ils se sont rasés* – they had a shave
> *elles se sont lavées* – they had a wash

A number of common verbs (including many which take *être*) have irregular past participles:

s'asseoir → assis	*lire → lu*
apprendre → appris	*mettre → mis*
avoir → eu	*mourir → mort*
boire → bu	*naître → né*
comprendre → compris	*offrir → offert*
conduire → conduit	*ouvrir → ouvert*
connaître → connu	*plaire → plu*
croire → cru	*pouvoir → pu*
courir → couru	*prendre → pris*
couvrir → couvert	*recevoir → reçu*
décrire → décrit	*rire → ri*
devenir → devenu	*savoir → su*
devoir → dû	*suivre → suivi*
dire → dit	*tenir → tenu*
écrire → écrit	*venir → venu*
être → été	*voir → vu*
faire → fait	*vouloir → voulu*

See Chapter 7

THE FUTURE TENSE

The future tense is generally used in French in the same circumstances as we do in English. However, it is also often used after *quand*, while in English it is never used after 'when':

> *Je lui parlerai quand elle arrivera.* – I shall speak to her when she arrives.

This is another tense which works through endings – the same endings for all verbs. You simply add the following endings to the infinitive of the verb (in the case of *re* verbs, first removing the *e*):

je	**-ai**	*nous*	**-ons**
tu	**-as**	*vous*	**-ez**
il/elle/on	**-a**	*ils/elles*	**-ont**

e.g. *je parlerai*
tu finiras
il vendra

Although the endings are always the same, some verbs are irregular in the future:

acheter → j'achèterai	*jeter → je jetterai*
aller → j'irai	*mourir → je mourrai*
appeler → j'appellerai	*pouvoir → je pourrai*
avoir → j'aurai	*recevoir → je recevrai*
courir → je courrai	*savoir → je saurai*
devenir → je deviendrai	*tenir → je tiendrai*

devoir → *je devrai*   *venir* → *je viendrai*
envoyer → *j'enverrai*   *voir* → *je verrai*
être → *je serai*   *vouloir* → *je voudrai*
faire → *je ferai*

THE CONDITIONAL TENSE

See Chapter **7**

CCEA and SEG
Understanding only

This is often used when the sentence contains *si* (if):
     Si j'avais beaucoup d'argent, – If I had a lot of money, I would
     j'achèterais une maison.   buy a house.
The most common conditional is Je *voudrais* (I'd like).

The conditional is formed in exactly the same way as the future, with the
following endings.

je	**-ais**	*nous*	**-ions**
tu	**-ais**	*vous*	**-iez**
il/elle/on	**-ait**	*ils/elles*	**-aient**

e.g. *je parlerais*
       tu finirais
       il vendrait

There are no exceptions.

THE PLUPERFECT TENSE

See Chapter **2**

NEAB and SEG
Understanding only

This tense moves one step further into the past than the perfect tense – it is
usually the equivalent of 'I had ...' in English. Its formation is the same as that
of the perfect tense, except that the imperfect of *avoir* or *être* is used:
     j'avais quitté – I had left
     tu avais choisi – you had chosen
     il/elle avait répondu – he/she had answered
     nous avions vu – we had seen
     vous aviez dit – you had said
     ils/elles avaient ouvert – they had opened

     j'étais arrivé(e) – I had arrived
     tu étais sorti(e) – you had gone out
     il était parti – he had left
     elle était tombée – she had fallen
     nous étions venu(e)s – we had come
     vous étiez allé(e)(s) – you had gone
     ils étaient descendus – they had gone down
     elles étaient entrées – they had gone in

THE FUTURE PERFECT TENSE

Understanding only

This tense is made up of the future of *avoir* or *être* and the past participle. It is
mainly used after:
quand:
     Quand ils seront arrivés, nous   – When they arrive, we will go out.
     sortirons.
dès que:
     Dès que j'aurai fini mes examens, – As soon as I have finished my
     je partirai en Italie.   exams, I shall go to Italy.

CCEA EDEX NEAB SEG
Understanding only

THE CONDITIONAL PERFECT TENSE

This tense is often used together with a *si* clause in which the verb is in the pluperfect. It is the equivalent of the English 'If something had happened, I would have ...'. Its formation is the same as that of the perfect tense, except that the conditional of *avoir* or *être* is used:

Si je t'avais vu, je t'aurais salué. – If I had seen you, I would have said hello.

Si j'avais su que tu étais malade, *je serais venu tout de suite.* – If I had known you were ill, I would have come straight away.

In the exams set by most boards, this tense will occur only in the Listening and Reading Tests.

Understanding only

THE PAST HISTORIC TENSE

This tense is not used in speech. It is most often found in literature and journalism, usually in the third person (*il/elle/on/ils/elles*). It will only occur in the Reading Test, and the verb is usually easily recognisable. You should probably not, therefore, spend time learning this unless you are confident that you can cope with everything else on the syllabus.

There are two types of endings:

er **verbs**		*ir* and *re* **verbs**	
je	*-ai*	*je*	*-is*
tu	*-as*	*tu*	*-is*
il/elle/on	*-a*	*il/elle/on*	*-it*
nous	*-âmes*	*nous*	*-îmes*
vous	*-âtes*	*vous*	*-îtes*
ils/elles	*-èrent*	*ils/elles*	*-irent*

Irregular verbs have the same endings as *ir* and *re* verbs:

je dis – I said
tu fis – you made
il s'assit – he sat down
elle vit – she saw
nous mîmes – we put on
vous prîtes – you took
ils/elles rirent – they laughed

CCEA NEAB SEG WJEC
Understanding only

THE SUBJUNCTIVE

This is not a tense, but a form of the verb which is used in certain kinds of structures which use *que*. Like the past historic, it is unlikely to occur except occasionally in the Reading Test, where the verb will be easily recognisable. There are a few irregular verbs where the subjunctive is not so easy to recognise:

aller → *j'aille*
avoir → *j'aie/il ait*
être → *je sois*
faire → *je fasse*

If you meet the subjunctive at all, it is most likely to appear in phrases beginning:

il faut que	it is necessary that
bien que/quoique	although
jusqu'à ce que	until
avant que	before

THE PASSIVE

See Chapter 10

CCEA MEG NEAB
SEG WJEC
Understanding only

When it is used in French, the passive is formed in more or less the same way as in English:

Elle a été piquée par une guêpe. – She has been stung by a wasp.

However, it is used much less frequently than in English, and is probably best avoided. There are a number of ways of doing this:

- Turning the sentence round so that it is no longer passive:
  'She has been stung by a wasp' becomes:
  Une guêpe l'a piquée. – A wasp stung her.

- Using *on*:
  'Her handbag has been stolen' becomes:
  On lui a volé son sac à main. – Someone has stolen her handbag.

- Using a reflexive:
  'Phone cards are sold at tobacconist's' becomes:
  Les télécartes se vendent dans les bureaux de tabac.

THE IMPERATIVE

See Chapter

The form used to tell someone what to do depends on who the person is:

- If it is someone you call *tu*, the imperative is the *tu* form of the verb without the pronoun:
  Viens ici! – Come here!
  Finis ton dîner! – Finish your dinner!
  Note: With *er* verbs, the final *-s* is omitted:
  Ne regarde pas ce film! – Don't watch that film!

- If it is someone you call *vous*, the imperative is the *vous* form of the verb without the pronoun:
  Venez ici! – Come here!

- If you want to say 'Let's ...', use the *nous* form of the verb without the pronoun:
  Allons au cinéma! – Let's go to the cinema!

If you are using a reflexive verb, the reflexive pronoun is still used. It comes after the verb, and is joined to it by a hyphen:

Dépêchons-nous! – Let's hurry up!
Dépêchez-vous! – Hurry up!
Dépêche-toi! – Hurry up!

Note that *te* becomes *toi*.

Object pronouns come **after** the imperative, and their order is different:

Donne-le-moi! – Give it to me!

For more details on this, see Position of pronouns on page 175.

THE NEGATIVE

See Chapter 10

The negative in French consists of two words:

ne ... pas	not
ne ... jamais	never/not ever
ne ... rien	nothing/not anything
ne ... personne	nobody/not anybody
ne ... plus	no more/no longer
ne ... que	only
ne ... guère	hardly/scarcely
ne ... ni ... ni	neither ... nor
ne ... aucun(e)	not any
ne ... nulle part	nowhere/not anywhere

It is important to know where these words fit in the sentence:

- Present tense:
  Je ne regarde pas la télé. – I don't watch TV.
  Je ne la regarde pas. – I don't watch it.

- Perfect tense:
  Je n'ai pas vu le film. – I didn't see the film.
  Je ne l'ai pas regardé. – I didn't see it.
  BUT *Je n'ai vu personne.* – I didn't see anybody.

- Reflexive verbs:
  Je ne m'ennuie jamais. – I'm never bored.

- *Personne, jamais* and *rien* can be used on their own.

- *Personne* can be the subject of the verb:
  Personne n'a gagné. – Nobody won.

See Chapter 3

EDEX NEAB WJEC
Understanding only

THE PRESENT PARTICIPLE

This is used to indicate that one action takes place at the same time as another. It is formed by taking the *nous* form of the present tense, removing the *-ons* and adding *-ant*:

Elle est tombée en descendant de la voiture.	– She fell as she was getting out of the car.
Elle est rentrée en chantant.	– She came home singing.
Je lis en regardant la télévision.	– I read while I am watching television.

See Chapter 5

THE INFINITIVE

In addition to being the form of the verb which often appears in the dictionary, the infinitive has five main uses. It always has one of three forms: the infinitive of all French verbs ends in *er*, *ir* or *re*. However, many infinitives which end in *ir* and *re* belong to irregular verbs (see pages 182–184).

1   If there are two verbs together in a sentence, the second will be in the infinitive.

- The following verbs are followed immediately by the infinitive:

adorer	to love
aimer	to like
désirer	to want to
détester	to hate
devoir	to have to /must
espérer	to hope
il faut	it is necessary
pouvoir	to be able to/can
préférer	to prefer
savoir	to know how to/can
vouloir	to want to

  e.g. *Il ne sait pas conduire.* – He can't drive.
  Elle peut venir à une heure. – She can come at one o'clock.
  J'espère aller à l'université. – I hope to go to university.

- After the following verbs, the infinitive has the word *à* in front of it:

aider	to help (someone to do something)
apprendre	to learn
commencer	to begin
continuer	to continue
se décider	to make up one's mind
hésiter	to hesitate
inviter	to invite
réussir	to succeed

e.g. *Je l'ai aidé(e) à faire la vaisselle.* – I helped him (her) to do the washing-up.

Il continue à regarder la télé. – He continues to watch TV.

Elle a réussi à trouver un apartement. – She succeeded in finding a flat.

- After the following verbs, the infinitive has *de* in front of it:

avoir besoin	to need to
avoir peur	to be afraid of
avoir le temps	to have time to
cesser	to stop
décider	to decide to
empêcher	to prevent from
essayer	to try to
finir	to finish
oublier	to forget to
promettre	to promise to
regretter	to be sorry to

e.g. *Je n'ai pas le temps de te parler.* – I don't have time to talk to you.

Elle a décidé d'aller au cinéma. – She decided to go to the cinema.

Je regrette de te déranger. – I'm sorry to disturb you.

2 The infinitive is used after *aller* to express a future idea:

Nous allons partir à onze heures. – We're going to leave at 11 o'clock.

3 The infinitive is used after *venir de* to express the idea of 'just':

- In the present:

Je viens d'arriver. – I have just arrived.

- In the imperfect:

Il venait de commencer. – He had just begun.

4 The infinitive is used after prepositions:

à   *J'ai quelque chose à te dire.* – I have something to tell you.

après   (with the perfect infinitive, i.e. *avoir/être* + past participle):

Après avoir mangé, elle est partie. – When she had eaten, she left.

Après s'être levée, elle a pris – When she had got up, she had
le petit déjeuner.   breakfast.

avant de   *Je veux te parler avant de partir.* – I want to talk to you before I leave.

pour   *Elle va à l'université pour* – She's going to university to
continuer ses études.   continue her studies.

sans   *Il est parti sans me dire au revoir.* – He left without saying goodbye to me.

5 When using an object pronoun with an infinitive, the pronoun comes first:

Je dois te parler. – I have to talk to you.

Il commence à m'énerver. – He's beginning to get on my nerves.

Nous avons oublié de te téléphoner. – We forgot to phone you.

LIST OF COMMON VERBS

Verbs marked * have minor irregularities – see Chapter 2.

COMMON ER VERBS

accepter	to accept	*allumer*	to light
accompagner	to go/come with	*améliorer*	to improve
accorder	to grant	*amuser*	to amuse
acheter	to buy	*s'amuser*	to have a good time
adorer	to love		
aider	to help	*annoncer*	to annonce
aimer	to like	*annuler*	to cancel
ajouter	to add	*appeler*	to call

*s'appeler	to be called	demeurer	to live
apporter	to bring	dépanner	to repair
approuver	to approve (of)	se dépêcher	to hurry
*appuyer	to lean/to press	dépenser	to spend (money)
arrêter	to stop (something else)	déposer	to put down
		déranger	to disturb
s'arrêter	to stop (oneself)	se déshabiller	to get undressed
arriver	to arrive/to happen	désirer	to want
		dessiner	to draw
attirer	to attract	se détendre	to relax
attraper	to catch	détester	to ate
augmenter	to add	deviner	to guess
avaler	to swallow	dîner	to have dinner
se baigner	to bathe	discuter	to discuss
*balayer	to sweep	distribuer	to deliver
bavarder	to chat	donner	to give
blesser	to injure	doubler	to overtake
bouger	to move	douter	to doubt
bricoler	to 'do-it-yourself'	durer	to last
briller	to shine	écouter	to listen (to)
bronzer	to get a sun-tan	écraser	to knock down
brosser	to brush	empêcher	to prevent
se brosser (les dents)	to brush (one's teeth)	emporter	to take away
		emprunter	to borrow
cacher	to hide	enfermer	to shut in
camper	to camp	*s'ennuyer	to be bored
casser	to break	enseigner	to teach
se casser (la jambe)	to break (one's leg)	entrer	to go/to come in
		*envoyer	to send
cambrioler	to burgle	*espérer	to hope
changer	to change	*essayer	to try (on)
chanter	to sing	*essuyer	to wipe/to clean
chercher	to look for	étonner	to surprise
classer	to sort	étudier	to study
cocher	to tick	éviter	to avoid
collectionner	to collect	expliquer	to explain
commander	to order	se fâcher	to get angry
*commencer	to begin	féliciter	to congratulate
composer	to dial (phone number	fermer	to close
		fêter	to celebrate
composter	to stamp	freiner	to brake
conseiller	to advise	frapper	to hit
consulter	to consult	fumer	to smoke
conter	to tell	gagner	to win
continuer	to continue	garer	to park
contrôler	to check	*geler	to freeze
se coucher	to go to bed	gonfler	to blow up (inflate)
couper	to cut		
coûter	to cost	goûter	to taste
crier	to shout	habiter	to live (in)
cultiver	to grow/to cultivate	s'habiller	to get dressed
		ignorer	not to know
danser	to dance	imaginer	to imagine
débarrasser	to clear away	indiquer	to indicate
se débarasser de	to get rid of	*s'inquiéter	to worry
se débrouiller	to cope/to get by	intéresser	to interest
décider	to decide	inviter	to invite
déclarer	to state	*jeter	to throw
décoller	to take off (aeroplane)	jouer	to play
		laisser	to leave
découper	to cut out	laver	to wash
décrocher	to lift the receiver (phone)	*se lever	to get up
		loger	to stay (accommodation)
déjeuner	to have lunch		
demander	to ask	louer	to rent/to hire
déménager	to move (house)	*manger	to eat

manquer	to miss		*remarquer*	to notice
(*il me manque* – I miss him)			*rembourser*	to refund
marcher	to walk/to work (equipment)		*remercier*	to thank
			rencontrer	to meet
marquer	to mark		*rentrer*	to return
*mener	to lead/to take		*renverser*	to knock over
monter	to climb/to get on		*réparer*	to repair
montrer	to show		**répéter*	to repeat
se moquer de	to make fun of		*se reposer*	to rest
nager	to swim		*réserver*	to book/to reserve
*nettoyer	to clean		*respirer*	to breathe
noter	to note down		*rester*	to stay/to remain
parler	to speak		*retourner*	to return
partager	to share		*se réveiller*	to wake up
participer	to take part		*rouler*	to travel (car, etc.)
passer	to pass		*saigner*	to bleed
se passer	to happen		*sauter*	to jump
penser	to think		*sembler*	to seem
persuader	to persuade		*séparer*	to separate
piquer	to sting		*serrer*	to shake (hands)
pleurer	to cry		*siffler*	to whistle
plonger	to dive		*signer*	to sign
porter	to wear/to carry		*soigner*	to take care of
poser	to put down		*souffler*	to blow
poser une question	to ask a question		*soulager*	to comfort
pousser	to push/to grow (plants)		*stationner*	to park
			supposer	to suppose
pratiquer	to practise/to take part in		*taper*	to type
			téléphoner	to telephone
préparer	to prepare		*se terminer*	to end
présenter	to introduce		*tirer*	to pull
presser	to squash		*tomber*	to fall
prêter	to lend		*toucher*	to touch
prier	to ask/to beg		*tourner*	to turn
*se promener	to go for a walk		*tousser*	to cough
proposer	to suggest		*travailler*	to work
protester	to protest		*traverser*	to cross
prouver	to prove		*se tromper*	to make a mistake
quitter	to leave			
raccomoder	to mend		*se tromper (de)*	to get the wrong (number/train)
raccrocher	to hang up (phone)			
			trouver	to find
raconter	to tell		*se trouver*	to be (situated)
ranger	to tidy		*tuer*	to kill
se raser	to have a shave		*utiliser*	to use
recommander	to recommend		*vérifier*	to check
refuser	to refuse		*visiter*	to visit
regretter	to regret/to be sorry		*voler*	to fly/to steal
			voyager	to travel

COMMON IR VERBS

choisir	to choose		*réussir*	to succeed
finir	to finish		*saisir*	to grab
remplir	to fill		*vieillir*	to grow old

COMMON RE VERBS

attendre	to wait (for)		*perdre*	to lose
descendre	to go down/to get off		*rendre*	to give back
			répondre	to answer/to reply
entendre	to hear		*vendre*	to sell

193

CHAPTER 1 L'ÉCOLE

F H LISTENING

Transcript

1

– Alain, ça te plaît, l'école?

– Ça dépend des jours. Le vendredi, j'ai deux heures d'EMT et deux heures de maths, alors c'est bon, car ce sont mes matières préférées. Mais le lundi, j'ai anglais, français et deux heures d'espagnol, et je ne suis vraiment pas bon en langues. Alors, le week-end, je pense que je déteste l'école, à cause des cours du lundi, mais du mardi au vendredi ça va.

– Et toi, Floriane?

– Oh oui! C'est super! J'y retrouve toutes mes amies, j'aime bien les profs, et les cours sont assez intéressants – à part la géographie. Ça va comme matière, mais j'ai horreur du prof.

Answers

	aime	n'aime pas	Attitude envers l'école
Alain	1 **l'EMT** 2 **les maths**	1 **les langues**	1 ② 3 4 5
Floriane	1 **retrouver ses amies** 2 **les profs**	1 **le prof de géographie**	① 2 3 4 5

Examiner's comments

You often have to work at extracting the right answer. Alain doesn't say in so many words *j'aime les maths* – you need to understand the whole of his first sentence. For Floriane, you need to pick out *à part* to be sure to gain the mark.

To work out the attitudes, you need to understand everything, and draw your conclusions. Floriane is quite straightforward – she only has one negative thing to say, and the word *super* rather gives it away. It's harder for Alain, and you might well be allowed to ring 2 or 3, and still get the credit.

Note that if you just wrote *la géographie* as Floriane's dislike, you wouldn't get the mark. You have to be as precise as you can, and she makes it quite clear that she doesn't dislike geography, just the teacher.

On this sort of question a Grade C candidate would get six or seven of the eight answers correct.

F H SPEAKING

Transcript

2

Teacher: Vous êtes en quelle classe?
Vous aimez les cours?
Et les profs, ils sont sympa?
Ça fait longtemps que vous apprenez le français?

Teacher: Vous êtes en quelle classe?
Student: (Je suis) en seconde.
Teacher: Vous aimez les cours?
Student: Mes matières préférées sont les maths et la chimie.
Teacher: Et les profs, ils sont sympa?
Student: Je n'aime pas le prof d'anglais.
Teacher: Ça fait longtemps que vous apprenez le français?
Student: (J'apprends le français) depuis quatre ans.

Examiner's comments

There is no reason not to answer naturally (you could, for example, leave out the words in brackets in the transcript, and still gain full marks). However, some of the questions will force you to reply in a sentence, and it's important to be accurate, especially with your verbs. You need to listen carefully to what your teacher says, especially for the unexpected part. You don't know what is coming, but you know from the prompts **when** it is coming.

Answers

Hélène: aime le vendredi; n'aime pas le jeudi.
Alexandre: aime le vendredi; n'aime pas le lundi.
Julie: aime le jeudi; n'aime pas le vendredi.

Examiner's comments

This question is simple enough to answer, and doesn't require any manipulation of French. However, you have to put together two sets of information (what you are told about the three people, and the timetable itself) to work out the answers. So, for Hélène's best day, you need to pick out a day when she has maths but not science, and for Alexandre's worst day, you need a day when he has languages.

A Grade C candidate would be expected to get all these answers correct, but many good candidates fail to score as well as they ought on the more straightforward questions. In the Reading Test, you should have time to go over what you have written and check for unnecessary errors.

CHAPTER 2   A LA MAISON/LES MEDIA

Transcript

1

- Tu aides beaucoup à la maison, Salim?
- Oui, mais c'est surtout mon père que j'aide dans le jardin ou avec le bricolage. Mais je m'occupe aussi de la cuisine de temps en temps. J'adore ça. Et toi, Noëlle?
- Non, moi, je ne fais rien.
- Et tes parents, qu'est-ce qu'ils disent?
- Ils ne disent rien.
- Et tu ne penses pas que tu devrais aider ta mère? Elle travaille, n'est-ce pas?
- Oui, elle travaille. Mais puisqu'elle ne me demande pas de l'aider, je ne vais pas lui demander du travail! Non merci, je suis bien contente comme ça! En tout cas, toi, Michel, tu ne fais pas grand-chose pour aider ta mère.
- C'est vrai. Mais moi, j'ai une raison.
- Ohhhh oui!
- Non, vraiment. Oui, c'est vrai, à la maison c'est mon frère qui aide mes parents – il fait un peu de jardinage, la vaisselle, il passe l'aspirateur.
- Et toi, alors?
- J'allais te le dire. Deux fois par semaine, je vais chez ma grand-mère et je fais tout son ménage. Et le samedi, je fais ses courses. Je m'entends bien avec elle, mon frère non. Alors, tout le monde est content.

Answers

1 Any 2 of: Il fait la cuisine/Il prépare les repas.
             Il aide son père.
             Il fait le jardinage.
             Il fait du bricolage.

2 Parce qu'elle est paresseuse/elle ne veut pas.

3 Any 2 of: Parce que Michel aide sa grand-mère.
             Parce que Michel fait le ménage pour sa grand-mère.
             Parce que Michel fait les courses pour sa grand-mère.

Examiner's comments

These answers are of Grade A standard because the questions give little help in finding the right information, and you have to answer in complete sentences. Clearly, there are alternative ways of answering, but you do have to give some quite precise details. Question 2 is particularly difficult because you have to draw a conclusion.

H READING

Answers

2
1 Marie regarde A2 à 20h40.
2 Alexandre regarde FR3 à 23h10.
3 Maryse regarde TF1 à 21h45.
4 Luc regarde FR3 à 19h30.

Examiner's comments

This question, which may appear quite simple, presents a number of problems. *Cultivez votre jardin* might appeal to Marie's interest in the environment, but not as much as a programme about the Brazilian forests. Alexandre would certainly rather watch highlights of the 1978 World Cup than a foreign film about a big match. Maryse would not be misled into watching a cartoon about an orchestra leader when she could watch a programme about French songs. Finally, Luc seems to have a lot of choice, but only one film really matches his taste for old French films: the film on TF1 is not old, and *Le Grand Match* is not French, it's subtitled. The fact that you need to understand so much of the detail to identify the right programme makes this quite a hard question – Grade A/B.

H SPEAKING

Transcript

3
Teacher: Où habites-tu?
Student: J'habite à Southampton. C'est une assez grande ville dans le sud de l'Angleterre. Southampton est sur la côte, et c'est un grand port.
Teacher: Tu habites dans le centre-ville?
Student: Non, j'habite dans la banlieue, à trois kilomètres du centre-ville.
Teacher: Parle-moi de ta maison.
Student: Eh bien, elle est assez petite. Il y a seulement trois chambres – une pour ma mère, une pour ma sœur, et la plus petite pour moi. J'habite ici depuis cinq ans. Avant, j'habitais à Newark.
Teacher: Et tu préfères habiter ici?
Student: Oui, parce qu'à Newark, nous habitions en ville, et il n'y avait pas de jardin.
Teacher: Décris ta chambre, s'il te plaît.
Student: Alors, elle est petite, comme j'ai dit, mais il y a assez de place pour une petite table où je fais mes devoirs. Les murs sont verts, et la moquette est grise. Aux murs j'ai mis toutes sortes de posters.

Examiner's comments

There's not much to say about that. It was a natural conversation, with the candidate volunteering lots of information without waiting for the teacher to ask specific questions – though importantly, it never turned into a monologue (which can often sound as if it's been learnt off by heart). The knack is to have in your head lots of things to say on all the topics, but to make them sound natural. When the teacher did ask a question, the candidate was able to answer without hesitation. Although this is only a short extract from a longer conversation, this is clearly an A Grade candidate.

Just one word of warning. This candidate managed to fit in a number of past tenses, but no future – because the topic doesn't really encourage it. However, to get the top grades, your conversation will probably have to have references to past, present and future. The candidate could have added at the end: E*t pour mon anniversaire, mes parents vont m'acheter une télévision.*

4 *Sample Student's Answer*

WRITING H

> Cher Dominique/Chère Dominique,
> Me voici enfin dans ma nouvelle maison. Elle est vraiment super! Elle est beaucoup plus grande que l'ancienne, et j'ai maintenant ma chambre à moi. Je ne partage plus avec mon frère! Elle est assez petite, mais j'ai une armoire et une petite table pour mon ordinateur. Le décor est plutôt moche, mais ma mère a dit que je pouvais la repeindre pendant les grandes vacances. Je vais aussi m'acheter une télévision – j'ai fait des économies!
> Il y a trois autres chambres, un salon et une salle à manger. Il y a aussi une grande cave où je vais jouer au tennis de table avec mes amis. Malheureusement, il y a un énorme jardin, et je suis sûr que je vais devoir aider mes parents.
> La nouvelle maison est plus loin du collège, mais il y a un car qui y va directement, alors ça va.
> Et toi, parle-moi un peu de ta maison. Elle te plaît? Pourquoi?
> A bientôt,

EXAMINER'S COMMENTS

- *This is everything this sort of answer should be.*
- *It reads like real French, with a number of colloquial expressions (Me voici enfin; plutôt moche; alors, ça va).*
- *It reads like a real letter, with information being given where it fits most naturally, not just slavishly following the order of the tasks set. (A word of warning, however: if you don't do the tasks in the same order as they appear in the question, you need to be even more careful to make sure you cover them all.)*
- *It goes into lots of detail, develops ideas and gives opinions as well as facts.*
- *It avoids the trap of simply listing items by adding descriptions and extra details. This means that there is a variety of vocabulary. There is also a variety of structure:*
  comparison – plus grande que l'ancienne
  negative – je ne partage plus
  que and qui clauses – je suis sûr que; il y a un car qui
  variety of tenses – ma mère a dit; je vais devoir
  And of course it is all very accurate.
- *Finally, it is a full reply. Even if you are not told how many words to write, this sort of question should produce between 120 and 150 words.*

CHAPTER 3   LA SANTE, LA FORME ET LA NOURRITURE

F H LISTENING

Transcript

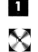

1   1   – Bonjour, docteur. Vous pouvez m'examiner le bras, s'il vous plaît?
          Ça fait très mal.
        – Qu'est-ce que vous avez fait?
        – Je suis tombé en jouant avec mon chien.
        – Ce n'est pas grave. Je vais vous donner une ordonnance.

   2   – Alors, qu'est-ce qui ne va pas?
       – J'ai mal au ventre, docteur.
       – Depuis combien de temps?
       – Depuis hier soir.
       – Et qu'est-ce que vous avez mangé hier?
       – Du poisson.
       – Alors, ne mangez rien pendant deux jours.

   3   – Aïe! J'ai vraiment mal au dos.
       – Vous avez fait du sport récemment?
       – Non, je ne fais jamais de sport, mais hier j'ai passé toute la
         journée à travailler dans le jardin.
       – Voilà le problème. Il faut vous reposer jusqu'à lundi prochain.

Answers

   1   C   Either *jouant avec chien* or *pas grave* or *ordonnance*
   2   A   Either *mangé (du) poisson* or *ne mangez pas 2 jours*
   3   E   Either *travaillé (dans) jardin* or *repos jusqu'à lundi*

Examiner's comments

The straightforward way to talk about symptoms (*j'ai mal à...*) is not always
exactly what you will hear in real life. In number 1, the phrase *ça fait mal* is
separated from the part of the body (*Vous pouvez m'examiner le bras*), and in
number 3, the addition of *vraiment* (really) might distract you.

The extra detail section is rather more difficult. In number 1, there are three
possibilities, of which two require more than just a single word, for example
chien alone would not carry any meaningful information. However, you do not
need a full sentence, nor a grammatically accurate phrase to gain the mark. In
numbers 2 and 3, both possibilities need a phrase, though in number 3,
jardinage would be a possible one-word answer. However, since it's not actually
heard on the recording, most candidates probably wouldn't produce it.

On this question, a Grade C candidate would probably gain 4 of the 6 marks,
while a Grade B candidate would expect to score full marks.

F H SPEAKING

Transcript

2   **Teacher:** Oui, mademoiselle?
        Student: Je voudrais un café, s'il vous plaît.
        Teacher: Voilà, mademoiselle.
        Student: Vous servez des repas?
        Teacher: Non, je regrette. Je peux vous faire un sandwich, si vous voulez?
        Student: Oui, donnez-moi un sandwich.
        Teacher: Qu'est-ce que vous voulez comme sandwich?
        Student: Un sandwich au jambon, s'il vous plaît.
        Teacher: Voilà, mademoiselle. C'est tout?
        Student: Oui. Où sont les toilettes, s'il vous plaît?

Examiner's comments

This went well. The candidate conveyed all the information politely and effectively, and she coped well with the unpredictable question. She could have said immediately what sort of sandwich she wanted, but the way it happened was perfectly natural. This is probably a Grade C performance, though a Grade A candidate couldn't have done much better.

Answers

3   **1** Le petit déjeuner; **2** Le déjeuner; **3** de bonne heure/pas tard/avant huit heures/pas après huit heures; **4** l'exercice

à éviter: biscuits, coca cola   **modérément:** vin   **important:** eau, lait

Examiner's comments

1 You have to deduce the answer from the gist of the paragraph.
2 Again, it's deduction; you have to put together what is said about *le déjeuner* and *le repas du soir* to work out the answer. The first mentions eating meat and vegetables, while the second mentions *légèrement* (lightly).
3 There are many different ways of expressing this answer.
4 Two difficulties here: you have to read the whole text to find the right section and you need to understand *vous dépasserez facilement les cent ans*.

The grid is not as easy as it might appear, as you have to work out the answers. For example, *plusieurs fois par jour* implies that drinking water is important, and *éviter excès de* implies that something is OK in moderation.

4 *Sample Student's Answer*

Monsieur

Malheureusement, moi, je ne mange pas sain. D'abord, je ne me lève jamais à temps pour préparer un vrai petit déjeuner. Ce matin, par exemple, je me suis levé à sept heures, alors j'ai tout simplement bu un verre de coca avant de sortir. Donc, à l'heure du café, j'avais vraiment faim, alors j'ai pris un paquet de biscuits. A midi, je n'ai pas le temps de prendre un bon repas - je bois un verre de bière et je mange des chips, c'est tout.
Le soir, c'est pareil. J'arrive chez moi vers huit heures, et je suis trop fatigué pour faire la cuisine, alors je mange du poisson-frites, avec de la bière.
Et en plus, je fume et je ne fais jamais de sport. Alors, je ne suis vraiment pas en forme. Mais, j'ai décidé de changer. Tous les matins je vais boire un verre de lait, et manger du pain grillé. A midi, je prendrai un sandwich, et le soir, je prendrai des légumes - pas toujours des frites!
Je vais aussi cesser de fumer, et essayer de boire moins de bière.

EXAMINER'S COMMENTS

- This is a real A* answer, so don't worry if you don't think you can match it, but there is a lot to learn from it. Even in a piece which doesn't seem to encourage use of the past, like this one, you can usually find a way of getting in a variety of tenses. Here, the past is introduced cleverly, by giving an example of what the writer has eaten today.

- There are lots of descriptive words (adjectives and adverbs) which add to the variety of the piece.

- There is a variety of structures – infinitives, different negatives, quite long sentences – and of vocabulary.

- The use of linking words makes it flow very smoothly.

CHAPTER 4 MOI, MA FAMILLE ET MES AMIS

H LISTENING

Transcript

1
– Eric, parle-moi un peu de ta famille.
– Alors, je suis fils unique; j'habite avec ma mère. Mon père est mort.
– Ça te plaît d'être tout seul comme ça?
– Ça va. Quelquefois je voudrais avoir quelqu'un de mon âge à qui je pourrais parler, ou pour emprunter des disques. Mais j'ai ma chambre à moi, ce qui est bien, et si j'ai besoin d'argent, ma mère m'en donne. Si nous étions deux, ce serait plus difficile, je crois.
– Et toi, Lorraine? Tu as des frères et sœurs?
– J'ai trois petits frères, hélas.
– Tu ne t'entends pas avec eux?
– Quelquefois ça va, mais il y a toujours du bruit à la maison – et en plus ils ne respectent pas mes affaires. Et puisque ce sont des garçons, mes parents ne leur demandent jamais de faire le ménage, mais moi...! Mais j'adore les émissions pour les enfants à la télé – et j'ai une excuse toute faite pour les regarder!

Answers

	Frères/Sœurs	Avantage	Inconvénient
Eric	Non/fils unique	propre chambre/chambre à lui/assez d'argent	seul/personne à qui parler
Lorraine	3 frères	aime regarder la télé pour enfants	bruit/ne respectent* pas ses affaires/n'aident* pas à la maison

Examiner's comments

* Here, it's the quality of your understanding that's being tested, not the quality of your written French. Even if you got the verb endings wrong, for example, and wrote *respecte* or *aide*, you would still get the credit.

A Grade C candidate would need to get all the answers in the first two columns right in this type of question. To score more highly you would need at least some of the information in the last column.

H SPEAKING

Transcript

2
Teacher: Alors, tu as des frères et sœurs?
Student: Oui, j'ai un frère et deux sœurs.
Teacher: Oui. Comment s'appellent-ils?
Student: Mon frère s'appelle Paul, et mes sœurs s'appellent Julie et Claire.
Teacher: Quel âge ont-ils?
Student: Paul a vingt ans, et Julie et Claire ont douze ans.
Teacher: Ce sont des jumelles alors?
Student: Oui.
Teacher: Tu t'entends bien avec eux?
Student: Paul est sympa, mais je n'aime pas mes sœurs.
Teacher: Pourquoi?
Student: Elles ne sont pas sympa.
Teacher: Qu'est-ce qu'elles font?
Student: Elles prennent mes vêtements.
Teacher: Et elles ne te demandent pas la permission?
Student: Non.
Teacher: C'est tout?

Student: Elles écoutent de la musique.

Teacher: Tu n'aimes pas la même musique qu'elles?

Student: Elles la mettent trop fort!

Teacher: Tu t'entends avec tes parents?

Student: Ça va. Mon père est trop strict.

Teacher: Par exemple?

Student: Je dois rentrer à la maison avant onze heures, même le samedi.

Teacher: Mais ta mère, ça va?

Student: Oui, j'aime bien ma mère.

Examiner's comments

It's a bit like hard work, isn't it? The teacher really has to try hard to get anything beyond the minimum, though the answers that are given are very accurate, and probably worth a Grade C. However, the teacher ends up saying too much, and the candidate doesn't say enough. Although this is a conversation, not a prepared monologue, the candidate should be prepared to volunteer some information without being asked. Here is another attempt at the same conversation.

Teacher: Alors, tu as des frères et sœurs?

Student: Oui, j'ai un frère et deux sœurs. Mon frère s'appelle Paul. Il a vingt ans. Mes sœurs s'appellent Julie et Claire. Ce sont des jumelles. Elles ont douze ans.

Teacher: Tu t'entends bien avec eux?

Student: Paul est sympa, mais je n'aime pas mes sœurs, parce qu'elles prennent mes vêtements sans me demander la permission. Et elles écoutent de la musique, aussi. J'aime la musique, mais elles la mettent trop fort.

Teacher: Tu t'entends avec tes parents?

Student: Oui, ça va, mais mon père est trop strict. Par exemple, je dois rentrer avant onze heures, même le samedi. Par contre, j'aime bien ma mère.

Examiner's comments

That was much better. Without adding any more information, and very little vocabulary, three things have happened:

- It's now a conversation, not an interrogation.

- The teacher's part has become much less dominant.

- Finally, because sentences have been linked together, it's a much more impressive display of French structures.

This sort of conversation is much more likely to get you a Grade A. Especially on a familiar topic like your family, where you must have something to say, it's important to take the initiative. If nothing else, it will stop the teacher getting stuck for things to ask, and perhaps coming up with a complicated question you can't cope with.

Answers

READING H

3 **1** V; **2** F; **3** ?; **4** F; **5** F

Examiner's comments

This exercise is graded at least B/C because of the difficulty of the French, because there is a lot of reading to do, and because you have to be able to make comparisons and draw conclusions to get to the right answer.

Remember, too, that this sort of exercise requires you to answer from the French you have read. There is no point in trying to answer just from your own point of view – your answer has to be justified in the text, For example, in question 4, you might be quite convinced that there was no entertainment in 1898, but the text states quite clearly that there was.

CHAPTER 5 **LE TEMPS LIBRE, LES LOISIRS, LES VACANCES ET LES FETES**

Transcript

H LISTENING

1
– Hé, Marie! On sort ce soir?
– Oui, je veux bien. On va où?
– Je ne sais pas. Il y a un assez bon film au cinéma.
– C'est quoi comme film?
– C'est un film de guerre – Le Train.
– Oh, je l'ai déjà vu.
– Bon. On va au complexe sportif, alors?
– Je voudrais bien jouer au tennis, mais je me suis fait mal au bras.
– Alors, on pourrait aller au café.
– Et tu sais ce qui va arriver? Tu vas me laisser toute seule pendant que tu joueras au baby-foot avec tes copains. C'est très amusant, ça!
– Alors, on va simplement se promener en ville?
– D'accord!

Answers

Marie	vrai/faux	raison
ne veut pas aller au cinéma.	V	(Elle a) vu le film.
veut aller au complexe sportif.	F	(Elle s'est fait) mal au bras.
ne veut pas aller au café.	V	(Elle sera) toute seule. OR: Il jouera/va jouer au baby-foot/avec (ses) copains. OR: (Ce n'est) pas amusant.

A la fin, ils décident d'aller se promener (en ville).

Examiner's comments

In the *vrai/faux* column, the answers are not as easy as they might seem, since Marie never actually says "no" in so many words – you need to work out her answer from what she says.

In the *raison* column, the parts in brackets are not needed to score the marks.

The first two answers can be supplied almost directly from what is heard on the CD, but if you attempt a sentence, remember that *je* on the CD must become *elle* in the answer, with the appropriate changes in the verb.

If the candidate had written *je me suis fait mal au bras*, it would not have scored the mark, since it would not have communicated the right idea.

There are a several possibles for the third answer, but only the most difficult (*toute seule*) can be lifted direct from the recording. The others both need some extra work – either changing the *tu* to *il*, or adding a negative. Although the irony is clear when you hear C'est très amusant, ça, it doesn't work as a written answer.

The final sentence is quite straightforward, and can be answered by directly quoting the recording.

The *vrai/faux* column and the final sentence are about Grade C, but the *raison* column can earn you a Grade B – perhaps even a Grade A for full marks.

2 Je vais vous parler de mon passe-temps préféré. Alors, je collectionne les timbres. Je fais ça depuis douze ans. J'ai commencé quand j'avais quatre ans, quand mon oncle m'a envoyé des cartes postales. Il travaillait en Europe, et il est allé en France, en Italie, en Belgique et en Allemagne. Plus tard, j'ai commencé à mettre les timbres dans un album – j'ai trouvé ça passionnant d'avoir des timbres de pays différents. Maintenant, j'ai une douzaine d'albums, avec à peu près six mille timbres. J'ai des timbres de tous les pays du monde – de l'Afrique du Sud, de la Chine, de l'Australie et des Etats-Unis.

Chaque fois que je mets un nouveau timbre dans mon album, je cherche son pays d'origine dans mon atlas – alors je fais de la géographie en même temps. Pratique, non?

Quelquefois mes amis m'envoient des cartes ou des lettres quand ils passent leurs vacances à l'étranger, mais je vais aussi dans des magasins spécialisés pour acheter des paquets de timbres. L'année prochaine, je vais aller aux Etats-Unis, mais je n'irai pas à Disneyland, comme tout le monde. Je vais aller dans le plus grand magasin de ·timbres du monde à New York, avec l'oncle qui m'a envoyé mon premier timbre étranger, il y a douze ans. Génial!

Examiner's comments

If your exam board allows you to do a presentation as part of the Speaking Test (check your syllabus), this allows you really to show off your French. You can prepare exactly what you are going to say in advance, so there should be no mistakes, and there is no chance of your being upset by being asked a question you don't understand. You should make sure that you get in as much variety of language as possible.

This candidate has certainly profited from the opportunities offered by the presentation. She has included a variety of tenses – perfect, imperfect, future and of course present. But there is much more. There are different time phrases (*depuis*; *quand*; *maintenant*; *en même temps*; *l'année prochaine*). There is some excellent vocabulary (*pays d'origine*; *spécialisé*) and some colloquial expressions (*j'ai trouvé ça passionnant*; *pratique, non*; *comme tout le monde*).

The delivery of the presentation is also very good. You really need to practise until you get it right, including the timing – the NEAB, for example, specifies about 1 minute 30 seconds.

This is clearly the presentation of a grade A/A* candidate, and is worth trying to learn from, even if you don't think you'll ever get to this level.

Answers

3 **1** c); **2** g); **3** a); **4** j); **5** f); **6** d); **7** h)

Examiner's comments

You can often use grammatical markers to help you in this sort of exercise. In Number 1, *un* tells you that the missing word must be a singular noun, while in Numbers 2 to 5, the figure, *des*, *les* and *vos* all indicate a plural noun. In Number 6, although you might be looking for a verb ending in *-ez* after *vous*, there isn't one in the list, and in any case the structure of the whole sentence means it must be another infinitive (after *faire* and *visiter*). Finally, the only possibility for Number 7 is an adjective.

Clearly, you also need to understand the vocabulary (for example, there are two feminine adjectives in the list, and six plural nouns), but don't forget you have a dictionary to check any words you don't know. Your dictionary will also give you some help with the grammatical markers, such as telling you whether a word you check is a noun, a verb or an adjective.

The level of vocabulary and structures in this text makes it quite hard, and even a Grade B candidate might make one or two errors.

F **H** WRITING

4 *Sample Student's Answer*

EXAMINER'S COMMENTS

● This is not a standard account of a weekend, but it shows imagination, is very well organised and sequenced, and contains some variety. There are perfect, imperfect and present tenses (the future wouldn't fit all that well into this title). There is a good use of negatives (n'a pas pu; il n'y avait rien; n'avait même pas; n'a pas cessé), a wide range of general vocabulary and some good clauses (pendant que ...; a annoncé que ...; car il n'a pas ...). A *good Grade A account.*

Le weekend dernier, je suis allé en Cornouailles avec ma famille. Nous sommes partis vendredi matin. Le soleil brillait. Mais pendant que nous nous reposions à Coventry, il a commencé à pleuvoir. Nous roulions sur une petite route de campagne quand mon père a annoncé que nous étions perdus. Ensuite, l'orage a commencé, et la voiture est tombée en panne.

Nous avons couru à la ferme la plus proche. Heureusement, le fermier nous a aidés. Nous avons passé la nuit à la ferme. Le lendemain, mon père a téléphoné au garage, mais le mécanicien n'a pas pu réparer la voiture avant lundi. Alors nous avons passé le weekend dans un petit hôtel près du garage. Il n'y avait rien à faire dans le village, et l'hôtel n'avait même pas la télé. J'ai dû jouer aux cartes avec ma sœur pendant des heures, car il n'a pas cessé de pleuvoir.

CHAPTER 6 **LES RAPPORTS PERSONNELS, LES ACTIVITES SOCIALES ET LES RENDEZ-VOUS**

F **H** LISTENING

Transcript

1

– Tu vas au concert ce soir?

– Bien sûr.

– On y va ensemble?

– D'accord. Où est-ce qu'on se retrouve?

– Le concert a lieu à la salle des fêtes, alors si on se retrouvait au bar? On aurait le temps de prendre un verre.

– Bien. A quelle heure?

– Le concert commence à neuf heures, alors disons huit heures.

– Ah! Ça, va être difficile. Je fais du baby-sitting jusqu'à sept heures et demie. Je dois surveiller mon petit frère.

– Pas de problème! Je passerai te chercher à huit heures moins le quart.

– Chez moi?

– Oui, bien sûr.

– Merci. C'est gentil.

Answers

1 A   **2** C   **3** C   **4** B   **5** A

Examiner's comments

1 This is very straightforward – simply a question of hearing the word in the recording, and picking the same word out in its written form.

2 *Salle des fêtes* is actually mentioned in the recording, so could mislead, but it shouldn't be too difficult to identify *café* (answer C) from *bar* on the recording.

3 A number of times are heard in the recording, including two of the possible answers. Times, and numbers generally, often cause problems in Listening Tests, and you need to concentrate both on hearing them correctly and on not being misled by irrelevant times.

4 You need to hear both *surveiller* and *frère* to get the right answer.

5 You need to be able to make the connection between *chez moi* (in the recording) and *à la maison* (in the answer) to gain the mark, and not to be distracted by *chez lui*.

On the whole, these questions should not be too difficult. A Grade C candidate would probably get all five answers correct.

Transcript

2 **Teacher:** Allô?

Student: Ici Claire. Tu veux venir au restaurant avec moi?

Teacher: Oui, je veux bien. Quand?

Student: On pourrait y aller mardi soir.

Teacher: Oh, je regrette, mardi je ne peux pas. Lundi, ça va?

Student: Non, le restaurant est fermé le lundi.

Teacher: Alors, je suis libre vendredi.

Student: Vendredi je travaille jusqu'à neuf heures.

Teacher: Alors, qu'est-ce qu'on fait?

Student: On y va vendredi à dix heures. D'accord?

Teacher: Oui, d'accord.

Examiner's comments

The candidate conducts this role-play with little difficulty, despite the unstructured nature of the candidate's role, which makes detailed preparation difficult. The most important thing when preparing a role-play like this is to look at all the information, and try to predict what you will need to say, but also to realise that you will also have to respond sensibly to what the teacher says.

In this example, you clearly need to issue an invitation. The information on the advertisement, and the fact that you are told that you work late on two days, tells you that the day and/or the time will be important, and that this will probably be the area for negotiation. You therefore need to prepare some ways of suggesting alternative days/times.

In this sample, the candidate's first two utterances are quite straightforward and predictable. In her third utterance, she had obviously predicted that there was going to be a problem with Sunday or Monday, and for her fourth utterance the other problem area – working late – had been foreseen, and she coped well with reaching a compromise.

Clearly, the end of the conversation could have gone in different directions: the candidate could have suggested Wednesday or Thursday, for example, or even next week.

Since this level of role-play is targeted at A*/A/B candidates, to do it as well as this would be worth at least a Grade A.

F H READING

Answers

3   1 B   2 F   3 A   4 C

Examiner's comments

Even at this level, the task will rarely be as simple as working out what word fits the picture, and then finding it in the sentence. Here, for example, the words *restaurant*; *bar/café*; *piscine*; *plage* – which are the obvious words for pictures A, B, C and F – do not appear anywhere. The candidate therefore needs to understand that *prendre un verre* means 'go for a drink', that *aller à la mer* means 'go to the sea-side', that an *invitation à dîner* would go with 'restaurant' and that *nager* goes with the swimming pool. However, a Grade C candidate should not have any difficulty with these items.

CHAPTER 7   LA VILLE, LES REGIONS ET LE TEMPS

H LISTENING

Transcript

1   1   Voici la météo pour aujourd'hui. Dans l'ensemble de la région, le brouillard va continuer jusqu'en fin d'après-midi. La visibilité sera de cinquante à cent mètres.

2   Ce matin s'annonce beau, mais un peu froid. Il y aura quelques nuages en début d'après-midi, mais il n'y aura pas de pluie avant la nuit.

3   Demain, il fera un temps chaud et ensoleillé, surtout sur la côte. La température maximale sera de vingt-neuf degrés.

4   Ce matin, il fera assez beau, mais le vent soufflera jusqu'à trente kilomètres à l'heure.

5   Ce matin, le ciel sera partout couvert, et il fera assez froid. Vers midi, la pluie arrivera du nord, et les averses deviendront de plus en plus fréquentes dans l'après-midi, avec quelques orages dans l'ouest de la région. Il y aura un vent assez fort.

Answers

1D   2E   3A   4B   5C

Examiner's comments

Here, you need to understand the gist of the whole forecast before making up your mind about which activity is most suitable. When tackling this kind of question, make sure first of all that you understand what is written, so that you can have an idea in advance about what conditions you are listening for (wind for wind-surfing, sun and warmth for sunbathing, etc.).

When listening to weather forecasts, you also need to listen for changes. For example, Number 5 starts off as quite suitable for a walk in the country, but gets worse as the day goes on.

A Grade C candidate would probably get most of these five answers correct.

Transcript

2

Teacher: Où habitez-vous?

Student: J'habite à Leeds. C'est une grande ville industrielle dans le nord de l'Angleterre.

Teacher: Il y a combien d'habitants, à peu près?

Student: Il y a environ cinq cent mille habitants.

Teacher: Parlez-moi un peu de Leeds.

Student: Il y a beaucoup de grands magasins dans le centre de la ville, et il y a aussi un nouveau centre commercial. Dans la zone piétonne, il y a aussi des cafés avec des terrasses, comme en France – mais ils sont très chers.

Teacher: Est-ce que vous allez souvent en centre-ville?

Student: Oui, au moins deux fois par semaine. Le samedi, j'y vais pour faire les courses, et le mardi soir, je vais au cinéma.

Teacher: Il y a beaucoup de cinémas?

Student: Oui, il y a trois grands cinémas avec plusieurs salles. Il y a aussi des théâtres, des boîtes de nuit et des salles de concert.

Teacher: Vous aimez habiter à Leeds?

Student: Oui. Il y a toujours quelque chose à faire. C'est une ville très animée, mais c'est aussi une ville très verte; il y a beaucoup de parcs et d'espaces verts. En été, il y a toujours quelques concerts de rock en plein air dans le parc. En plus, la campagne autour de Leeds est très belle, et on est à seulement trente kilomètres de York, une vieille ville historique qui attire beaucoup de touristes.

Examiner's comments

Many of the topics which might occur in the Speaking Test will be personal (hobbies, family, school) and you will have things to say about them without having to think too much. However, other topics might require you to find out some information before you can talk about them. You may not go to town very often; you may not know much about its facilities, its history and so on. This is one topic where preparing information in advance will help greatly. It's worth checking your syllabus to see if there are any other topics which might come up which you don't know much about. This candidate clearly either knows a lot about the topic, or has prepared very thoroughly, and the conversation certainly benefits from this.

As far as the French is concerned, there is little to say. The candidate does much more than simply respond to the questions, and uses a wide variety of structures and vocabulary.

However, it would have been quite easy to add a little variety of tense, for example: *je vais aller à un concert de rock en plein air dans le parc la semaine prochaine; je suis allé(e) à York l'été dernier avec mes parents*. When preparing any topic it's a good idea to try to fit in at least one past and one future tense – and it's quite easy, even if the topic doesn't seem to lend itself particularly to different tenses, or if the teacher's questions don't specifically encourage them.

Assuming that different tenses had been used in other areas of the conversation, this is clearly the work of a Grade A candidate.

3 *Sample Student's Answer*

- This is a clear A* piece of work, fulfilling the main requirements of this level.

- The French is accurate, and the candidate's grasp of grammar and French structures is excellent.

- It reads like French, and not like English translated into French.

- There is a variety of sentence construction and vocabulary.

- The candidate uses present, imperfect, perfect, future and conditional tenses, and a number of colloquial expressions (ça me plaît d'habiter; c'est à Nottingham que se passaient; A part).

- The information is varied and interesting, and all the questions are answered.

> J'habite à Nottingham, qui est une assez grande ville dans le centre de l'Angleterre. C'est une ville moderne, avec beaucoup de nouveaux bâtiments, mais il y a aussi un vieux château. Nottingham est la ville anglaise la plus éloignée de la mer (130 km). C'est à Nottingham que se passaient les aventures de Robin des Bois.
>
> ● Nottingham est située sur une grande rivière, et on peut pratiquer toutes sortes de sports nautiques – le ski nautique, l'aviron, etc. La rivière est aussi très jolie.
>
> Le climat de la région centrale de l'Angleterre est assez doux, mais comme partout il pleut souvent. En été, il est quand même très agréable de se promener au bord de la rivière. La semaine prochaine je ferai un pique-nique avec mes amis s'il fait beau.
>
> ● A part le sport (il y a deux équipes de football et une équipe de cricket) il y a des cinémas, des théâtres et des musées. J'habite à Nottingham depuis trois ans, mais je n'ai jamais visité le château. J'aimerais bien y aller un jour.
>
> Enfin, ça me plaît d'habiter ici. Il y a beaucoup de distractions pour les jeunes, et ce n'est pas aussi cher qu'à Londres.

Answers

4 1 f) chaud   2 h) plusieurs   3 j) l'eau   4 a) température
5 d) perdre   6 e) prouve   7 b) changer

Examiner's comments

This kind of exercise can seem a little daunting at first, because you need to understand two passages in French. However, remember that you do have a dictionary to help you, and also that there are grammatical clues – in some blanks only an adjective will fit, in others only a verb, etc. However, there will sometimes be two solutions which appear to fit. In this case, blank 2 could be filled by *plusieurs* or *quatre*. Either would make sense, but by referring back to the original article, you will see that *quatre* would in fact be wrong; the original says *deux mois*, which cannot be four weeks.

When faced with a task like this, don't be tempted to use your dictionary to look up every word. It would take far too long. Try to get as much of the gist of the original article as possible without using the dictionary, then put in any answers you are sure of. Use your dictionary first to check the meanings of the alternatives offered, if you need to, then of unknown words in the gapped passage.

The problems of comparing two texts make this a Grade A/B task, though a Grade C candidate should get at least some of the answers right.

CHAPTER 8 **LES COURSES ET LES SERVICES PUBLICS**

Transcript

LISTENING H

1

– Qu'est-ce qu'on va acheter pour l'anniversaire de maman, cette année?
– C'est difficile. Je ne sais jamais ce qui lui ferait plaisir.
– Elle disait hier qu'elle venait de casser encore une assiette, et qu'il n'en reste que quatre maintenant.
– Voilà une bonne idée. On va lui acheter quelque chose dont elle a besoin.
– Mais non! On ne va pas lui acheter de la vaisselle, quand même. C'est son anniversaire. Il faut lui donner quelque chose de personnel!
– Oui, tu as raison. Mais quoi?
– Une nouvelle montre, peut-être. Elle a sa montre depuis des années.
– Oui, mais c'était un cadeau de papa. Il la lui a donnée à l'occasion de leur dixième anniversaire de mariage, alors elle y tient vraiment. Elle n'en porterait pas d'autre, je crois.
– C'est vrai. Mais qu'est-ce qu'on va lui acheter enfin? Des fleurs?
– Oui, elle les adore. Mais elles se fanent si vite. Huit jours après, il n'y en a plus.
– Bof! Que c'est difficile.
– Moi, j'ai trouvé!
– Quoi?
– Des billets!
– Comment, des billets? Des billets de train?
– Mais non, des billets de théâtre. Elle ne sort pas assez – et ça fait longtemps qu'elle n'est pas allée voir une pièce.

Answers

		cadeau	parce que
Ils décident de ne pas acheter	1	**assiettes OR vaisselle**	**pas assez personnel**
	2	**montre**	**aime sa montre OR sa montre était un cadeau de papa**
	3	**fleurs**	**se fanent vite OR ne durent pas**
Enfin ils décident d'acheter		**billets de théâtre**	**elle ne sort pas souvent/assez OR longtemps qu'elle n'est pas allée (au théâtre)**

209

Examiner's comments

There are two things which make this a difficult exercise. First, it is quite long. You should get into the habit of making brief notes as you listen – not trying to answer the questions particularly, but getting the key points down so you don't forget them. Secondly, conversations where people express different views – even contradictory ones – can be quite hard to follow. Here it doesn't matter who is saying what, but it's not always easy to spot when they agree with each other (though in this sort of discussion, it's almost certain to be the last thing mentioned).

The items (*assiettes, montre, fleurs, billets de théâtre*) are not in themselves difficult, but the reasons for buying or not buying them are quite hard to express in French. This is especially true of the third one, where you have to either use a French verb you are not familiar with (*se faner*) or produce your own answer which was not on the CD.

When you are asked to answer in French, only the hardest (A/A*) questions will ask you to produce more than a short phrase, and there will often be an example to indicate roughly how much you need to write. Answers in French will be marked according to whether they communicate the correct information, not how accurate they are. In the answers here, spelling mistakes in the first column would not be penalised as long as it is clearly the correct item. In the second column the same principle about spelling would apply but the construction of the phrase, while not necessarily perfect, would have to convey the correct meaning. For example, *aime la montre* would not score, since it clearly doesn't refer to the one she already has. If the phrase includes a verb in the wrong tense, or leaves out a negative, it would almost certainly give the wrong message and so not score.

A Grade C candidate would probably identify some of the items discussed but a Grade A candidate would get most of the reasons as well.

H READING

Answers

2　**Amir:** D; **Pascale:** A; **Elodie:** B

Examiner's comments

Amir uses lots of negatives, which tend to make it harder to work out what he thinks, especially in a phrase like *ce n'est pas que je ne trouve rien*. He also talks about spending all his money *d'un seul coup*, which sounds like Elodie.

Pascale talks mainly about shopping with her mother, and it's only at the end that we realise that even shopping with her friends gives her no pleasure.

Elodie talks of having no money left, but everything she says reinforces the fact that she can't resist spending. The fact that she uses a number of colloquial phrases which you may not find in your dictionary means that you have to understand the gist of what she says.

This exercise is harder than it looks, and to get all the answers right is a Grade A perfomance.

**H SPEAKING**

Transcript

3　**Teacher:** Oui, mademoiselle? Je peux vous aider?
　　Student: Oui. J'ai acheté ce pull hier.
　　Teacher: Il y a un problème?
　　Student: Oui, il y a un trou, là, dans le dos.
　　Teacher: Ah oui, je vois.
　　Student: Est-ce que vous pouvez me le changer?
　　Teacher: Je regrette, mademoiselle. Il n'y en a plus.

Student: Alors, vous pouvez me rembourser?
Teacher: Oui, mademoiselle. Vous avez le reçu?
Student: Oui, voilà.

Examiner's comments

Apart from knowing that you have bought a sweater and there's something wrong with it, you have to invent the rest of this role-play for yourself. This can be difficult, but at least you can choose what to say for yourself, and are not forced into phrases you're less than comfortable with. You can decide when you bought the sweater, and what is wrong with it (it could be torn, or even the wrong size or colour).

However, you do have to try to predict what is likely to happen. So, you need to ask yourself: 'If I take something back to a shop, what is likely to happen?'

You also need to be aware that in this kind of role-play, the shop-assistant probably won't agree to your first suggestion. You need to prepare to ask for a replacement or your money back, or in the end to see the manager, so that you have alternatives ready. This candidate had done all that was necessary, and would have got an A for this role-play. Even the request for the receipt at the end was well, if simply, handled.

4 *Sample Student's Answer*

Ce matin, je suis allée en ville pour faire des courses. J'ai acheté des cadeaux pour ma famille. Puis j'ai rencontré Marie au café. Nous avons pris un coca et un sandwich, et nous avons bavardé. Mais quand le garçon nous a donné l'addition, je ne trouvais plus mon sac. Comment allais-je payer? Heureusement, Marie avait assez d'argent, et c'est elle qui a payé.

"Où as-tu perdu ton sac?" a-t-elle demandé.

"Je n'ai aucune idée," ai-je répondu, "Qu'est-ce que je vais faire?"

Nous sommes retournées aux magasins où j'avais fait mes achats, mais sans succès. Personne n'avait trouvé mon sac. Enfin, nous sommes allées au commissariat.

"Alors, il est comment votre sac?" a demandé l'agent.

"Il est en cuir noir, avec les initiales AF dessus. Dedans, il y a à peu près quatre cents francs et ma carte d'étudiant. Mais le pire, c'est qu'il y avait aussi les clés de ma voiture."

"Ne vous inquiétez pas," a dit l'agent. Je vous téléphonerai dès que j'aurai des nouvelles."

EXAMINER'S COMMENTS

- *The important thing to remember when you are basing your writing on a series of pictures, is that the pictures only give the bare bones of the story. You have to add the details yourself.*

- *This sort of exercise is very good for showing off what you can do. Use the opportunity to include a wide variety of structures, and if possible put in some dialogue – this enables you to vary your tenses more.*

- *The underlined phrases would count highly towards any mark for range of language.*

- *Notice that the account includes present, imperfect, perfect, pluperfect and future tenses.*

- *This piece of work would gain a Grade A because of its variety and accuracy.*

CHAPTER 9 **LA ROUTE, LES VOYAGES ET LES TRANSPORTS**

F H LISTENING

Transcript

1 1 Il y a trois kilomètres de bouchons sur l'autoroute A26 entre La Chapelle et Lille. Il vaut mieux éviter cette région si possible.

2 Si vous allez vers Avalon, il faut faire bien attention. Il y a du brouillard dans toute la région, alors ralentissez, et allumez vos phares. Sur la RN6 à Vallou, la visibilité est de trente mètres.

3 A la suite d'une chute de pierres, la D973 est bloquée entre Chevagne et Les Voisins. Il faut emprunter la D238 et la D299 pour éviter ce problème.

4 Ce matin il y a un convoi exceptionnel qui va de Brionne à Bernay sur la RN138. Cet engin roule à 8km/h, et il sera très difficile de le doubler.

Answers

1 A26; bouchons/embouteillages
2 RN6; brouillard/visibilité limitée
3 D973; chute de pierres/pierres sur la route
4 RN138; convoi exceptionnel/véhicule (camion) lent

Examiner's comments

This is a fairly straightforward exercise, but which still might cause some problems. Place names, (which you do not need to understand unless they are very well-known places) can be very distracting. Another frequent difficulty in the Listening Test is identifying numbers, and here the numbers are a little 'hidden' by being combined with a letter (A, D, RN). Also, in the third question, there are several numbers given, and you have to pick out the appropriate one.

Some of the vocabulary might be a bit tricky, too. In Question 4, you should be able to work out the problem, even if you don't understand *convoi exceptionnel*. In Question 3, *pierres* might confuse you if you've only met the word as a boy's name. These are the sorts of words you might find it useful to check in your dictionary, if you are allowed five minutes reading time at the end of the Test.

H SPEAKING

Transcript

2 Je me suis levée à sept heures. Il faisait beau. J'ai pris mon petit déjeuner, et j'ai téléphoné à Céline. "Tu veux faire une promenade à vélo?" "Oui, d'accord." J'ai préparé des sandwichs et je suis allée chez Céline.

A dix heures, nous étions dans la campagne. Je suis tombée de mon vélo. J'avais mal à la jambe. Céline a téléphoné pour appeler une ambulance. Quand l'ambulance est arrivée, je suis allée à l'hôpital. Ma mère est venue me voir à l'hôpital.

Examiner's comments

This is a solid, accurate account of the incident described by the pictures. However, it is limited in terms of structures, full descriptions and longer sentences. For example, in the second part, the second and third sentences could become *Soudain, un chat a traversé la route devant moi et je suis tombée de mon vélo. Je me suis fait mal à la jambe, et je ne pouvais pas marcher*. And in the last sentence, it would be better to avoid the repetition of *hôpital* by saying *je suis allée à l'hôpital, où ma mère est venue me voir*.

In theory, you need to refer to past, present and future to get a Grade C, but this account would make it, in spite of the absence of a future tense, partly because this candidate would have been encouraged to use other tenses in the general conversation. However, you should do your best to make sure that you get in past, present and future references in every part of the exam. With a bit of imagination, it is usually possible, even in the most unlikely topic. For example, in a topic which seems entirely based in the future, such as your career, you can always talk about a similar thing in the past, such as a job you have done. And in the same way, if talking about an event in the past, such as a disastrous weekend, you could always add *Je n'irai jamais plus à Blackpool*, or wherever you might have been.

So this candidate, who clearly is very able, doesn't really do herself justice. Her account covers most of the events shown, but only briefly. She doesn't add to them, nor does she give any full descriptions. With her good knowledge of structures, she could have done much better, as she shows in this next attempt.

Transcript

Samedi, je me suis levée de bonne heure. J'ai regardé par la fenêtre, et j'ai vu qu'il faisait beau. Alors je suis descendue. J'ai pris mon petit déjeuner, et j'ai téléphoné à Céline, qui habite pas loin de chez moi. "Dis, ça te dit de faire une promenade à vélo?' Céline était d'accord, donc j'ai préparé quelques sandwichs, et je suis partie chez Céline.

A dix heures, nous étions dans la campagne. Je roulais assez vite, en regardant le paysage. Mais je ne regardais pas la route. Soudain, j'ai vu le virage – mais trop tard. J'ai quitté la route, et je suis tombée de mon vélo. Céline s'est arrêtée, et m'a demandé si j'avais mal. J'avais mal à la jambe, et je ne pouvais pas marcher. Céline est montée sur son vélo, et est allée téléphoner pour appeler une ambulance.

Une heure après, l'ambulance est arrivée, et m'a emmenée à l'hôpital. Ma mère m'y attendait, car Céline lui avait téléphoné après avoir appelé l'ambulance.

Heureusement, je ne m'étais pas cassé la jambe, mais la prochaine fois, je regarderai bien la route.

Examiner's comments

Here is the same level of accuracy, but it is a much more interesting account, adding a lot of detail and a little imagination to the outline contained in the pictures.

Note the longer sentences, often containing a link word, as well as the wider variety of structures (*j'ai vu que; qui habite; Dis...; en regardant; m'a demandé si j'avais mal; m'y attendait*).

Note also the pluperfect and future tenses introduced in the final sentence.

This account is now of Grade A/A* standard.

Answers

3
1 seule femme [1]; seule grand-mère [1] (**Seule** is only needed once.)
2 traversée des mers/au dessus de l'eau [1]
3 tomber à l'eau [1] **plus** EITHER problème technique OR mauvais temps [1]
4 90 jours [1]
5 1 000km [1]
6 déserts; glaciers; forêts (tropicales) [3]
7 (pour gagner/récolter) de l'argent [1]; pour Sauvons les Enfants [1]

Examiner's comments

This passage is targeted at Grades A/B, partly because of its length, but also because it contains some unusual vocabulary. However, all the questions can be answered by following the gist of the article, without necessarily checking the meaning of every unknown word.

Notice also that the answers can be expressed quite simply, with familiar words or words taken directly from the text. There is no need for complete sentences.

The main difficulty, even though the questions are asked in chronological order, lies in identifying the right part of the article to find the answer, since the form of the question does not give a direct link to the passage. For example, in Question 1, the word *unique* does not appear in the article, nor does the word *dangereux* from Question 2.

While a Grade C candidate might get some of the answers correct (probably 4 and 5, and possibly part of 6), only a good Grade A candidate would score all 12 marks.

CHAPTER 10 L'ENSEIGNEMENT SUPERIEUR, LA FORMATION ET L'EMPLOI

H LISTENING

Transcript

1

– Qu'est-ce que tu vas faire, Marika, l'année prochaine?

– Je ne sais pas encore exactement, mais si tout va bien, l'année prochaine, je serai en seconde au lycée.

– Tu vas prendre quelles options?

– Je choisirai probablement la filière maths-sciences.

– Oui, toi, tu es bonne en maths et en sciences. Moi, ce n'est pas mon fort!

– Qu'est-ce que tu vas faire alors, Léo?

– Je voudrais faire un bac lettres-langues.

– Pourquoi?

– Parce que ça m'intéresse, et aussi parce que je veux peut-être devenir journaliste, et les langues me seraient sûrement utiles.

– Tu voudrais voyager, alors?

– Oui, je voudrais aller aux Etats-Unis – pas pour travailler, mais pour perfectionner mon anglais. Toi, Vestine, tu voudrais rester en France pour travailler?

– Non, j'ai envie de rentrer en Guadeloupe après le bac.

– Et qu'est-ce que tu vas y faire?

– Mon oncle a un studio là-bas, et je voudrais travailler avec lui. Il est photographe, et moi aussi, je voudrais l'être. Et toi, Marika, tu as décidé d'un métier?

– Décidé, non. Mes parents veulent que je devienne médecin, mais je ne sais pas si ça m'intéresse vraiment. Et en plus, il faut être très doué, ce que je ne suis pas.

– Oh si!

– Non, mais je crois que je voudrais travailler dans un laboratoire.

Answers

1 V; **2** M; **3** (blank); **4** L; **5** V

Examiner's comments

1 This is quite hard, because each of the speakers mentions at least one specific job, and it's only by listening very closely that you can work out that only Vestine has made a real decision. Léo says "*je veux peut-être devenir journaliste*" and Marika says "*je crois que je voudrais travailler dans un laboratoire*".

2   This answer is a little easier to arrive at, but only if you know that the *bac* allows candidates to choose their specialism.

3   Marika explains carefully that it's her **parents** who want her to become a doctor.

4   You need to understand the colloquial expression M*oi, ce n'est pas mon fort* to work out that Léo isn't good at science.

5   You have to make the link between M*on oncle est photographe* and *moi aussi, je voudrais l'être*. This is not too hard if you have already eliminated **3**, but more difficult if you are still hesitating.

It is very useful, when doing this sort of exercise, to know that you are only going to use four of the five possibilities. If the question doesn't tell you that, the number of marks allocated to the particular question (here 4 marks) often will.

A Grade C candidate would find this exercise quite hard, and even a Grade B candidate might well score only three of the four marks.

Transcript

SPEAKING   H

2   **Teacher:** Alors, tu étudies quelles matières en ce moment?

      Student: Je fais maths, anglais, sciences, français, histoire et dessin.

      Teacher: Et laquelle préfères-tu?

      Student: Je préfère les maths et les sciences.

      Teacher: Pourquoi?

      Student: Je trouve ça intéressant.

      Teacher: Tu as eu de bonnes notes à tes examens?

      Student: Oui.

      Teacher: L'année prochaine, tu vas continuer tes études?

      Student: Oui, je vais retourner à l'école.

      Teacher: Et quelles matières vas-tu étudier?

      Student: La biologie, la chimie et les maths.

      Teacher: Et quel métier vas-tu faire plus tard?

      Student: Je ne comprends pas.

      Teacher: Qu'est-ce que tu vas faire comme travail?

      Student: Ah. Je ne sais pas.

Examiner's comments

This was an accurate, fairly competent conversation. The first question obviously invites a list, and the candidate did well to put it into a full sentence, with a verb in the present tense. Don't forget that to get a Grade C you need to refer to past, present and future, and to do that you need to use verbs. You should get into the habit of answering in a sentence whenever possible, as this almost forces you to use verbs.

However, the second answer could have been extended to include the reason, and this would have decreased the teacher's input. Your aim should be to try to say more than the teacher!

Try never to answer just O*ui* or N*on*. It's nearly always possible to go on to give an example, such as O*ui, surtout en chimie – j'ai eu dix-neuf sur vingt.* (In Britain, of course, we usually get marks out of a hundred, but the French system of marks out of twenty involves smaller numbers!)

These hints would transform a very ordinary Grade C performance into a B, or even an A.

Finally, all is not lost if you don't understand a question. If you let the teacher know, he or she will repeat or rephrase the question so that you can answer it. However, prompt response does count towards the marking, so you can't afford to do this too often. Make sure you learn as much vocabulary as possible – certainly everything in the syllabus – so that you're not caught out like this. You're not allowed to use your dictionary during the actual Speaking Test, so although it will help you in preparing the role-plays, it's no use in the conversation.

 **H READING**

Answers

3
1	les yeux	**5**	l'exploitation
2	minimes	**6**	famille
3	adultes	**7**	intellectuel
4	épouvantables	**8**	suffisant

Examiner's comments

This is a difficult passage, and the fact that many of the words in the list are familiar won't help unless you can follow the gist of the article. When using your dictionary in this sort of exercise, it is better to concentrate on making sure you understand the words in the list so that you can fit them in with the gist of the article, as you won't have time to check all the words in the article itself. However, make sure you understand the title, since it can be of enormous help with understanding the gist.

Do make sure that you use your grammatical knowledge to help. In this case there are enough 'extra' words to mean that you can't rely on this entirely, but it still helps you to avoid mistakes.

 **H WRITING**

EXAMINER'S COMMENTS

- This candidate has answered all the questions in the original letter, without producing a boring series of responses.

- The whole letter flows naturally, and the candidate has made use of material from the original letter without copying it – this is a very useful skill to develop. For example, she has changed *les examens sont finis* to *j'ai fini mes examens*, added *assez* to *avoir de bonnes notes*, and changed *comme mon père* to *comme mes parents. The stimulus letter in this kind of question will not only give you some useful phrases (though you need to adapt, not copy, otherwise you will get no credit for them) but also some ideas about what to say.*

- Particular good points about this letter are:
  - *Il y en a que j'ai trouvés très difficiles,* which makes the sentence more interesting
  - giving a reason for finding history difficult
  - *J'espère avoir* – infinitive constructions add variety
  - the use of the colloquial *J'ai de la chance, non?*
  - the use of a less common negative: *je n'ai aucune idée*
  - the use of *sauf que* and *je crois que* – *que* clauses always add interest

- A candidate who could write like this would clearly get A* in the exam.

4 Sample Student's Answer

> Chèr ...
>
> Moi aussi, j'ai fini mes examens. Il y en a que j'ai trouvés très difficiles – par exemple l'histoire, parce que notre prof d'histoire a été malade, alors on n'a pas eu beaucoup de temps pour faire les révisions. Mais à part l'histoire, et la physique, où je ne comprends rien, ils se sont bien passés, je crois. J'espère avoir d'assez bonnes notes, surtout en langues – je fais français et allemand – et en anglais.
>
> Mes parents, heureusement, sont très sympa – ils m'ont aidée beaucoup avec mes études, mais ils n'ont jamais essayé de me forcer. J'ai de la chance, non? Pour l'avenir, je ne sais pas. Je vais étudier les langues à l'université, mais après, je n'ai aucune idée – sauf que je ne veux pas être prof comme mes parents. Mais je crois que tu as raison – pour être comptable il faut aimer les maths, et moi, je préfère d'autres matières.

CHAPTER 11 LA PUBLICITE, LES COMMUNICATIONS ET LES LANGUES AU TRAVAIL

1

– Qu'est-ce que tu penses des pubs à la télé, Caroline?
– Quelquefois elles sont amusantes, mais c'est presque toujours des pubs pour la nourriture, et elles me donnent envie de manger.
– Mais elles ne t'énervent pas?
– Comment ça, Matthieu?
– Euh, il y a un bon film. Tu arrives à un moment vraiment passionnant, et toc. Une publicité pour un shampooing!
– Oui, tu as raison, Matthieu.
– Moi, il me semble que toute publicité est mauvaise.
– Tu ne peux pas dire ça, Elise.
– Si, parce que la publicité encourage les gens à dépenser trop d'argent, et à acheter des choses dont ils n'ont pas besoin.
– Oui, tu as raison, surtout quand c'est une pub pour des jouets. Les parents trouvent difficile de résister à leurs enfants. Qu'en penses-tu, Luc?
– Je trouve que les femmes sont souvent stéréotypées, surtout dans les pubs pour les produits ménagers. Mais je dois dire que quelquefois les pubs m'amusent plus que les émissions.

Answers

1 E   **2** M   **3** L   **4** C

Examiner's comments

Although what you hear is fairly straightforward, in that each person only expresses one opinion, there is some overlap in what they say, so you have to listen to the whole thing before you can make up your mind. For example, both Caroline and Luc say that adverts are sometimes amusing, but their basic opinions are quite different. Matthieu uses the word *mauvaise* but answer 3 clearly does not fit in with his views.

Answers

2   **1** a)   **2** c)   **3** a)   **4** b)

Examiner's comments

The first two questions simply rely on interpreting the statistics, and the fact that there are a lot of percentages should guide you to the right section of the article. You then simply have to match the ages with the words (eg *moins de 15 ans = enfants*).

Question 3 is harder, since it requires you to deduce the point of the advert. However, various references to racism clearly point you to answer **a)**.

In Question 4, you are again clearly guided to the right part of the article by the names which are the answers. You should know *sondage* but you may have needed to look up *prévu* (not easy, because first of all you have to realise that it's a past participle, then work out the infinitive (*prévoir*) in order to use your dictionary effectively. Then it should be clear that the only comment to do with the survey (*sondage*) was Jérôme's.

Although aimed at Grade C, this is a difficult Grade C question, and only the best C candidates would get all four marks.

F H SPEAKING

Transcript

3

Student: Allô.

Teacher: Je voudrais parler au directeur, s'il vous plaît. C'est de la part de Mme Dupuis.

Student: Le directeur n'est pas là en ce moment.

Teacher: Quand est-ce qu'il sera au bureau?

Student: Cet après-midi à trois heures.

Teacher: Oh, c'est dommage.

Student: Je peux vous aider?

Teacher: Il pourra me téléphoner ce soir?

Student: Quel est votre numéro de téléphone?

Teacher: C'est le zéro-trois, quarante-six, quatre-vingts, onze, cinquante et un.

Examiner's comments

Much of the difficulty here is that the candidate has to take the initiative. Usually, you would be the one asking to speak to someone, giving your phone number, and so on. However, in this particular area of 'language at work', you might well be asked to imagine that you are working in France. You need to learn simple telephone phrases such as those in this role-play.

You also need to prepare for the unpredictable question, and work out what it might be. Here, it was quite likely to be 'When will he be in?'. This candidate gave all the information required, and gained maximum marks.

H WRITING

EXAMINER'S COMMENTS

- This is an adequate answer, which because of its accuracy would certainly get a Grade C.

- The first three sentences are fine. However, in the next sentence, there is scope for a little more detail – the question does talk of jobs in the plural. Perhaps add something a little more relevant to the job, such as *Je travaille dans le café de mon cousin le samedi comme serveuse. Je l'aide aussi à préparer les repas.*

- The real problem area is asking the questions. Rather than asking two abrupt direct questions, it would be better (and more polite) to say: *Pourriez-vous me donner des détails sur le salaire et sur les heures de travail? Est-ce que j'aurai un jour de libre? Je commencerai à quelle heure, et je travaillerai jusqu'à quelle heure le soir? Est-ce que je serai payée par semaine, ou par mois?* Just some of these additions would make the letter more interesting, and allow a wider variety of structure and vocabulary. This would make a B, or even an A, possible.

4 *Sample Student's Answer*

> Monsieur,
>
> Je m'appelle Marie Martin. J'ai seize ans, et j'habite à Portsmouth, en Angleterre. Je voudrais être serveuse dans votre restaurant, parce que je veux travailler en France pendant les vacances. J'ai déjà fait du baby-sitting pour ma tante - elle a deux enfants, et j'ai préparé leurs repas. Je suis travailleuse, et je ne suis pas timide. J'étudie le français depuis cinq ans, et je veux le parler pendant les vacances. Quelles sont les heures de travail? Quel est le salaire? Je peux travailler du 2 au 28 août.
>
> Je vous prie d'agréer, monsieur, l'expression de mes sentiments distingués.

CHAPTER 12 LA VIE A L'ETRANGER, LE TOURISME, LES COUTUMES ET LE LOGEMENT

Transcript

1

– Qu'est-ce que tu aimes comme vacances, Nathalie?

– En principe, j'aime voir des choses différentes - j'adore aller à l'étranger, mais pas pour bronzer sur les plages espagnoles plutôt que françaises. Non, je préfère visiter les villes ou les villages typiques du pays, de préférence quand il n'y a pas beaucoup de touristes. Par exemple, l'année dernière, je suis allée en Allemagne passer quelques semaines chez des cousins. J'ai trouvé très intéressant de vivre comme une Allemande, et de voir comment la vie était différente là-bas.

– Et toi, Antoine, qu'est-ce que tu aimes faire en vacances?

– Ben, moi aussi, j'aimerais visiter différents pays, mais je ne suis pas comme Nathalie. C'est la vie qui m'intéresse, mais c'est la vie des bêtes. J'ai visité presque toutes les réserves naturelles françaises, mais je voudrais aller dans les grands parcs nationaux du Canada ou des Etats-Unis pour photographier les bêtes sauvages dans leur habitat.

– Et pour terminer, Sophie, quelles sont tes vacances idéales?

– Alors je ne suis pas comme les autres, car je travaille tellement pendant l'année qu'en vacances j'aime être très paresseuse. Je n'aime pas trop le soleil, alors un mois sur une plage ne me tente pas, mais je n'ai besoin que d'une petite cabane sans voisins, sans télévision ni téléphone, de la bonne nourriture (j'aime bien faire la cuisine) et tous les livres que je n'ai pas eu le temps de lire. Voilà mon rêve.

Answers

Nathalie: D; voir comment vivent les autres/vie de famille
Antoine: A; animaux/nature/jolies photos
Sophie: C; loin des autres/loin de la ville/tranquille/pas de téléphone, etc.

Examiner's comments

Although you can answer the questions by using words from the recording, it's not easy to get to the right words. Indeed, there is quite a lot of difficult language.

Nathalie uses quite a lot of familiar vocabulary, but she also uses a number of awkward negatives, and missing these could lead you in the wrong direction.

Antoine uses a lot of unfamiliar vocabulary, such as *parcs nationaux*, *réserves naturelles*, *bêtes sauvages* and *photographier*, though much of it is quite similar to English.

Sophie uses one or two more difficult words (*paresseuse*, *tenter*, *cabane*), and you would be misled if you didn't hear *sans*. Also, she throws in the 'red herring' of *la cuisine*.

Only quite careful listening, and a willingness to ignore unnecessary information, will enable you to get the gist of what is said. Once you've identified the appropriate destination, giving the reason is not too hard – but there is a lot to do in the course of only two hearings.

This is a Grade B question, but probably only a Grade A candidate would get all the answers right.

2 *Sample Student's Answer*

EXAMINER'S COMMENTS

- This is an A* answer, with lots of variety of tense and vocabulary, and a number of good expressions (je vous ai écrit; pour nous réserver; le lendemain [a very useful word in accounts – you can't really use demain in this situation, though you could have used dimanche of course]; à partir de).

- The candidate uses his/her imagination, and adds a comment about the weather based on the fact that a lot of time was spent on the beach.

- It is also good, in an account of this sort, to include some direct speech. Not only does this add variety, it also allows you to introduce present and future tenses in a piece of work which would otherwise be entirely in the past. This is important for gaining a Grade C or above, as is the inclusion of opinions and attitudes.

Nous sommes arrivés dans notre hôtel à six heures du soir, après un long voyage. Mon père est entré, et a donné son nom à la réceptionniste. "Je regrette, monsieur," a-t-elle dit, "mais je ne trouve pas votre réservation."

"Je vous ai écrit il y a trois mois," a répondu mon père. Mais elle n'a pas trouvé la réservation. Malheureusement, l'hôtel était complet, mais la réceptionniste était très gentille, et elle a dit "Je vais téléphoner à un autre hôtel pour vous réserver des chambres." Le problème, c'était que l'hôtel était à soixante kilomètres.

Enfin, vers huit heures, nous avons trouvé nos chambres. Nous étions tous très fatigués – les vacances avaient mal commencé. Alors, le lendemain, nous n'avons pas fait grand-chose. Nous nous sommes reposés à l'hôtel, qui était très bien.

Lundi, nous avons fait une excursion à un magnifique château, c'était parfait. A partir de mardi, il a commencé à faire très beau, alors nous avons passé nos journées sur la plage.

Quand nous sommes partis, samedi matin, nous étions tous bien bronzés. Le voyage s'est très bien passé, et nous sommes arrivés chez nous à cinq heures.

3 **Teacher:** Oui, monsieur, je peux vous aider?

Student: Oui. La douche dans ma chambre ne marche pas.

Teacher: Je suis désolé, monsieur. C'est quelle chambre?

Student: La chambre deux cent quarante-quatre.

Teacher: Alors j'enverrai un plombier demain matin.

Student: Mais j'ai besoin d'une douche maintenant.

Teacher: Voyons. Il y a une chambre avec salle de bains de libre au troisième étage.

Student: C'est plus cher?

Teacher: Non, monsieur, je vous l'offre au même prix.

Student: Merci. C'est quel numéro?

Examiner's comments

These Higher Level role-plays are tricky because there is so little you can predict. Here, you can predict your first utterance quite confidently, but from there on it is less clear. Will the receptionist be helpful? You don't know.

However, you can predict possible outcomes. If the receptionist is helpful, he or she might offer you another room, or the use of a shower, or to get it fixed. If not, you might have to threaten to go to another hotel. In your preparation time, you can work out roughly what you would say in these circumstances.

You should also look closely at the visual, if there is one. Usually, if it is there, it is to give you helpful information. This role-play didn't quite follow any of the predicted alternatives (they rarely do!) but you should perhaps have thought that the price of the room might be relevant in some way, as it is there in the visual. However, when you have prepared all the possibilities you can think of, you still need to be ready to think on your feet, to listen carefully to what the teacher says and to respond as promptly as possible. Did you prepare to say what the number of the room was? It was a fairly likely question!

Answers

4 1 vol/voyage + long OR coûteux

2 entrée gratuite (moins de 12 ans)

3 plus grand écran de France

4 encourager de nouveaux clients

5 trop cher/les prix

6 moins cher [1 mark]; plus français [1 mark]

Examiner's comments

The difficulty of the passage makes this a Higher Level question. However, the answers aren't too hard to find, and a Grade C candidate should do quite well. It is usually simply a question of finding the right words from the text and copying them, but you still have to get from the question to the right part of the article.

In handling a text like this, don't be tempted to look up all the words in the article that you don't know – you won't have time. The gist of the article is quite easy, so concentrate on that, and on understanding the questions. The hardest question is number 5, where you have to work out that when Isabelle says she can't go because her father's unemployed, and Christophe says that Parc Astérix is cheaper, they are agreeing with Fabienne that it's *très cher*.

CHAPTER 13 LE MONDE

Transcript

1 – Alors, aujourd'hui je vais discuter avec quatre jeunes des plus grands problèmes de nos jours. D'abord, Julien.

 – Moi, c'est le manque d'eau douce qui m'inquiète le plus.

– Comment ça, Julien?

– On dit que d'ici trente ans il n'y en aura pas assez.

– Non, je ne suis pas tout à fait d'accord.

– Salim?

– Le problème, c'est que l'eau n'est pas toujours au bon endroit. Elle est souvent loin des grandes villes et il est difficile de la transporter.

– Qu'est-ce que tu en penses, Karine?

– A mon avis, il faut faire quelque chose avant qu'il n'y ait un problème. Par exemple, on peut développer certaines techniques pour enlever le sel de l'eau de mer.

– Véronique, tu n'as rien dit jusqu'ici.

– Mais ce n'est pas que l'eau qui va peut-être manquer. C'est aussi la nourriture. Car si, comme prévu, la population du monde double en cinquante ans, il n'y aura pas de quoi manger pour tout le monde.

– Oui, mais ....

– Oui, Salim?

– Mais aussi, tous les autres problèmes sont la faute de l'homme – la déforestation, le réchauffement de la planète, la désertification. Alors, deux fois plus d'hommes, ça veut dire deux fois plus de problèmes.

– Karine, tu allais dire quelque chose?

– Je suis d'accord avec Salim. Hier, j'ai lu dans le journal que dans les écoles de Lyon, on a dû interdire toutes les activités de plein air à cause de la forte concentration de dioxyde de soufre dans l'air. C'est effrayant.

Answers

1 (blank); **2** J; **3** V; **4** K; **5** S; **6** K; **7** S

Examiner's comments

Any discussion of this topic is sure to be hard. It will often contain technical words, and though these often look similar to English words, the similarity is not so easy to spot when you are listening. In this conversation, there were *la déforestation, la désertification, le réchauffement de la planète, le dioxyde de soufre.* However, you often only need a vague idea of their meaning – and not necessarily of all of them. It's the gist of what people are saying which is important.

Another difficulty with this sort of question is keeping up with who says what. Even when, like here, each speaker is introduced by name, you need to really keep on your toes while you are listening. Indeed, it may be a good idea to try to jot down a provisional answer on the first hearing, so that you can use the second hearing to confirm your first impression, and to make changes where necessary.

One final general point about this kind of question. Before you listen, look carefully at the mark allocation. Here, there are six marks available, and seven boxes. This must mean that one of the boxes will be left blank. Also, you will clearly have to use some letters more than once.

This is one of the questions where you will find your dictionary invaluable, if your exam board allows you to use it before and after you listen. The sentences printed on the question paper are quite complex, so check any words you need to be sure that you understand them in detail. Then you can really concentrate while you are listening.

The topic alone makes this a Higher Level question. Because of the length of the item, it is at Grade A/B.

2 **Teacher:** Alors, vous allez me parler de la Belgique, n'est-ce pas? Pourquoi la Belgique?

Student: Je vais parler de la Belgique parce que j'y suis née. Mon père travaillait à Bruxelles. La Belgique est située au nord de la France, sur la mer du Nord. C'est un assez petit pays, avec dix millions d'habitants. En Belgique, il y a deux langues officielles; le français et le flamand (une langue qui ressemble au hollandais). A Bruxelles, où j'habitais moi, on parle les deux, car c'est la capitale, mais normalement la langue dépend de la région. Souvent, les gens qui parlent français et les gens qui parlent flamand ne s'aiment pas beaucoup.

Comme les Pays-Bas, la Belgique est un pays plat, alors on y voit beaucoup de bicyclettes. Quand j'étais petite, j'allais à l'école à bicyclette, comme tout le monde.

Je retourne en Belgique de temps en temps, car nous avons beaucoup d'amis là-bas, mais j'ai oublié tout mon flamand, car nous sommes revenus en Angleterre quand j'avais neuf ans.

J'étais contente de vivre à Bruxelles, mais je n'y retournerais pas pour travailler – je préférerais travailler en France.

Examiner's comments

A presentation is quite different from the other parts of the Speaking Test. You can prepare it in detail in advance, which makes it easier – and even if your teacher asks you questions about it, it's fairly easy to predict what they might be.

However, although you might actually have written the whole thing out, so that you can practise it, you should not attempt to read it. Your pronunciation will certainly suffer if you do. Once you have written your presentation and worked out timings – you should aim at 1 to 1½ minutes – try to make some cue cards which will remind you of what comes next. These should be just phrases, or even single words. Some people even think that visual cue cards are best, so that they don't interfere with pronunciation at all.

The other important thing is fluency. You will be expected to have thoroughly prepared, and so to deliver your presentation without too many hesitations. However, don't rush it. Take it at a smooth pace that you can cope with. If you try to go too fast, you will spoil your intonation and fall over your words.

Don't try to make your presentation too complicated, but bear in mind the requirements for Grade C, and make sure you put in a variety of tenses and some personal opinions, as well as some interesting vocabulary and some longer sentences.

Though the presentaion is only a small part of the Speaking Test in those boards which use it, this candidate is a clear Grade A.

Answers

3 Tick boxes 2, 3, 4 and 6.

Examiner's comments

As in the Listening, look at the mark allocation. Here, there are four marks available, so you know that four of the statements are true.

Also like the Listening, you should probably concentrate on getting the gist of the article, and use your dictionary to make sure that you understand all the statements. There is no word-for-word match between the article and the statements. Indeed, in this case, when a word does occur in a statement and in the article, the statement is not correct. You have to work at putting together *les sacs en plastique ne sont pas facilement biodégradables* and *les sacs en plastique peuvent mettre des centaines d'années à s'autodétruire*. This makes this question Grade A/B.

CHAPTER 14 **LISTENING AND RESPONDING**

TRANSCRIPTS OF RECORDINGS FOR CHECK YOURSELF EXERCISES

Check yourself 1

Q1 **a)** Le train part du quai numéro huit à dix heures vingt-trois. Alors, ça fait soixante-quinze francs, s'il vous plaît.
b) Bon. Je vous verrai demain à vingt heures trente.
c) Dis, il y a un match de foot cet après-midi au stade. On y va?
d) Mon anniversaire, c'est le vingt-neuf avril.
e) Rendez-vous mardi soir devant la mairie.

Q2 **a)** Je ne trouve pas ça très facile, et en plus le prof de maths n'est pas sympa. Alors, il faut le dire, il y a d'autres matières que je préfère.
b) Il n'a pas fait un temps splendide, mais j'étais avec des copains, alors on s'est bien amusé.
c) Pour mon anniversaire, mes parents m'ont acheté une veste en cuir. C'était très gentil, mais je préfère acheter mes vêtements moi-même, tu sais.
d) Ce matin, il n'y avait pas de car, alors j'ai dû venir au collège à pied. Ça fait seulement cinq kilomètres, mais je ne suis pas en forme.
e) Mon frère a peur des chiens, et il est allergique aux chats, alors nous n'avons pas d'animal à la maison. C'est bien dommage.

Check yourself 2

Q1 **a)** Ça fait quatre-vingt-neuf francs.
b) Trente-quatre francs soixante, s'il vous plaît.
c) Au collège, il y a mille trois cents élèves.
d) Le train arrive à seize heures quarante.
e) Mon frère est né en mille neuf cent soixante-treize.

Q2 **a)** Ils étaient tous très fatigués.
b) Tu entends cette musique?
c) Allez vous asseoir dans la salle d'attente.

Q3 **a)** 1) paix   2) paix   3) baie   4) paix
b) 1) moi   2) noix   3) noix   4) noix
c) 1) fend   2) fend   3) fend   4) vend
d) 1) tant   2) dans   3) tant   4) tant

Check yourself 3

Q1 **a)** Cet après-midi il y aura des averses partout dans la région, mais demain il fera beau. Notre prévision pour le week-end: la pluie va revenir!
b) – J'aime bien mon petit frère, tu sais, mais ses jeux sont toujours si bruyants. C'est difficile quand j'essaie de travailler.
– Moi, par contre, ma soeur aînée me critique tout le temps. Heureusement, dans deux mois elle part faire des études à l'université.
– Vous avez de la chance. Moi, j'ai deux frères et trois soeurs. Alors, impossible de prendre une douche sans faire la queue.
c) – Mes parents me donnent pas mal d'argent de poche, mais je dois acheter mes vêtements avec, alors il ne m'en reste pas beaucoup pour sortir.
– Moi aussi, je sors très peu, car mon père est au chômage. J'ai un petit job, mais je ne gagne pas assez pour aller au cinéma ou en discothèque.

– Moi, j'ai un salaire suffisant, mais je vais aller à l'université l'année prochaine, donc je dois faire des économies. Il n'est pas question de sortir tous les soirs.

Q2 a) L'école, c'est très important pour moi. Je veux réussir. Je ne trouve pas toujours ça facile, mais je fais des efforts.

b) Je voudrais bien trouver un petit emploi, mais … je ne sais pas … je ne suis pas très doué, et je ne sais jamais quoi dire.

c) Moi, je ne fais rien pour aider à la maison. Le week-end, je fais la grasse matinée jusqu'à onze heures, midi, puis je sors avec mes copains.

Check yourself 4

Q1 a) J'ai de la chance. Mon oncle est propriétaire d'un garage, et il m'a offert un emploi.

b) Si je fais des économies, dans deux ans, j'aurai ma propre voiture.

c) Oui, ce serait bien. Mais moi, je ne vais pas quitter l'école.

d) Mes parents sont tous les deux professeurs – mais moi, j'aurais horreur de ça!

Q2 a) Moi, tu sais que j'adore les sports nautiques, surtout la planche à voile.

b) On s'est bien amusé l'année dernière, hein? Et je me suis fait beaucoup d'amis au camping, qui seront encore tous là cette année.

c) Oh, moi, j'en ai marre d'aller toujours au même endroit. Cette année on va louer une villa à la campagne.

d) Ben moi, j'ai déjà décidé. Un camping ou une villa, pour moi, c'est pareil. Toujours la cuisine et la vaisselle. Cette année, on va à l'hôtel.

ANSWERS TO EXAM PRACTICE AND TRANSCRIPTS OF RECORDINGS

Transcript

1 Vous pouvez dîner entre sept heures et demie et neuf heures.

2 Avant de quitter l'hôtel, voulez-vous rendre la clé à la réception, s'il vous plaît.

3 Dans le nord, il y aura de la pluie un peu partout.

Dans l'ouest, la température maximale sera de treize degrés.

Dans l'est, il fera un temps ensoleillé.

Dans le sud, le vent soufflera jusqu'à quarante kilomètres-heure.

4 Moi, j'aime les vacances actives, tu sais, et puis j'habite pas loin des Alpes, alors je prends plutôt mes vacances l'hiver. Je n'aime pas trop voyager.

5 Ce soir à vingt et une heures trente sur la place du marché, grand cirque russe. Achetez vos billets jusqu'à quinze heures au syndicat d'initiative – adultes soixante francs, enfants quarante francs – ou à l'entrée – adultes soixante-quinze francs, enfants cinquante francs. Nous vous informons qu'aucun animal sauvage ne fait partie de ce cirque.

6 Allô. Est-ce que je peux laisser un message pour Mme Lucas, s'il vous plaît? Ici M. Dupond – D U P O N D. Pouvez-vous lui dire que je l'attendrai à l'office du tourisme à seize heures quinze? Merci.

7 – Tous les ans, on va au bord de la mer. J'adore les sports nautiques.
– Mais Jeanne, je croyais que ton frère ne savait pas nager.
– Oui, c'est vrai. Et alors?

– Mais qu'est-ce qu'il fait?
– Ben ... il me regarde, quoi!

– Oui, je voudrais bien partir en vacances avec toi, mais l'année prochaine je passe mon bac, alors je n'ai pas le temps de m'amuser.
– Mais Amélie, tu as bien le temps de prendre deux semaines de vacances, quand même.
– Euh ... non ... euh ... non vraiment, je ne crois pas.

8 Nous avons passé des vacances super. Nous avons trouvé un camping à deux cents mètres de la mer. C'était formidable.

9 – Hier soir, j'ai fait une boum chez moi.
– Et tes parents, qu'est-ce qu'ils ont dit?
– Ils sont allés voir ma grand-mère qui est malade.

10 Pour être médecin, il faut faire plusieurs années d'études, alors c'est ce que je vais faire, j'espère.

11 J'ai choisi la filière maths-sciences, parce que je ne suis pas forte en langues.

12 – On a eu pas mal de problèmes en vacances, tu sais?
– Comment ça?
– Ben, d'abord l'hôtel n'a pas trouvé ma réservation, alors ils nous ont donné une chambre au troisième et l'autre au cinquième. Mais en plus, l'ascenseur ne marchait pas. Je me suis plaint, naturellement, mais sans succès – et il n'était pas question de changer d'hôtel. Tous les hôtels de Nice étaient complets. Alors, nous sommes tous en forme maintenant, je t'assure.
– Alors, t'as pas passé de bonnes vacances?
– Oh si, quand même. Il a fait très beau, et le restaurant de l'hôtel était vraiment extra!

Answers

1 B

2 B

3 i) C; ii) A; iii) D; iv) F

4 C

5 A + C

6 ~~Dupuis~~ Dupond; ~~hôtel de ville~~ office du tourisme; ~~6h15~~ 16h15

7 égoïste J   sérieuse A

8 près de la mer/plage OR (à) 200m de la mer/plage

9 (allés) chez grand-mère/à la maison de grand-mère/allés visiter grand-mère.

10 Il veut/désire/va être médecin.

11 Elle est forte en maths OR Elle n'est pas forte dans les autres matières/en langues.

12 **a)** Hotel had lost booking + Rooms a long way apart/on different floors + lift not working (ANY TWO)
b) Hotel(s) full
c) Everyone got fit
d) (i) enjoyed it/had a good time
(ii) good food/restaurant + good weather

Examiner's comments

This is a little awkward, as you need to get both times right.

Again, all the alternatives mention the key, but you need to understand the link between the word *donner* heard on the CD, and the word *laisser* in B.

Once more, there are two tasks in one. You need to understand the points of the compass and the weather – which is not expressed in its simplest form.

4 Here you need to eliminate the possibilities as you hear extra information. For example, you can eliminate **D** when you hear *Je n'aime pas trop voyager*.

5 In quite a long utterance, it's not easy to keep both sets of prices in your head, and to pick out a very short word – *russe* – and link it with *étranger*.

6 The time could be difficult (*six/seize*).

A Grade C candidate would probably not have dropped any marks so far.

These are both quite hard gist items, with colloquial expressions, hesitations, etc. to make them more difficult. In addition, you never hear on the CD the words in the question, nor even single words which have the same meaning.

You need to be careful with your expression in French. *Sur la plage*, for example, would not be correct.

9 Again, *grand-mère* alone would not do; you have to be more precise.

A Grade B candidate would only have dropped one or possibly two marks so far.

10–11 You have to produce meaningful sentences which answer the questions – but minor spelling errors won't make any difference to the mark.

12 **a)** There are many different ways of expressing these ideas – it's the facts which matter, not the exact words used.

b) Like **a)**, these are fairly straightforward factual answers, but you have to identify them within quite a long conversation. However, the questions will almost always come in the same order that you hear the information – except of course when it's a gist question.

c) Here you have to make the link between the lift not working and the result.

d) (i) You have to connect the question with the answer (and understand *si* meaning 'yes' after a negative question) to get the answer.

(ii) Two more factual details, but there is some colloquial French (*extra*) to understand.

An A* candidate would probably score very close to full marks – say at least 22/23 out of 25.

CHAPTER 15   SPEAKING

TRANSCRIPTS OF RECORDINGS FOR CHECK YOURSELF EXERCISES

Check yourself 2

Q1   a) A quelle heure est-ce qu'on se retrouve?
   b) C'est pour quel jour?
   c) Quel est votre numéro de téléphone?
   d) C'est à quel nom?
   e) Où l'avez-vous perdue?

Check yourself 3

Q2   a) Vous avez déjà travaillé?
   b) Qu'est-ce-qu'il y a à faire dans la région?
   c) Où étiez-vous exactement?
   d) Tu as un petit job?
   e) Qu'est-ce qu'il aime, votre frère?

SAMPLE STUDENTS' ANSWERS TO EXAM PRACTICE AND TRANSCRIPTS OF RECORDINGS

ROLE-PLAYS

Transcript

1   **Teacher:** Oui, mademoiselle?
   Student: Je voudrais jouer au tennis.
   Teacher: Vous êtes combien?
   Student: Il y a quatre personnes.
   Teacher: Voilà, mademoiselle.
   Student: C'est combien?
   Teacher: Vous voulez jouer combien de temps?
   Student: Deux heures.
   Teacher: Alors, c'est trente francs par personne.

Examiner's comments

Although sometimes at this level it is possible to answer quite adequately with a single word (this candidate could have just said *quatre* in the second utterance), sometimes you have to use a sentence. *Tennis* alone would not have been enough to begin with, and to ask a question you almost always need to use a verb.

Transcript

2   **Student:** Bonjour, madame.
   Teacher: Bonjour, mademoiselle. Vous désirez?
   Student: Je voudrais un café et un croissant, s'il vous plaît.
   Teacher: Oui, mademoiselle.
   Student: Ça fait combien?

Teacher: Seize francs.
Student: Merci beaucoup.
Teacher: Merci, mademoiselle.
Student: Au revoir.

Examiner's comments

In this style of role-play, the greetings and saying thank you are part of the set tasks, and you would lose marks if you left them out.

Transcript

3

Teacher: Je peux vous aider?
Student: Je voudrais des pommes, s'il vous plaît.
Teacher: Vous en voulez combien?
Student: Un kilo.
Teacher: C'est tout?
Student: Je voudrais une bouteille d'eau minérale.
Teacher: Voilà.
Student: Donnez-moi trois paquets de chips.
Teacher: C'est tout?
Student: Oui. Ça fait combien?

Examiner's comments

Remember that polite phrases are expected. This candidate introduces a little variety by using *Donnez-moi*, though *Je voudrais* would do as well. Remember also that, especially when asking for the total cost of a number of items, it is usual to ask *Ça fait combien?*.

Transcript

4

Teacher: Salut, John.
Student: Bonjour.
Teacher: Que fais-tu le week-end?
Student: Je fais du cyclisme.
Teacher: Et le soir?
Student: Je regarde la télé.
Teacher: Tu écoutes des disques?
Student: Je n'aime pas la musique.
Teacher: Moi, je l'adore.
Student: Au revoir.

Examiner's comments

Although in answer to the question *Que fais-tu le week-end?* the answer *le cyclisme* would just about be adequate (though the sentence is better), the other replies do need a verb. Since you do not know exactly what the teacher's question is going to be, it is probably better to plan your answers in sentence form.

Transcript

5

Teacher: Bonjour, mademoiselle.
Student: Bonjour, monsieur. Je voudrais une serviette, s'il vous plaît.
Teacher: Oui, mademoiselle. De quelle couleur?
Student: Bleue.
Teacher: Vous la voulez en quelle taille?
Student: Je voudrais une grande, s'il vous plaît.
Student: Je voudrais aussi un T-shirt rouge, en quarante-deux.
Teacher: Voilà. Ça fait cent vingt-cinq francs.
Student: J'ai seulement un billet de cinq cents francs.
Teacher: Pas de problème, mademoiselle.

Examiner's comments

At Foundation/Higher level, you have more decisions to take. Although instruction 3 tells you to decide on the size of the towel, it does not tell you what size to choose. In addition, there is the unpredictable item – but quite often, you can predict two or three strong possibilities. Here, being asked to choose the colour of the towel was obviously one of the most likely. The problem at the end gave two possible ways of explaining. The candidate could equally have said *Je n'ai pas de monnaie*.

Transcript

6 **Teacher:** Oui, monsieur.

Student: Le train pour Nice part à quelle heure?

Teacher: A onze heures trente.

Student: Je voudrais un billet aller-retour, s'il vous plaît.

Teacher: Vous payez comment?

Student: J'ai une carte de crédit.

Teacher: Merci, monsieur.

Student: Le train part de quel quai?

Teacher: Du quai numéro huit.

Examiner's comments

This role-play indicates the importance of understanding the symbols which your exam board uses for certain common ideas. The question mark – which tells you that you should ask a question – is particularly important, as is the exclamation mark to indicate the unpredictable element. This particular one is perhaps not very predictable, but as long as you are listening carefully to the question, it is not too difficult.

Transcript

7 **Teacher:** Bonjour, mademoiselle.

Student: Bonjour, madame. Je voudrais une chambre pour une personne, s'il vous plaît.

Teacher: C'est pour combien de nuits?

Student: Pour une nuit.

Teacher: Bon, c'est la chambre numéro quinze.

Student: La chambre est à quel étage?

Teacher: Au premier.

Student: C'est combien avec petit déjeuner?

Teacher: Cent quatre-vingts francs, mademoiselle.

Examiner's comments

This role-play is quite tricky, because it requires two questions (which candidates often find hard) and quite a long sentence, but it is all familiar material, and the unpredictable element is not really very hard to guess.

Transcript

8 **Student:** Bonjour.

Teacher: Bonjour, Paul. Tu as un petit job en Angleterre?

Student: Oui, je travaille dans un supermarché après le collège.

Teacher: Quelles sont tes heures de travail?

Student: Je travaille de quatre heures à huit heures le soir.

Teacher: Et qu'est-ce que tu achètes avec l'argent?

Student: J'achète des vêtements.

Teacher: Tu gagnes combien?

Student: Je gagne soixante livres par semaine.

Teacher: Merci, Paul. Au revoir.

Student: Au revoir, monsieur.

Examiner's comments

This candidate answers quite fully. In fact, all his utterances could have been much shorter and still scored well. However, as was said earlier, it is probably best to prepare your replies in sentences. It was not hard to predict that the unknown question might be about how much the candidate earned.

Transcript

9

Teacher: Alors, qu'est-ce que tu as fait en Normandie?

Student: D'abord, nous sommes allés dans un petit bar pour prendre le petit déjeuner. Nous avons mangé des croissants, et moi, j'ai pris du chocolat chaud.

Teacher: C'était bon?

Student: Oui, c'était excellent. Après, puisqu'il faisait assez froid, nous avons fait des courses.

Teacher: Qu'est-ce que tu as acheté?

Student: J'ai acheté des souvenirs. Pour mon père, j'ai acheté des chocolats, et pour ma mère j'ai choisi du parfum.

Teacher: Elle l'a aimé?

Student: Oh oui, elle adore le parfum. J'ai aussi acheté des cadeaux pour mes amies. J'ai dépensé cent cinquante francs.

Teacher: Et qu'est-ce que tu as fait d'autre?

Student: Nous sommes allés à la cathédrale, et nous avons visité le musée.

Teacher: C'était intéressant?

Student: Non, je n'aime pas beaucoup les musées, alors j'ai trouvé ça un peu ennuyeux.

Teacher: Et l'après-midi?

Student: Nous sommes allés à la plage, où nous avons mangé un pique-nique, et nous avons joué au volley. Le soir, nous avons dîné au restaurant, puis nous sommes allés en discothèque. Nous nous sommes couchés très tard.

Teacher: Merci, c'était très intéressant.

Examiner's comments

This is a different sort of role-play, and most of the comments are equally appropriate to the Presentation or the General Conversation. This has to be a narrative in the past, and the candidate takes full advantage to include a variety of different kinds of past tense, using *être*, *avoir* and a reflexive verb. He adds in a lot of extra detail, but is careful to leave nothing out. He answers the teacher's questions well and without hesitation.

Transcript

10

Teacher: Bonjour, monsieur. Je peux vous aider?

Student: Bonjour. J'ai acheté cette radio ici.

Teacher: Ah oui? Il y a un problème?

Student: Elle ne marche pas.

Teacher: Vous l'avez achetée quand?

Student: Mardi matin.

Teacher: Vous avez le reçu?

Student: Oui, voilà.

Teacher: Alors, je peux la faire réparer.

Student: Ah non. Vous pouvez la remplacer?

Teacher: Je regrette, il n'y en a plus.

Student: Alors, je voudrais un remboursement, s'il vous plaît.

Teacher: D'accord, monsieur.

Examiner's comments

At Higher Level, you can't really begin to write yourself a script, because you don't know how the teacher is going to conduct his/her role. However, as here, you can often predict in some detail what your opening sentence is going to be in the given situation. One of the main difficulties is that you have to invent not just the French, but the basic information. You really do need to be on the ball to invent very quickly an appropriate answer to *Vous l'avez achetée quand?*. You also need to be prepared to negotiate the best deal for yourself – as long as you do it politely.

Transcript

11 **Teacher:** Vous parlez quelles langues, mademoiselle?

Student: Je parle anglais, français et un peu allemand.

Teacher: Vous avez des questions à me poser?

Student: Oui. Le salaire, c'est combien?

Teacher: Soixante francs de l'heure.

Student: Et quelles sont les heures de travail?

Teacher: Du mardi au vendredi de dix-huit heures à vingt heures, et le samedi matin de huit heures à midi.

Student: Et le travail commence quand?

Teacher: Le sept août. Nous avons besoin de quelqu'un du sept août au quinze septembre.

Student: Je ne peux pas travailler en septembre. Je rentre au collège le cinq.

Teacher: Ce n'est pas un problème.

Examiner's comments

The stress in the advert on *étrangers* and *européenne* should have warned you that there would be a question about languages spoken. The scene-setting tells you to ask about hours and how long the job is for, and this might suggest to you that the problem – and there is always some sort of problem at this level – might be in this last area, and encourage you to prepare accordingly.

PRESENTATION AND DISCUSSION

Transcript

Teacher: Alors, tu vas me parler de ta famille, n'est-ce pas?

Student: Oui. J'ai une assez grande famille. J'ai deux frères et une sœur, et j'ai aussi deux demi-frères, car mes parents sont divorcés, et mon père s'est remarié. J'habite avec ma mère et mes frères et sœur dans une petite maison. Mes frères partagent une chambre, et moi, je dois partager une chambre avec ma sœur. D'habitude, ça va, car nous nous entendons assez bien. Elle s'appelle Louise, et elle a deux ans de moins que moi. Nous nous parlons de tout – de l'école, des garçons, du cinéma, de la musique. Heureusement, nous avons les mêmes goûts – nous aimons les mêmes vêtements. Louise est assez grande pour son âge, alors elle m'emprunte mes robes, et moi, je fais pareil. Quelquefois c'est difficile, parce que j'ai des examens, et elle n'en a pas, mais normalement elle me laisse la chambre, et elle va écouter ses disques dans le salon. Après les examens, on va passer quinze jours ensemble à Londres, chez ma tante.

Mes frères, par contre, ne sont pas sympa. Ils ont onze ans – ce sont des jumeaux – et ils sont vraiment casse-pieds. Ils sont stupides et égoïstes. Quelquefois, ma mère doit nous séparer. La semaine dernière, par exemple, Tony a pris un de mes cahiers pour écrire une lettre. C'était mon cahier d'histoire, et j'avais un examen deux jours après. Heureusement, Louise l'a vu, et elle me l'a rendu.

Teacher: Tu t'entends bien avec ta mère?

Student: Oui. Elle est très sympa. Elle travaille dans une banque, et elle est souvent fatiguée, mais si j'ai un problème elle m'écoute toujours.

Teacher: Et ton père?

Student: Oh, ça va. Je vois mon père presque tous les week-ends, et on va au cinéma. Mais ma sœur, elle, ne s'entend pas du tout avec lui. Quelquefois elle refuse de venir avec moi quand je vais le voir.

Teacher: Merci.

Examiner's comments

The aims here are the same as in the General Conversation – for the candidate to show off a variety of structures, tenses and vocabulary. This candidate does exceptionally well. She speaks fluently and confidently, and has clearly thought about what she wanted to say, learned the vocabulary and phrases, and prepared the delivery thoroughly. She is careful to include a reference to the future and a number of past tenses, and her sentences are quite long and complex. Her vocabulary is wide – she even uses the colloquial *casse-pieds* to describe her brothers. When the teacher asks questions, her responses are full and prompt.

GENERAL CONVERSATION

Transcript

a) Teacher's questions:
- Où habites-tu?
- Qu'est-ce que tu as fait pour aider à la maison la semaine dernière?
- Parle-moi de ta chambre.
- Qu'est-ce que tu vas faire ce week-end?
- Quels sont tes loisirs?
- Qu'est-ce que tu as fait hier soir?
- Parle-moi de ton collège.
- Qu'est-ce que tu vas faire l'année prochaine?
- Tu as déjà choisi un métier?

b) Conversation

Teacher: Où habites-tu?

Student: J'habite à Portsmouth, dans le sud de l'Angleterre. J'habite dans une grande maison près du centre-ville. Il y a quatre chambres et un grand jardin. C'est une assez vieille maison, alors les pièces sont grandes, mais en hiver on a toujours froid, car on n'a pas le chauffage central.

Teacher: Qu'est-ce que tu as fait pour aider à la maison la semaine dernière?

Student: Samedi j'ai lavé la voiture de mon père. J'ai aussi fait un peu de jardinage. J'ai fait la vaisselle tous les jours, et mardi j'ai préparé le repas du soir, car ma mère est sortie. J'ai aussi rangé et nettoyé ma chambre.

Teacher: Parle-moi de ta chambre.

Student: Elle est assez petite. Il y a juste la place pour mon lit, une armoire, et la table où je fais mes devoirs. J'adore ma chambre. Les murs sont bleus, et les rideaux sont jaunes. Je l'ai décorée moi-même.

Teacher: Qu'est-ce que tu vas faire ce week-end?

Student: Samedi après-midi, je vais aller en ville avec mes copines. Nous allons faire des courses. Je vais m'acheter une jupe et peut-être un pull. Après, nous irons au café pour retrouver Paul et John, et le soir nous allons à une boum. Dimanche, je ferai la grasse matinée jusqu'à onze heures. L'après-midi, j'irai voir ma grand-mère, qui habite à la campagne.

Teacher: Quels sont tes loisirs?

Student: J'aime le sport – je joue souvent au tennis et au volley. J'adore aussi la lecture. Je préfère les romans policiers, mais je lis aussi des magazines. Mais ma passion, c'est la natation. Je vais à la piscine au moins deux fois par semaine, et en vacances, je passe tout mon temps à me baigner. Ce que je n'aime pas beaucoup, c'est regarder la télé. Je trouve ça ennuyeux.

Teacher: Qu'est-ce que tu as fait hier soir?

Student: Il y avait un film à la télé que je voulais voir, mais il n'était pas très bon, alors je me suis couchée de bonne heure.

Teacher: Parle-moi de ton collège.

Student: Il est grand. Il y a mille cent élèves et soixante profs. Ce n'est pas mal comme collège. Je trouve les cours assez intéressants, et les profs sont sympa. En plus, j'ai beaucoup d'amis au collège.

Teacher: Qu'est-ce que tu vas faire l'année prochaine?

Student: Je crois que je vais retourner au collège pour continuer mes études, mais ça dépend des résultats de mes examens. Si c'est possible, je voudrais étudier les sciences et les maths.

Teacher: Tu as déjà choisi un métier?

Student: Non. J'avais pensé devenir médecin, mais maintenant je ne sais plus. Je crois que je voudrais travailler dans l'informatique – mais on verra. D'abord, il faut réussir aux examens, puis je voudrais aller à l'université.

Examiner's comments

This is an example of what can be done. No one candidate ever (or anyway very rarely) performs like this, but a good candidate can produce some sections of this quality. It's not so much the individual bits which make it so good – you will find all the phrases and vocabulary in the first 13 chapters of this book – it's the way they're put together, and particularly the way the candidate never stops at the minimum answer, but always goes on to add extra details, give opinions and examples, and respond fluently and naturally. Of course, there is a wide variety of tenses and some complex structures such as *qui* and *que* clauses.

If you don't think you can sustain this sort of performance, don't worry. This candidate would have scored an A* with plenty to spare – what you should do is to make sure that at least one or two of your answers are of this sort of length and complexity. If you do that, you could be well on the way to an A* yourself!

CHAPTER 16 READING

1 B   [1]

Examiner's comments

If you had to, you could use a dictionary, though it shouldn't be necessary. *Gare routière* is, of course, a bus station.

 a) children [1 mark] from 3 to 13 [1 mark]   [2]
b) Mondays   [1]
c) touch (the animals)   [1]

Examiner's comments

Make sure you give all the information required. In **a)**, 'children' and the age-range are both important.

	Julie	Alexandre	Aurélie
Je suis fils/fille unique.		✔	
Je m'entends bien avec ma sœur.			✔
J'ai une assez grande famille.	✔		

Examiner's comments

When you have to compare a number of passages, as here, there is always rather more work to do, but it can be done fairly quickly. You can eliminate Julie and Aurélie from being only children, as they both mention brothers and/or sisters. If Alexandre is an only child, the second and third statements can't apply to him. Aurélie talks a lot about her sister, while Julie has three brothers and two sisters. You need to do this sort of calculation quite quickly at this stage.

4 Chambre E; Cuisine F; Salon B; Jardin A; Salle de bains C; Salle à manger D   [6]

Examiner's comments

Like Question 1, this is simply a vocabulary exercise, with words which you should know, and therefore it should not be necessary to use the dictionary.

5 **a)** mauvais
　　 b) contente
　　 c) dans un village
　　 d) bien dormir   [4]

Examiner's comments

It's useful to realise that there are four questions and four paragraphs.
a) is fairly clear, since Amélie makes three separate complaints about the journey.
b) too is quite clearly complimentary.
c) is a little more difficult, since traffic noise might lead you to think of a town, but *loin des autres maisons* combined with traffic noise can only fit *dans un village*.
d) Amélie is clearly more concerned with getting a good night's sleep than with going to the beach!

6 2 océan; 3 découvertes; 4 cuisines; 5 s'échapper; 6 sautant; 7 requins; 8 cachées   [7]

Examiner's comments

Don't forget to use your knowledge of grammar in this sort of exercise. 2, 4 and 7 have to be nouns (after the definite or indefinite article), while 3 and 8 must be past participles (after the auxiliary *a* or *sont*). After *à* the only possibility in the list is the infinitive *s'échapper*.

7 **a)** FAUX; **b)** VRAI; **c)** FAUX; **d)** VRAI   [4]

Examiner's comments

The second and fourth statements are quite tricky. The *depuis* in the passage is followed by *quatre ans*, which might lead you to FAUX, but in fact *depuis* with a period of time means 'for' and this is quite correct if you work it out. The fourth statement relies on putting together the last two sentences of the passage ('That's what he paints').

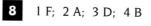

 8 1 F; 2 A; 3 D; 4 B [4]

Examiner's comments

To begin with the easy options, only E and F could follow 1, and *Europe* is too limited for what Martine says. Number 4 can't logically be followed by an infinitive, which leaves B as the best answer, since C is not true. You can then start to work out answers for 2 and 3 – not too hard when you've eliminated some of the possibilities already.

9 1 D; 2 F; 3 A; 4 C; 5 G; 6 E; 7 B [4]

Examiner's comments

It is helpful here that every third answer is given as an example, so it is less likely that one error will lead to a number of others. It's just a question of looking at number 1, and working out which is the only possibility for number 2, and so on. The important thing is to approach this sort of item in a cool manner, and take it step by step.

10 1 Olivier; 2 Sandrine; 3 Tiphaine; 4 Sandrine [4]

Examiner's comments

Don't forget, these questions all relate to what the people actually say. Make sure you understand the questions first, then go through the text until you find someone who definitely fits.

11   **a)** They have become illegal/they have had to hide [1]
    b) The police used force/tear-gas [1]
    c) People are afraid/
        People think immigrants cause unemployment/
        People think immigrants are responsible for street violence
          ANY ONE [1]
    d) Immigrants are the victims/
        Immigrants suffer most from unemployment/
        Immigrants suffer most from street violence
          ANY ONE [1]
    e) Sympathetic to (problems of) immigrants [1]

Examiner's comments

Each of these questions requires you to understand the gist of a section of the article. Once you have decided where to look for the answer, the task becomes quite a lot easier. Remember, you are really being asked for a summary here, so you need to do more than just translate one or two details. In addition, the last question requires you to give an impression of the overall tone of the whole passage, not just to concentrate on one paragraph.

[Total: 46 marks]

A Grade A candidate would gain most of the marks on this paper. A Grade C candidate would gain most of the marks on questions 1 to 6, with a few others from questions 7 to 11.

CHAPTER 17 WRITING

Questions 1–6 are Foundation Level tasks, and are aimed at Grades E, F, G. To get a Grade E, candidates need to complete all or almost all the tasks in a way which would communicate the ideas to a sympathetic native speaker who knows no English.

▌ *Sample Student's Answer*

1	crème solaire
2	sandales
3	shorts
4	maillot de bain
5	t-shirts
6	matelas pneumatique
7	ballon
8	tente
9	lampe électrique
10	livres

EXAMINER'S COMMENTS

● *These lists are simply vocabulary exercises, but the more you can do at this early stage without your dictionary, the less time it will take. However, don't be tempted to put down any 10 words – they have to fit with the instruction, in this case things that you would want to take on a holiday to France. You will find that if you can put yourself into a precise situation, ideas will come more easily. Here, once you think of a camping holiday, the possibilities are almost endless.*

▌ *Sample Student's Answer*

8h30	aller à l'école
12h	prendre le déjeuner
16h	rentrer à la maison
19h	regarder la télé
22h30	se coucher

EXAMINER'S COMMENTS

● *Look carefully at the example. It will tell you roughly how much you are expected to write. In this case, it will also tell you (as does the word* activités *in the instruction) that you will need at least some verbs, if only in the infinitive. This student has chosen to answer entirely with verbs, but he/she could have put simply* déjeuner *for the second answer (this is in fact a verb [to have lunch] as well as a noun, anyway), or* au lit *for the last answer, and still scored the marks.*

▌ *Sample Student's Answer*

Je suis au Barcarès, dans le sud de la France.
On est dans un camping.
Il pleut et il fait du vent.
On va au cinéma et à la piscine.
Je rentre en Angleterre le 15 août.

EXAMINER'S COMMENTS

● *This sort of question limits your choice about what to say, since if in the first part you put* Le Barcarès *in the wrong part of France, or if in the third part you had the weather as hot and sunny, you would not get the marks.*

● *If you are asked to write a postcard or a letter, remember that, even when you are answering questions, you need to write complete sentences to score full marks. What you write has to be understandable to someone who hasn't got the original questions available.*

EXAMINER'S COMMENTS

- Clearly, a candidate would only choose one of the three possibilities in each case, and since the illustrations are only examples he/she might easily choose a different one – for example, if the word for 'German' escapes you in the exam, you could put espagnol or any other school subject.

- The beginnings of the sentences don't leave much room for alteration, but even at this early stage, there is no reason not to introduce a bit of variety, as this candidate does, by using Elle instead of repeating L'école at the start of the third sentence.

4 Sample Student's Answer

Je vais dans une école	de garçons	de filles	mixte.
Mon école est	grande	de taille moyenne	petite.
Elle est	en ville	à la campagne	au bord de la mer.
Je vais à l'école	en autobus	en voiture	à pied.
Je préfère	la géographie	les sciences	l'allemand.

EXAMINER'S COMMENTS

- In this sort of question, it can be hard to keep down to the required number of words, especially if you have been concentrating on trying to add detail and variety to your writing. This answer, although over the 'limit', is fine but don't get carried away, because the timing of the test assumes you are writing more or less the recommended number of words. If you write too many more, you are taking time away from later questions which do need more words, and therefore more time. This would still score full marks without et jouer du violon and une ville touristique.

5 Sample Student's Answer

J'ai un frère qui s'appelle Peter. J'aime lire et jouer du violon. J'habite à York, une ville touristique dans le nord de L'Angleterre. Je n'aime pas l'école. L'année dernière, j'ai passé deux semaines à Nice, dans le sud de la France.

6 *Sample Student's Answer*

Lundi Matin: Excursion	*Nous allons au musée du château.*
Mardi Matin:	*On va en ville pour faire des courses.*
Après-midi:	*On peut aller à la piscine s'il fait beau.*
Soir: grands-parents	*Je vais chez mes grands-parents*
Mercredi Matin: Départ en vacances	*Nous partons au bord de la mer.*

EXAMINER'S COMMENTS

● *This task does not actually require full sentence answers. However, if you left out the verbs and wrote your answer in note form (au musée du château, etc.), you would need to add some extra detail to get up to the 30 words suggested.*

● *This sort of task tends to encourage repetition – for example, all the verbs could easily come out as nous allons. This candidate has avoided repetition quite cleverly, by using different parts of the verb aller, and by replacing it in the last sentence by partir.*

Questions 7 – 11 are Foundation/Higher tasks, and are aimed at Grades D and C.

7 *Sample Student's Answer*

Cher Rachid,

Moi aussi, j'ai un emploi. Je travaille dans un supermarché le vendredi soir, de six heures à neuf heures, et le dimanche de huit heures à cinq heures. Je n'aime pas le travail, car c'est ennuyeux, mais je gagne 40 livres par semaine!

Avec l'argent, j'achète des vêtements et des livres, car j'adore lire. Mais mon passe-temps préféré, c'est le cyclisme.

A' l'école, j'aime l'histoire et la géographie.

Qu'est-ce que tu aimes comme musique?

A bientôt

EXAMINER'S COMMENTS

● *This is a competent piece of work. It is accurate, and it answers all the tasks. It goes beyond the minimum in a number of ways, most of them quite simple. In the first paragraph aussi, and the use of car and mais are refinements which would be expected at Grade C. The use of car again in the second paragraph would obviously not gain as much credit.*

● *However, this piece of work would not get more than a Grade D, in spite of some good points and its excellent accuracy, because it does not contain any references to past or future events.*

● *The addition of a past (e.g. Le week-end dernier je suis allé(e) à la campagne à vélo avec mes copines at the end of the second paragraph) and a future (e.g. Est-ce que tu vas jouer de la guitare dans un groupe? at the end of the last paragraph) would immediately make this a Grade C answer. Avoiding some of the repetitions would also help; you could add après l'école instead of the times after vendredi soir, and you could change one car to parce que.*

- Because it is very accurate, and it contains references to past, present and future, this piece of work is of Grade C standard. A candidate entered for Foundation Level, where this would be the last question, could feel well pleased with it.

- However, there are few signs that this is the work of a Grade A/B candidate, and improvements could be made in a number of areas:
  - The first paragraph is good. There is a variety of structure (Moi, ... je fais; je dois nettoyer; j'ai préparé, and it is a full answer to the first task.
  - The next section does not flow quite as well. Perhaps it needs something to indicate why it's unfair (e.g. ... et mes parents ne disent rien; ... mais si je veux regarder l'athlétisme, je ne peux pas). It would also add interest to explain why the brother's age is mentioned (e.g. Mais il a dix-huit ans, alors c'est normal qu'il rentre plus tard.). Adding comme d'habitude after minuit would also make better sense with the future tense.

  The last paragraph is a little thin. Don't forget this is the third task, not just an extra detail, and the piece does not yet have much expression of personal opinion. You could continue: C'est plus facile pour tout le monde (surtout la mère) si on partage les tâches, et tout le monde aura besoin de faire le ménage plus tard dans la vie.

8 Sample Student's Answer

> Moi, à la maison, je fais la vaisselle, et j'aide aussi mon père dans le jardin.
> Le week-end, je dois nettoyer ma chambre.
> Vendredi dernier, j'ai préparé le repas du soir.
> Mais mon frère ne fait rien à la maison.
> Je suis d'accord avec Nathalie : ce n'est pas juste. Sa chambre est toujours en désordre.
> Le soir, s'il y a du football à la télé, on le regarde. Je déteste le football. Moi, je dois rentrer avant onze heures le soir, mais lui, samedi soir il va rentrer à minuit. Il a dix-huit ans.
> Je pense que les garçons comme les filles doivent aider leurs parents à la maison.

- There are few opportunities in this task for developing ideas, but the candidate does add bits beyond the minimum response to the question where possible, by adding an explanation in the second paragraph and extra details in the others.

- Don't forget, if the number of words you should write is printed on the paper, it is to help you, and though you don't need to keep an exact word count, you probably won't get a good mark for a question in which you fall much short of this number.

- There is not much chance for a really good candidate to shine here, but there is reference to past, present and future, and a personal opinion, so it is of Grade C standard.

9 Sample Student's Answer

> Monsieur
> Je m'appelle   , j'ai seize ans, et je suis anglais(e).
> Je peux travailler du 15 juillet au 4 septembre. Je dois rentrer en Angleterre, car les cours commencent le 7 septembre.
> J'ai travaillé dans un magasin pendant les vacances l'année dernière, et maintenant je travaille dans un café.
> J'aime le foot et la natation, j'adore faire la cuisine.
> Est-ce que je travaillerais le soir, ou à midi aussi ?

10 *Sample Student's Answer*

Cher Sébastien

Hier, vendredi, j'ai passé une journée formidable.
Après le collège, je suis allé au café pour rencontrer mes
copains. Puis, à huit heures moins le quart, nous sommes
allés au cinéma pour voir le dernier film de James
Bond, qui était super.

Après le film, je suis allé chez Laura, car c'était
son anniversaire. Nous avons dansé toute la nuit,
jusqu'à une heure et demie. Cool, non?

● Demain, je vais faire la grasse matinée, parce que
je suis tellement fatigué!

EXAMINER'S COMMENTS

- This piece of work does all that could be expected in so few words. It gives full accounts of the activities (including past and future references), and it gives the writer's impressions, which are specifically required by the question — formidable; super; cool. It also includes a variety of structures (pour rencontrer; qui était; car; parce que) and expressions (passer une journée; le dernier film; toute la nuit; faire la grasse matinée).

- In itself, this piece of work is worth a Grade C, but it shows clear indications of ability to go beyond that level.

11 *Sample Student's Answer*

Le matin, je ne me lève pas avant onze heures.
Je prends le petit déjeuner au lit, et puis je
prends une douche. A midi, je vais en ville
dans ma Ferrari rouge, et je mange dans le
meilleur restaurant. Je passe l'après-midi
à faire les magasins. Tous les soirs, je vais à
une boum, ou au cinéma, avec mon petit
copain, et le week-end on va à Paris. Je
collectionne tous les CD de mes chanteurs
préférés, et j'achète tous les vêtements que
je veux – la semaine dernière j'ai dépensé
cinq mille livres!

Il y a un mois, j'ai gagné à la loterie
nationale, mais maintenant, je m'ennuie.
Je voudrais retourner à ma vie normale.

EXAMINER'S COMMENTS

- This sort of task can be rather difficult to handle. Before you begin, you need to decide how you are going to approach it. Are you going to write 'If I was rich I would ...' all the time? After 100 words it can seem a bit clumsy. Or are you going to write a straightforward account as if you were already rich? This works fine, but it can be hard to get in a variety of tenses. One good way might be to write in the past about what you did last week (with a sentence or two about what you will do next week).

- This candidate took a different approach, writing in the present, but making sure he/she got in a past and a future reference. It fulfils all the tasks, and gets in a fair variety of structures (e.g. Je ne me lève pas avant).

Questions 12–15 are Higher Level tasks, and are aimed at Grades B, A and A*. To get these grades, candidates must produce work which is generally accurate in spelling and grammar and in which they express opinions and justify points of view in longer sentences, using a range of vocabulary and structures, including time references.

EXAMINER'S COMMENTS

- To get the best marks at this level, you have to demonstrate a variety of language, even within a fairly small number of words. Although you could write more, you may not have time. This candidate is clearly aware of the need to include as much as possible:
  - There is a regular procession of 'good' phrases: assez tôt; après avoir; ce que nous avons fait; pour nous baigner; il a commencé à pleuvoir; avant d'arriver; complètement; toutes les deux; ne … jamais plus; on risque de … .
  - All the sentences are quite complex, either with two parts or with added details.
  - There is a variety of tenses – past, present (on risque de) and future (Nous ne ferons). The past participles are made feminine where appropriate.

- This would certainly be an A*.

12 Sample Student's Answer

Le week-end dernier, ma copine Laura et moi, nous sommes allées faire du camping près de Windermere, dans la région des lacs dans le nord de l'Angleterre. Nous sommes parties à vélo assez tôt samedi matin, et nous sommes arrivées au camping vers midi.

Après avoir dressé la tente, ce que nous avons fait très vite, nous avons préparé le déjeuner, puis nous sommes descendues au lac pour nous baigner. Mais après une demi-heure, il a commencé à pleuvoir. Avant d'arriver à la tente, nous étions complètement trempées.

La pluie a continué toute la nuit, et nous sommes rentrées dimanche matin. Nous étions toutes les deux enrhumées. Nous ne ferons jamais plus de camping au mois de mai — certainement pas en Angleterre – on risque d'être malade.

EXAMINER'S COMMENTS

- This is another A* piece of work. Don't be depressed if you think 'I could never write like that'. The point is that, although you might not be able to sustain it for 150 words, you are quite capable of producing some of the good things in this piece of work, as long as you know what is needed. Often, the difficulty at this level is not so much the language, it's having the imagination to know what to say, and the confidence to use the French that you know.

- There is no need to think out in English what you want to say – there is nothing in this piece of work which you have not learnt in Chapters 1 to 13.

- These sample answers should provide you with some ideas for introducing different tenses into what you write, and using a variety of language. Using the words underlined should ensure that your sentences are sufficiently long and complex.

13 Sample Student's Answer

Quand j'étais en troisième, j'ai passé un mois dans une famille française. Ils habitaient près de Perpignan, dans le sud-est de la France. Leur maison était très grande, alors j'avais ma propre chambre. Il y avait deux enfants, une petite fille de douze ans, et un garçon de mon âge. Ils étaient tous très sympa, et j'adore la cuisine française, alors c'était très bien.

Il n'y avait personne dans la famille qui parlait anglais, alors j'ai dû parler français tout le temps. A la fin du mois, donc, je parlais très bien le français, mais j'ai trouvé ça fatigant, quand même. Le meilleur moment, ça a été quand ils ont invité tous leurs amis à une boum pour me dire au revoir.

Je ne pense pas que je voudrais passer un mois en Allemagne – c'est trop long, et je ne parle pas bien allemand.

14 *Sample Students' Answers*

Le week-end dernier j'ai visité Paris. J'ai pris le train, et je suis arrivée à dix heures. Le train a traversé la mer par le tunnel. C'était très rapide. J'ai mangé au restaurant. J'ai pris du potage aux légumes, du poulet avec frites et une tarte aux pommes. C'était délicieux. J'ai rencontré des amis au restaurant. Après le déjeuner, nous avons fait une promenade en bateau sur la rivière. C'était très intéressant. Nous avons vu la cathédrale de Notre Dame. Elle est très belle. Nous avons vu aussi la Tour Eiffel.

Le week-end dernier, je suis allée à Paris avec des copains. Nous avons pris l'Eurostar à la gare de Waterloo, à Londres. C'était la première fois que je prenais le tunnel sous la Manche, et j'avais un peu peur. Mais le voyage a passé très vite, et nous sommes arrivés à Paris vers dix heures.

Nous avons trouvé notre hôtel, et nous y avons laissé nos bagages. Nous avons pris un sandwich à la terrasse d'un café. L'après midi, nous avons vu l'Arc de Triomphe et nous sommes montés au sommet de la Tour Eiffel- La vue est vraiment impressionnante!

Le soir, nous avons mangé à l'hôtel. Le repas était excellent, mais très cher. Après le dîner, nous nous sommes promenés dans les rues de Paris.

Dimanche matin, nous avons visité la cathédrale de Notre Dame, et après, nous avons fait une promenade sur la Seine en bateau-mouche. C'était très bien de voir Paris de l'eau.

J'ai passé un week-end formidable, et je retournerai certainement à Paris un jour.

EXAMINER'S COMMENTS

● First, the good points. This is a very accurate piece of work, which contains a variety of verbs (perfect, imperfect and present tenses), and which expresses an opinion for almost every fact. However, there is no flow. The sentences are not always very short, but they are all simple, almost basic. There is no Higher Level vocabulary, and the opinions are tacked on at the end, almost as afterthoughts. It has clearly been written on the basis of 'What can I say about this picture?', with little attempt to impose a story-line on what is written.

● Although its accuracy is of Grade A standard, it has neither the variety, the complexity nor the length (it is not much more than half the recommended length, though it does superficially cover all the tasks) to merit more than a Grade C, and without a reference to the future, it is probably only worth a D.

● Compare it with the next account, which maintains the accuracy of the first but combines it with a real story, with more complex sentences, a much wider vocabulary, and that all-important range of tenses. Again, you might not think you are capable of writing the second piece, but you can certainly take some of the good things from it to improve on the bare bones of the original account. The underlined phrases show how it is possible to add to an account, and the use of vocabulary specific to Paris (Arc de Triomphe; bateau-mouche; Seine) is quite impressive, since it could probably not have come from a dictionary.

243

15 *Sample Student's Answer*

- This piece demonstrates yet again what is possible within the structures and vocabulary contained in Chapters 1 to 13. This candidate has clearly begun by working out the overall shape of his account – in other words what he wanted to say. Once you have done that, you can weave in the vocabulary and structures you know to fill out your account.

- One final piece of advice. The Foundation and Foundation/Higher tasks are rarely open-ended. In other words, you are told fairly precisely what you are to say – though you may have to supply out of your head simple things like the name of a job, or your favourite hobby/school subject. However, if the Higher task is open-ended – so that you have to invent almost the whole situation and the shape of your account yourself – you need to get into the habit of doing this fairly quickly. You can't afford the time to agonise for too long about the sort of job you are going to pretend you've done. When you've decided on the outline, sketch it out with a few phrases and vocabulary items (in French, of course) before you start to write.

L'année dernière, j'ai travaillé dans un complexe sportif pendant l'été. Je travaillais du lundi au vendredi, de sept heures et demie à six heures, et le samedi ou le dimanche. J'ai choisi cet emploi parce que je suis très sportif, j'aime surtout la natation. J'ai donc pensé que je pourrais aider les autres jeunes, et pratiquer mon sport favori en même temps.

Mais malheureusement, je voyais seulement la piscine à la fin de la journée, pour la nettoyer. Le directeur m'a donné plusieurs tâches. J'ai dû travailler à la caisse. J'ai été serveur au bar. J'ai été vraiment déçu, mais j'ai gagné un peu d'argent.

Après l'école, je voudrais trouver un emploi dans le sport – mais je ne veux pas travailler dans un complexe sportif. J'ai l'intention de devenir professeur de gymnastique.

Published by HarperCollins*Publishers* Ltd
77–85 Fulham Palace Road
London W6 8JB

www.**Collins**Education.com
On-line support for schools and colleges

ISBN 0 00 711200 9

British Library Cataloguing in Publication Data

A catalogue record for this book is available from the British Library.

Edited by Sue Chapple

Production by Kathryn Botterill

Language consultant: Marie-Thérèse Bougard

Cover design by Susi Martin-Taylor

Book design by Rupert Purcell and produced by Gecko Limited

Printed and bound by Scotprint

Acknowledgements
The Author and Publishers are grateful to the following for permission to reproduce copyright material: Mon Quotidien: pp. 72, 86, 148

Photographs
Tim Booth: 4, 23, 57, 69, 88, 98; Rex Features: 84 (bottom); Telegraph Colour Library: 36, 76, 84 (top), 96; Travel Ink: 52, 90.

Illustrations
Kath Baxendale; Richard Deverell; Hilary Evans; Gecko Ltd; Sarah Jowsey; Dave Poole; Nick Ward.

Every effort has been made to contact the holders of copyright material, but if any have been inadvertently overlooked, the Publishers will be pleased to make the necessary arrangements at the first opportunity.

Audio CD
The audio CD was recorded at Post Sound Studios, London and was produced by the Language Production Company with the voices of Jérôme Ambroggi, Laetitia Ambroggi, Jean-Pierre Blanchard, Juliet Dante, Alexandre Pageon, Katherine Pageon, Sarah Sherborne.

Production by Marie-Thérèse Bougard and Charlie Waygood.

Music by Nigel Martinez and Dick Walter.

You might also like to visit:
www.**fire**and**water**.com
The book lover's website

INDEX

accommodation 88–92, 219–21
accounts (type of writing), in Writing Test 157
adjectives 29, 168–9
    comparative 53, 173
    demonstrative 84, 169
    indefinite 99, 171
    possessive 170
    superlative 83–4, 174
adverbs 61, 172–3
    comparative 53, 173–4
    indefinite 99, 171
    superlative 84, 174
advertisements, in Reading Test 145
advertising 81–7, 217–18
air transport 65
animals 27
announcements 112
annual holidays 34
articles (grammar) 22, 168
articles (type of writing), in Writing Test 156–7

body, parts of the human body 19
breakdowns, transport 67

camping 88
car breakdowns 67
ce qui/ce que 46
chemist 21
cinema 42
clothes 58
commands 5, 189
communication 81–7, 217–18
comparison (grammar) 53, 173–4
complaints 21
conditional perfect tense 188
conditional tense 54, 187
conjunctions 4, 180–1
consonants, pronunciation 107, 119, 120
containers 61
conversation, general, in Speaking Test 127, 133
cooking methods 21
counting 60–1
countries 96
    flags 27
    Great Britain 57
countryside, features 50
crockery 18
cue–cards 126
customs 88–92, 219–21
cutlery 18

dates 4
    annual holidays 34
    numbers 61
definite articles 22, 168
demonstrative adjectives 84, 169
demonstrative pronouns 84, 170

depuis 5
dialogues 112
dictionary, using 135–6, 153–4
directions 65
dishes 19
dress 58
driving 67

education
    further education 74–80, 214–16
    school 1–8
emphatic pronouns 46, 175–6
employment 74–80, 214–16
en (pronoun) 45, 175
energy sources 98
entertainment 34–41, 81, 202–4
environment 98
er verbs 13, 191–3
excursions 90
eye colour 27

family 26–33, 200–2
    members 26
farm animals 50
ferries 65
films 42
finding the way 65–80, 212–14
fitness 18–25, 198–9
flags, national 27
food 18–25, 198–9
foreign countries, life in 88–92, 219–21
free time 34–41, 202–4
friends 26–33, 200–2
furniture 11
further education 74–80, 214–16
future perfect tense 187
future tense 53, 186–7

games 34
getting around 65–80, 212–14
greetings 42

hairstyles 26
health 18–25, 198–9
higher level, Speaking Test 123, 124
his/her (personal pronouns) 29
holidays 34–41, 202–4
home life 10–17, 195–7
home town 50–6, 206–9
hotel 90
housework 10
how long for 5
human body 19

imperative 5, 189
imperfect tense 91, 185
impersonal verbs 184
indefinite adjectives, adverbs and pronouns 99, 171–2
indefinite articles 22, 168
infinitive (verbs) 37, 190–1

intensifiers 172–3
interrogatives 68–9, 181
introductions 42
ir verbs 13, 193
irregular verbs 182–4
    common 14
    er verbs 13
    future tense 53

jobs 74–80, 214–16
    languages at work 81–7, 217–8

language patterns 108
languages 96
    at work 81–7, 217–8
leisure 34–41, 81, 202–4
lessons 2
letters
    in Reading Test 145
    in Writing Test 156
letters of the alphabet, pronunciation
    see pronunciation
life abroad 88–92, 219–21
local environment 50–6, 206–9
lui/leur pronouns 174

magazines, in Reading Test 145
materials 60
meals 10, 19
measurement 61
media 10–17, 195–7
meetings 42–50, 204–6
menus 19
monologues 112
months 1
motorways 67
multiple-choice questions 112–13, 142–3
my/your (personal pronouns) 29

nationalities 27
negatives 76–7, 107, 189–90
newspapers, in Reading Test 145
notices, in Reading Test 145
nouns 21–2, 167
numbers 60–1, 107, 176–7

object pronouns 45, 174–5
offices 83
opinions 12, 43

parts of the body 19
passive 77, 189
past historic tense 92, 188
past participle 38
past tenses 37–9, 91–2
percentages 60
perfect tense 37–9, 185–6
personal characteristics 83
personal relationships 42–50, 204–6
pluperfect tense 91–2, 187

246

possessive adjectives 170
possessive pronouns 170–1
prepositions 5, 179–80
present participle 23, 190
present tense 13–14, 181–4
prices 34
pronouns 44–6, 174–6
    demonstrative 84, 170
    indefinite 99, 171–2
    order of 46, 175
    personal 29
    positioning 46, 175
    possessive 170–1
    relative 99, 177
pronunciation
    consonants 107, 119, 120
    language patterns 108
    in Speaking Test 119–20
    vowels 119
public services 57–64, 209–11

quantity 61, 177–8
questions, asking 68–9, 181
qui/que (pronoun) 46

radio 12
re verbs 13, 193
recipes 90
recorded messages 112
reductions in shops 59
reflexive verbs 14, 39
relationships with other people 42
relative pronouns 99, 176
restaurant
    courses 19
    menu 19
    ordering in 21
road transport 65, 67
role-plays, in Speaking Test 122–3,
    129–33
rooms 10

school 1–8, 194–5
    types of school 3
school years 3
self 26–33, 200–2
shopping 57–64, 209–11
shops 50, 57, 59
signs
    associated with travel 65
    road directions 67
skimming (reading) 140
small ads 81
social activities 42–50, 204–6
special occasions 34–41
sports 35
stars (film, theatre) 97
subject pronouns 44–5, 174
subjunctive 92, 188
superlative 83–4, 174

telephones
    telephone calls 112
    using public telephones 81
television 12

theatre 42
time 4–5, 179
times of day 2
tourism 88–92, 219–21
    see also travel
towns, home town 50–6, 206–9
training 74–80, 214–16
transport 65–80, 212–14
    methods of transport 65, 66
travel 65–80, 212–14
    see also tourism

understanding, strategies for, in Reading
    Test 136

vehicles 65
verbs 181–93
    conditional perfect tense 188
    conditional tense 54, 187
    er verbs 13, 191–3
    future perfect tense 187
    future tense 53, 186–7
    imperative 5, 189
    imperfect tense 91, 185
    impersonal 184
    infinitive 37, 190–1
    ir verbs 13, 193
    irregular 13, 14, 53, 182–4
    negative 189–90
    passive 77, 189
    past historic tense 92, 188
    past tenses 37–9, 91–2
    perfect tense 37–9, 185–6
    pluperfect tense 91–2, 187
    present participle 23, 190
    present tense 13–14, 181–4
    re verbs 13, 193
    reflexive 14, 39
    in Speaking Test 122
    subjunctive 92, 188
    venir de + infinitive 92

weather 50–6, 206–9
weights and measures 61
word separation, listening practice 108
work
    jobs 74–80, 214–16
    languages at work 81–7, 217–18
workplaces 74
world problems 98
world, the 96–103, 222–3

y (pronoun) 45, 175
your/my (personal pronouns) 29
yourself 26, 200–2
youth hostel rules 88

DEX